ETHNIC DILEMMAS

ETHNIC DILEMMAS 1964–1982

Nathan Glazer

HARVARD UNIVERSITY PRESS
Cambridge, Massachusetts
and London, England
1983

LIBRARY OF CONGRESS CATALOGING IN PUBLICATION DATA

Glazer, Nathan.
    Ethnic dilemmas, 1964–1982.

    Bibliography: p.
    Includes index.
    1. United States — Ethnic relations — Addresses, essays,
lectures.   2. United States — Race relations — Addresses,
essays, lectures.   3. Minorities — United States — Addresses, essays, lectures.   4. Ethnicity — United States —
Addresses, essays, lectures.   I. Title.
E184.A1G56 1983   305.8′00973   82-23396
ISBN 0-674-26852-0

To Dan and Pearl Bell

Acknowledgments

THE PAPERS that make up this book have been selected from among those I wrote during the years 1964 to 1982 to form a running commentary on and analysis of issues of racial and ethnic conflict. Many were solicited by editors of journals or of books, or by organizers of conferences; I thank them all for their invitations. The journals and books where these chapters originally appeared are listed in the Credits on page 354.

Martha Metzler has typed just about every one of the chapters in this book, working from manuscripts others would have found indecipherable. Her meticulousness and sense of responsibility have saved me from many errors. I wish to express my appreciation to her.

My wife, Lochi, read all these essays carefully, in draft and in proof, at a time when the manuscript had become too familiar to me, and discovered many errors, obscurities, and inelegancies. I am deeply grateful to her for her willingness to undertake this chore. The book reads better because of it.

I have dedicated this book to my good friends of many years, Dan and Pearl Bell. Dan and Pearl have not often written directly about ethnicity in America, but when they have they have shown, with insight and brilliance, how ethnic influences are worked into the fabric of American society and culture. We have talked about matters discussed in this book over the years, but more commonly we seem to have understood each other even without talking.

Contents

ETHNIC DILEMMAS

Introduction

BETWEEN 1964 AND 1982 the American approach to racial and ethnic discrimination, and the range of problems that a multi-ethnic society must confront, underwent a strange and unexpected series of somersaults. Intending in 1964 to create a color-blind America, we discovered to our surprise in the 1970s that we were creating an increasingly color-conscious society. Voting for an administration that campaigned against these policies in 1980, we discovered that it could do nothing against them in 1982. The two years, 1964 and 1982, clearly bound a distinct epoch in American race relations and group relations.

There will be no dispute over the significance of 1964 as the beginning of a new stage in race relations in America. In that year the Civil Rights Act seemed finally to have set the course that the United States would henceforth follow in race relations, and it was to be, as blacks and their defenders had long demanded, a "color-blind" course: Public authorities and private individuals, insofar as they wielded substantial power, would have to treat each individual as an individual, regardless of race or ethnic background. In the ringing language of the Civil Rights Act, there was to be no discrimination or segregation "on the ground of race, color, religion, or national origin" in places of public accommodation, or in the distribution of federal benefits; "on account of race, color, religion, or national origin" in public facilities; "by reason of race, color, religion, or national origin" in public education; "because of [an] individual's color, religion, sex or national origin," in employment. The

Civil Rights Act followed the language and spirit of the Thirteenth, Fourteenth, and Fifteenth Amendments. It spoke of "citizens," "individuals," "persons"—not of blacks, Hispanic Americans, American Indians, Asians, or any other group that might be subject to discrimination. It was designed to vindicate the rights of blacks, but its language insisted that race, color, religion, national origin were to limit no one's rights. Just as the language of the post–Civil War amendments permitted in time other groups than freed slaves to come under their protection, so the language of the Civil Rights Act provided an equally broad and general protection—even, and this was no surprise, to whites.

The Civil Rights Act was the centerpiece of a series of acts that drove discrimination out of public life. One must add to it the Voting Rights Act of 1965, and the Immigration Act of 1965, which eliminated quotas based on ethnic origin and race.

These were to be no paper rights. The Civil Rights Act created a powerful agency, the Equal Employment Opportunity Commission, which was in time to deploy a staff of thousands. The President joined in with a powerful executive order not only banning discrimination among federal contractors but requiring "affirmative action" to ensure that even inadvertent discrimination would not occur. And that action was in time to lead to the growth of another powerful agency, the Office of Federal Contract Compliance Programs. Other civil rights agencies, in the Department of Justice, the Department of Health, Education, and Welfare, and the Department of Housing and Urban Development, were also strengthened. In time armies of officials were deployed to root out discrimination, and by 1980 $550 million dollars were budgeted by the federal government for civil rights enforcement.[1]

To those who fought for these measures, to those who voted for them, to the mass media which supported them, to the federal officials who initially implemented them, it seemed clear that we were entering into a new epoch in which Justice Harlan's famous dissent in *Plessy v. Ferguson* would finally become law: "Our Constitution is color blind," he had written. Seventy years later it finally became true. Or so it seemed.

But to characterize the eighteen years that followed as an

era of color-blind policy would be grossly mistaken. For something quite unexpected followed upon this burst of legislation. What happened was the very rapid institution and steady expansion of methods of enforcement of the new array of civil rights legislation and the executive order that surprisingly enough *required* local, state and federal public authorities, major private employers, public and private institutions of higher education, and varied institutions that were recipients of federal aid or subject to government regulation, to pay an increasingly exact attention to race and ethnicity. The new measures, the enforcing officials decreed, made it necessary to count how many of each group were interviewed, promoted, hired, admitted, served, enrolled.

Today crucial documents in American history are not necessarily to be found in legislation, executive action, or even the court orders of our powerful judiciary. The modest reporting forms issued by regulatory agencies may be as consequential as any of these. Standard Form 100 (EEO-1) of the Equal Employment Opportunity Commission required regular reporting from employers on their "Negro," "Oriental," "American Indian," and "Spanish American" employees. Colleges and universities were required to report on the numbers of their students in each of these categories. These figures, the relevant agencies had decided, were necessary to determine whether discrimination was taking place. The terms that were applied eighteen years ago to the four groups that had been selected — by a bureaucratic process that is still unclear — as the special beneficiaries of civil rights legislation have since changed. There have been many disputes as to who should be included among the "Spanish Americans" and "Orientals" in particular. A new burst of immigration, of enormous significance, has changed radically the composition and size of these two groups. But the principle was set: Simultaneously with the commitment, clearly enshrined in legislation, that this was to be a color-blind America, we set a course marked by a diametrically opposed principle, that of color consciousness. Every institution that dispensed education, jobs, money, power, at least for the four groups (or, in the case of the "Spanish Americans" and "Orientals," groups of groups) that were chosen as the specific concern of the enforcement agencies, would have to be aware of the color or ethnic background of every person benefited or harmed.

The next eighteen years were marked by a struggle between the two principles to determine just how far the principle of color-consciousness in government policy would be allowed to go. The stages of the struggle were marked by a series of major constitutional cases, trying to determine whether the Constitution, and the legislation that had been passed to enforce it, was indeed "color-blind": *DeFunis, Bakke, Weber, Fullilove* . . .

By 1964, I had already been writing on race and ethnicity in America for twenty years.[2]

As an editor of *Commentary*, I wrote frequently on prejudice and discrimination, ethnicity and race. Inevitably, I had developed a point of view, and one that at the time was indistinguishable from the position embraced by all who fought for an end to prejudice and discrimination, and the full incorporation into American life, of blacks and other groups that faced discrimination, without regard to color or ethnicity. The new developments that followed the passage of the Civil Rights Act of 1964 surprised me; and many of the essays in this book trace my response to and analysis of them.

I discussed the recurrent rise and fall of ethnicity as an issue in American politics and culture (Chapter 1); the unexpected rift that opened between two great allies in the civil rights struggle, blacks and Jews (Chapter 2); whether something in black family structure was a problem for black achievement (Chapter 3); the contrasts between blacks and white ethnic groups, which became one key ground for moving beyond policies that deal with individuals to "group-conscious" policies (Chapters 4 and 5); and, as affirmative action developed into a policy that tested the justice and the effectiveness of action against discrimination by statistical results, I analyzed the difficult issues it raised (Chapters 9, 10, 11).

As color-blind approaches receded and color-conscious ones succeeded them, new issues arose, particularly in the sphere of education. How were the schools to respond to the new black consciousness, and to the rising white ethnic consciousness that it helped give rise to? How were they to respond as Hispanic groups raised their own demands for an education shaped to their needs and their culture? How was American education to take account of multiethnicity — and were there dangers in an increasing governmental role in determining just how it was to be taken into account? (Chapters 6, 7, 8.)

A common theme seemed to underlie a variety of issues that agitated the country in the 1970s. A term like affirmative action, which was first used to specify employment policies for government contractors, could migrate to be used to define admissions policies for colleges, universities, and professional schools. It could be stretched to describe educational policies in which group differences and color were not to be ignored but accentuated, even to the point of incorporating into curricula material designed to enhance distinctive group pride and maintain group commitment. In all these areas, the underlying issue could be summed up: color-blind or color-conscious? Assimilation, or something different — cultural pluralism, rights distributed by group, group consciousness maintained and enhanced?

With the onset of the 1980s it appeared that this struggle was to take a decisive turn. For in 1980 the first presidential candidate who directly and openly attacked color conscious measures — specifically, busing for racial integration, goals or quotas for employment, and the requirements of bilingual education for children of non-English-speaking background — was elected. Surely, the color-conscious policies could no longer survive, in view of the overwhelming opposition to them among whites, the very substantial opposition to them among blacks, the ideological and political complexion of the administration, and the fact that these policies were in such large part the product of executive agencies under the thumb of the President. Those who favored these approaches, insisting they were the only means to achieving equality for minorities who had faced prejudice and discrimination, waited in horror for the axe to fall on regulations and agencies; those who saw them as a denial of the equal protection of the laws and the promise of a color-blind America expected that it would indeed fall.

By 1982, as congressional mid-term elections approached, these fears and hopes had receded. The Reagan administration can do, or will do, almost nothing against these policies, and they are fixed as part of American life. (Even the withdrawal of the proposed bilingual regulations of the Carter administration represents less of a change than many believe; the previous *Lau* regulations — see Chapter 7 — remain in force.) The reasons why it could not act are spelled out in Chapter 9 of this book, where I describe a similar period when the administration of Gerald Ford, apparently opposed to these policies, as was the great majority of the American people, also found it impossible to act. It is now clear that the Reagan administration, which is weaker after two years in office than when it began, will not try to act against the elaborated provisions of an executive order requiring racial and ethnic goals that is fully within its power to change, and will not act against the policies created by the Justice Department and the courts that in effect require quota hiring in many areas by major private firms and by major public employers. Undoubtedly the laws and regulations will not be enforced with the vigor the Carter administration brought to them; undoubtedly we will see a slackening of federal energy in pursuing busing policies that are almost totally discredited and bilingual requirements whose effectiveness is now doubted; the government, in particularly egregious cases, may try to limit the spread of race-conscious policies. But even that is in doubt. The administration could not act decisively against a strengthening of the Voting Rights Act in 1982 that makes more likely judicial imposition of race and ethnic quotas for political representation. Is it likely to act in areas that are further from the heart of American government and American democracy than the electoral process?

The battle over affirmative action assumed such significance not only because it seemed to challenge the principles all liberals had accepted in 1964 but because the problem to which it was addressed, against all expectations, retained its awesome size and significance. This problem was of course that of the depressed condition of a large part of the black population. After 1964, blacks rapidly entered higher positions in government, business, and the universities, and the gap between black and white earnings narrowed. But at the same time, high black unemployment persisted and increased, the rate of family dissolution rose, black communities were afflicted with drugs and crime. I touch on these matters (in Chapters 5 and 9), but scarcely to the degree their importance requires. One reason is that during this period it became almost impossible for either blacks or whites to discuss these matters. The facts were known, but significant research almost ceased, and analysis was dumb. The common wisdom was that more vigorous pursuit of the fight against discrimination, plus huge expenditures on social problems, would help. I argue in this book that the fight against discrimination chose the wrong solution. Discrimination was less and less relevant as an explanation of these problems. And huge expenditures on social problems were made, but did not help. Now we are cutting back on the social expenditures and beginning to look more frankly at the problems.

So there is good reason in 1982 to take stock. One phase in the long effort to deal with discrimination and the condition of minorities seems to have come to an end: we have lost faith in our ability to target large social expenditures to overcome the problems of the black community, and we have come to a compromise, for the moment, on the kinds of policies to be pursued in the fight against discrimination. But now new issues appear on the horizon, which are bound to unsettle the temporary settlement of 1982.

For there was a second contradiction that marked the great period in the mid-1960s when we set a public course for a color-blind America and discovered that the executive and the courts had instead steered us in the direction of an increasingly color-conscious America. This second contradiction was created by the Immigration Act of 1965, which abandoned national quotas and preferences. This was intended to create a color-blind America, in the area of immigration policies, as the Civil Rights Act was to create a color-blind America in domestic policies. But the effects of the Immigration Act guarantee that the new color-consciousness that evolved in policy after 1964 cannot remain stable, and pose a greater threat to it than the ideology of the Reagan administration. The reason is a simple one: Because of the shift in the sources of immigration after 1965, the benefited classes under the new color-conscious policies of the later 1960s and the 1970s have greatly expanded in a way that no one intended and no one expected. The Immigration Act eliminated quotas because the descendants of those who were discriminated against under these quotas—Italians, Jews, Greeks, East Europeans—had always opposed them and with increasing political power and in a period of liberal reshaping of our laws they were able to do away with these insulting limitations. But as it turned out it was not *their* relatives and countrymen who were the beneficiaries of the quota eliminations. The beneficiaries have been Latin Americans and Asians, whose political weight in this country would never have been sufficient to change the Immigration Act in their favor if that had been its purported intention.

European immigration fell off rapidly after 1965; Latin American, West Indian, and Asian immigration grew. The facts are startling. In the 1960s more than one-third of our immigrants still came from Europe, a mere 13 percent from Asia, and the rest from Latin America, the West Indies, and Canada. In the 1970s only 18 percent came from Europe, more than one-third from Asia, and those from the Western Hemisphere were overwhelmingly Latin American and West Indian. Under the new Immigration Act, even the minuscule immigration from Africa doubled. At the turn of the 1980s, new waves of refugees from Asia and Cuba swelled the immigration totals. One million five hundred thousand immigrants entered the country in 1980 and 1981, numbers that had not been reached since before World War I. And these new immigrants are the beneficiaries of decisions that were not made with them in mind but that place them in protected classes. Certainly those who voted for both the Civil Rights Act and the Immigration Act never dreamed that the two would intersect to place the new immigrants in a privileged class as compared with most native Americans.

A strange development indeed! And one that guarantees that these policies must be reexamined in years to come. In Charles Keely's words:

[New] problems were created by . . . the new dominance of immigrants from Asian and Latin countries. The first problem was that the new immigrants became eligible for programs seeking to bolster equality of access as measured by equality of achievement. If affirmative action is to right past wrongs, why should a recent immigrant qualify? In addition, many of the recent immigrants have been skilled and professional people . . . On what basis can one justify their being categorized as a disadvantaged minority   solely because of ethnic ancestry?

Second, the concentration of new immigrants from Asian and Latin countries. which are also the areas of origin of the bulk of the illegal migrants and the preponderance of refugees, has raised the issue of the absorptive capacity of the American society . . . What is different from the past is that the very groups focused on by policies to foster equality are augmented in considerable numbers by new residents within an atmosphere of government-sponsored emphasis on ethnicity.[3]

A little bureaucratic story, although of no great consequence in itself, illustrates the problems we have created for ourselves by defining some groups as requiring special protection. Almost all federal agencies — as well as state and local agencies — that give out benefits must now be concerned with how those benefits are distributed among recipient groups. One agency that must define groups worthy of special consideration is the Small Business Administration (SBA). Section 8(a) of the Small Business Act is a program to "foster business ownership by individuals who are both socially and economically disadvantaged." But who are they? One begins inevitably with the four groups or groups of groups that had been determined to be especially worthy of attention by the Equal Employment Opportunity Commission (EEOC). When these groups were established in 1965, "Orientals" consisted mostly of Japanese and Chinese. Since then, substantial immigration from Asia has added many Filipinos, Koreans, Vietnamese, and Asian Indians. The question arises, do Indians belong in the category "Orientals," or "Asian Americans"? At first they were consistently excluded (see Chapter 10). But many among them have demanded to be included among the disadvantaged because that is the route to advantage. This despite the fact that Indians are overwhelmingly a community of professionals and businessmen. We should not blame them. After all, if the equally prosperous Chinese and Japanese are deserving of special assistance as against the "white" majority, why not Asian Indians? One imagines the Indian engineer who has started his small business seeking government contracts in Silicon Valley looking enviously at his Chinese or Japanese competitors who are considered "disadvantaged" while he is not. On May 18, 1982, a notice was published in the Federal Register of a petition to SBA requesting minority-group designation for Asian Indians. It was the work of Jan Pillai, a professor of law at Temple University and President of the National Association of Americans of Asian Indian Descent (NAAAID). Professor Pillai predicted, *India Abroad* reported, that approval of the petition by the SBA was "certain to lead to disadvantaged minority group status for Indians by both the Health and Human Services (HHS) and the Environmental Protection Agency (EPA), thus opening up other avenues of aid." The HHS had previously denied the designation to Indians.

Apparently when the law was passed, the SBA had designated as one of its beneficiary groups "Asian Pacific Americans" and had excluded Asian Indians. Two congressmen — Parren Mitchell, Chairman of the House Small Business Committee, and Joseph P. Addabbo, a member of the committee, had written to the SBA explaining that they had not intended to exclude Asian Indians from the 8(a) program when the bill was passed (indeed they could not possibly have been thinking of them), and supported the group's designation by the SBA as socially disadvantaged.[4]

Indians were not universally happy with this petition. *India Abroad* published letters of protest over the next two months, but the comments the SBA received in response to this notice were overwhelmingly in favor: Only six comments were received opposing the designation, five from Indians, one from a black. The SBA then determined that Asian Indians were a socially disadvantaged group, and Professor Pillai's NAAAID said it would communicate this important decision to other federal agencies, defense procurement agencies, educational institutions, and state and city agencies.

The ironic conclusion of the story is that the Reagan administration, whose agency had approved the designation, decided to take credit for it: "Peter Terpeluk, deputy national administrator of SBA, addressing the third national convention of NAAAID, announced that 30 billion dollars had been set aside for small business of disadvantaged minorities under the 8-A program."[5] The story is of no great consequence except as a symbol: The road to preference, once entered upon, is not easy to get off. Preference spreads from one area of governmental largesse to another, from one group to another. I believe that developments of this sort cannot long remain buried in the Federal Register and the pages of specialized community newspapers, but will become a matter for general concern. Developments of this type are foreshadowed in many of my essays from 1964 onward: Their full emergence, the conflicts that will inevitably take place around them, and their resolution must be matters for the 1980s and beyond. And certainly one of the most significant problems that will be raised is why certain immigrant groups are progressing more rapidly than a large part of the black community.

The question of how the United States is to build a unified country out of peoples from all over the world is one that can never for long be ignored. A dynamic nation whose place in the world, whose sources of immigration, whose self-image constantly changes, must again and again address itself to this great question and ponder what its answer is to be.

Nor is the United States any longer unique in dealing with these issues. The dream of ethnic homogeneity — one nation for each country, a country for each nation — which dominated the settlement of World Wars I and II is now seen to be illusory (see Chapter 12). The countries of Europe have become more mixed because their economic energy has drawn in people from the less-developed parts of Europe, from Asia, and from Africa; the heritage of empire has led to the same consequences. The empire builders of the nineteenth century could never have dreamed that the results of their work would be large populations of Indians and Pakistanis in England, of Vietnamese, North Africans, and Africans in France (see Chapter 15). But so it has happened, and American problems are no longer America's alone.

Are there broad general principles that can guide us to the establishment of multiethnic polities and societies that are simultaneously just to racial and ethnic groups and to individuals? This is an issue many nations now struggle with, and one in which the experience of the United States may be of value. Does attention to group disadvantage, and concern to overcome it, inevitably mean that individuals must see their rights abridged or strengthened on the grounds of race and ethnic background? Despite my participation in the debates that have been fought over this question, I do not believe that there is only one democratic and decent path to a multiethnic society, the one for which I have argued in the United States. I would place individual rights at the center, and groups would then exist only as the result of the free choice of individuals, and the existence of a group would derive no advantage in public law for its members.

But certainly other courses are possible, and in Part IV of this book I explore two such approaches from the perspective of international experience. One approach to group rights in multiethnic societies is that of federalism, establishing subunits of the society in which various groups have special rights. American federalism, as I point out, is of a very different order, and although it offers some help in easing interethnic conflict it is no basic solution (Chapter 14). Another approach is the straightforward distribution of rights on a group basis, by way of a national interethnic or interracial compromise (Chapter 13). A number of our fellow-democracies have taken that route, and perhaps we will too. One can see the beginnings in embryo (Chapter 16). But it is my conviction that the United States, in defining its essence as a multiracial and multiethnic society, has been for generations working toward something different — toward a society in which there is sufficient respect for human dignity, regardless of race or ethnic background, that no special protection is required for any group, even those which have suffered severely from prejudice and discrimination. We already have remarkable examples of how, under a regime of color-blindness and individual rights, groups that once suffered discrimination affecting their capacity for education, for occupations of high status and high return, and for social equality have changed their position rapidly, and have shown leaps in one generation that would be impossible were we the racist and prejudiced society that so many people think we are. Is there in this a model for all groups that have suffered from prejudice and discrimination? Is it possible for all groups to take the route of individual rights, trusting to the opportunities offered by a free and open and tolerant society? Or are we doomed, now that we have abandoned the state exercise of discrimination to keep groups down, to the state exercise of discrimination to prop them up? That, it seems to me, is the key issue that will have to be debated in the United States in the 1980s and beyond.

I

BLACKS, JEWS,

AND OTHERS

1

The Peoples of America

THE HISTORY of ethnicity and ethnic self-consciousness in this country has moved in waves; we are now, in 1965, in a trough between two crests, and the challenge is to describe the shape and form of the next crest. That there will be another crest it is hardly possible to doubt. Since the end of European mass immigration to this country forty years ago we have waited for the subsidence of ethnic self-consciousness, and often announced it, and it has returned again and again. But each time it has returned in so different a form that one could well argue it was not the same thing returning at all, that what we saw was not the breakthrough of the consciousness of common origin and community among the groups that made America, but rather that ethnicity was being used as a cover for some other more significant force, which was borrowing another identity.

During the early years of the depression, ethnicity withdrew as a theme in American life. Both those who had urged the "Americanization" of immigrants and those who had advocated the acceptance of "cultural pluralism" now had more important concerns. Immigration was matched by a counteremigration back to the countries of origin; one episode of American history, it seemed, had come to an end. Then with the rise of Hitler the ethnic texture of American life began to reassert itself. First Jews; then Germans; then Czechs, Poles, Italians, and even the "old Americans," remembering their origins in England, all were spurred to action and organization by Hitler and the great war that he began. Samuel Lubell has traced how support for Franklin D. Roosevelt in the great cities shifted from class to ethnicity, as the international conflict developed and various groups responded to, or against, Roosevelt as he displayed his sentiments and allegiances.[1]

In 1945 this great crest began to withdraw. True, there was the continuing impact on ethnic groups of the confrontation with Russia and communism, but with the passage of time this began to lose its ethnic coloration. Catholics in general were more anti-Communist than others, Poles still more so, Jews much less so. But the international conflict was so sharply colored by ideology, rather than national antagonism, that with the passage of time it no longer served to set group against group (as it had in the Hitler years). Soviet opposition to Israel and Soviet anti-Semitism; the rise of a measure of cautious Polish independence; de-Stalinization in Russia—all these developments softened the sharp conflicts which had created a powerful resonance among immigrants and their children in this country.

The Eisenhower period thus marked a new trough, and it was possible to conclude that the workings of the melting pot had been retarded only slightly by the Neolithic tribal ferocity of Hitler and the counterreactions he evoked. But now a new wave began to gather force, a wave that had nothing to do with international affairs. Will Herberg interpreted the increased religious activity of the postwar years as a half-embarrassed means of maintaining group identity in a democratic society that did not look with favor on the long-continued maintenance of sharply distinguished ethnic groups.[2] The "triple melting pot" theory of Ruby Jo Reeves Kennedy, along with her data on intermarriage, suggested that old ethnic lines were being replaced by new religious lines. The chameleon-like force of ancestral connection, one could argue, was being transmuted into the forms of religion.[3] Those who were concerned for religion could of course take no comfort in this analysis, even if the religious denominations benefited from higher collections and new buildings. If our major religions were replacing ethnic groups, one could not yet herald the creation of a homogeneous and undivided American group consciousness, but at least our divisions no longer paralleled those of old Europe — something that had deeply troubled our leaders from Washington to Woodrow Wilson — but the more acceptable divisions of religion, which ostensibly had an older and more respectable lineage and justification. Thus, if Herberg could still discern the forces of ethnic identity at work in the new clothes of religious denominationalism, at least they no longer expressed themselves openly.

But once again an unabashed ethnicity reasserted itself, in the campaign of John F. Kennedy and his brief Presidency. In his cabinet, for the first time, there sat a Jew of East European origin, an Italian American, a Polish American. If the Jews were no longer being appointed primarily to represent a group there was no question that this was the explanation for the appointment of an Italian American and a Polish American. The Catholic President was reminded by everyone that he was an Irish President. He was the first President to be elected from an immigrant group that had suffered discrimination and prejudice, and that still remembered it — and those of us from later immigrant groups, who had experienced the lordly position of the Irish in the cities of the East, discovered only with some surprise that the Irish did remember their days as a degraded minority. Those who stemmed from the new immigration now realized that the Irish shared very much the same feelings of resentment at past treatment, of gratification in present accomplishment and recognition. But the old Americans too responded to the realization that they had an Irish President, as well as a Democratic, Catholic, and intellectual President. Certainly it is hard to explain otherwise the mutual antagonism that rapidly sprang up between the new administration and such a large part of the big business establishment, the seat of the old Americans, the WASP power. The administration's policies were not antagonistic to big business. There was of course the President's violent response to the steel price rise, but was not that, too, a reflection — at least in part — of old ethnic images and conflicts? No one who spoke to anyone close to those events could doubt it.

I would suggest a gentle recession, if not a trough, in the period since the assassination of President Kennedy. Two events to my mind suggest the retreat of an open and congratulatory ethnic self-assertiveness, and they are related. One is the new concern with the poor, which complementarily marks all the non-poor as members of the same group, with the same social task laid upon them; and the second is the steady radicalization of the civil rights movement and Negro opinion,* and this increasingly places all the whites in the same category, without distinction. And once again a symbolic political event marks the recession of ethnic self-consciousness: the accession of President Johnson, who, like President Eisenhower, comes from a part of America that was relatively unaffected by European immigration.

I have marked recurrent crests and troughs of ethnic self-consciousness by political events, but the political events have of course paralleled social events. The crisis of the depression erased for the moment ethnic memories and allegiances. The agony of the European peoples reawakened it. Prosperity and the rapid rise of the new immigrant groups to upper working-class and middle-class status again reduced their sense of difference. The security that came with long sustained prosperity made it possible for the descendants of despised immigrants to again take pleasure in their origins and their differences. One of the less observed effects of affluence is that it leads people to their real or hopefully reconstructed origins. In Europe and among Americans who look to the European upper classes this may mean acquiring crests, forebears, and antiques. Among the American descendants of European peasants and artisans, it meant, in a surprising number of cases, a new interest in the culture of the old country. But in the most recent period, the rise of the joint problems of poverty and the assimilation of the Negro raises a new set of questions. For the moment, ethnic self-assertiveness is in eclipse and even in bad odor. And the eclipse is directly related to the new problems.

---

*I retain the usage of the times, and thus it is "Negro" in the essays of the middle 1960s, "black" in later essays.

Michael Harrington put the matter quite directly when he said in a recent speech that the accumulated wisdom of the great European immigrant groups in this country had become irrelevant, for it will not help the current poor and it will not help the Negroes. In varying degrees, we are hearing the same from Louis Lomax, from James Baldwin, from Nat Hentoff, and from other supporters and defenders of Negro militancy. Inevitably the next wave of ethnic self-consciousness must reflect one of the most remarkable and least expected consequences of the Negro revolution — the growing estrangement between European ethnic groups and the Negroes. Its beginnings were studied by Samuel Lubell in the early postwar period, and we have seen the estrangement develop to the point where the fear of the white backlash — and this meant generally the backlash from recent white immigrant groups in the cities — became one of the major issues of the Goldwater-Johnson campaign. The separation, first the barest of lines, has deepened through conflicts over the adoption and administration of fair employment laws, fair housing laws, measures to combat *de facto* school segregation. The patterns under which and through which the European ethnic groups have lived — the trade unions and branches of industry dominated by one or a few ethnic groups, the ethnically concentrated neighborhoods with their distinctive schools and churches and organizations — all have come under increasing attack. And thus the distinctive social patterns of the North and West, which the immigrant and the ethnic groups helped create, are now being slowly but surely turned into a southern-like confrontation of white and black. The varied, more balanced, and more creative ethnic conflicts of the North are now in danger of being transformed into the monolithic confrontation of the South.

In the South northern heterogeneity never developed. One great division dominated and smothered all others — the division between black and white. In this area, the European immigrant of the later nineteenth and early twentieth century never penetrated. All he had to offer generally was unskilled labor, and in the South the unskilled labor was the work of Negroes. The white immigrant laborer refused to enter an area in which the laborer was degraded not only by his work but by a caste system, where wages were low, and where racial conflict hindered trade union development and social legislation. The immigrant worked in the parts of the country where work had greater respect and was better rewarded. If he entered the South, it was more often as a merchant than as a worker.

But in northern cities, where almost half the Negroes now live, it was not inevitable that the same line of division should be imported from the South. The entry of the Negroes into the northern cities in great numbers during and after World War I and again during and after World War II raised a critical question: were they the last of the great immigrant groups? Would their experience parallel that of the Irish and the Poles and the Jews who had arrived as exploited and unskilled workers and had moved upward, at varying speeds, into middle-class occupations, the professions, business? How would those who were themselves children and grandchildren of recent immigrant waves view them? How would the Negroes view themselves and their prospects? Against whom would they measure their circumstances? And would the inevitable conflicts between the poorer and the more prosperous resemble the conflicts between Yankees and Irish, Irish and Italians—or would they take the form of the far more deadly and longer established conflict between black and white? I feel the answers are still not given. They will be shaped both by the established ethnic groups and the Negro migrants. But I fear the answer from both sides will be . . . yes, the Negro is different.

It is impossible for the history of ethnic self-consciousness to escape from the impact of Negro urban migration, for all the waves of immigration have affected the self-consciousness of waves that came before. The old Americans reacted to the first great waves of immigrants of the 1840s and 1850s with an exaggerated sense of their own high status and aristocratic connections. The early immigrants from each group withdrew from later immigrants, but were generally forced together with them because the old Americans imposed a common identity on them. The history of ethnic self-consciousness, it is clear, has not worked itself out independently of social and economic and political events. If anything, it has been a reaction to these events: the rise of one group, the occupancy of the bottom by another, the political conflicts of Europe, the sequence of immigration in each town and city and section. All these have helped mold ethnic self-consciousness, and its reflection in social activity, in political choice, in economic history.

But on the whole this self-consciousness, whatever its· stages, had been marked by optimism and hope. I have described the Kennedy mood among the more recent and more sharply defined American ethnic groups as self-congratulation. Indeed it was that, though each of the groups might have found some basis for resentment rather than pride. The Irish had reached the heights of political success, and the Jews were prosperous, but both were still in large measure excluded from the pinnacles of economic power—the great banks, insurance companies, corporations. The Italians still were remarkably poorly represented in high political posts, and had a much smaller share in every establishment—economic, political, cultural—than the Jews, who had come at the same time and were less numerous. The Poles were even poorer. And yet such invidious comparisons—which the census made clear—were rarely made. All the new groups seem to have escaped from the difficult period of second-generation self-depreciation and exaggerated Americanism. All seemed to wear ethnic connection with self-assurance. Certainly the growing prosperity of Europe, the increased trade with Europe, the wide acceptance of its consumer goods here, the large influence of European culture, all made the acceptance of one's ethnic connections easier—for by doing so, after all, one was no longer acknowledging poor relations. It was fascinating to remark upon the change in the image of the homeland among the more self-conscious and better educated descendants of the immigrants. Ireland was no longer the home of potatoes and cabbage, but of Joyce and the Abbey theatre, good Irish whiskey and Georgian architecture, horse-racing and tweeds. Italy became the land of chic, while Israel and Poland, if they could not compete in the arts of affluent consumption, became now paragons of political independence and heroism.

Every group fortunately found something to admire in the old (or new) country, and found it easy to acknowledge the connection that had once been obscured.

But if this characterizes the most recent mood of ethnic self-consciousness, it is now challenged by the new Negro militancy and the theory on which it is reared. The self-congratulatory expressions are strangled in the throat. For a while, in the 1940s and 1950s, when Jewish and Catholic groups worked effectively with the Urban League and the NAACP, with Negroes proud of having achieved middle-class status, the older ethnic groups and their representatives could present themselves as models and elder brothers—in community organization, in group defense work, in cultural and political activity. But the radical Negro mood, and its growing reflection among intellectuals, turns all whites into exploiters, with old Americans, old immigrants, and new immigrants lumped together. The success of the ethnic groups—limited as it is for many—now becomes a reproach. Their very history, which each group has been so busy writing and reconstructing, now becomes an unspoken (and sometimes spoken) criticism of the northern Negro. Both sides see it, and rush to explain themselves.

What after all is the history of the American ethnic groups but a history of group and individual adaptation to difficult circumstances? All the histories move in the same patterns. The immigrants arrive; they represent the poorest and least educated and most oppressed of their countries in Europe and Asia. They arrive ignorant of our language and customs, exploited and abused. They huddle together in the ghettos of the cities, beginning slowly to attend to their most immediate needs—organization for companionship, patterns of self-aid in crisis, churches for worship, schools to maintain the old culture. American society and government are indifferent to their needs and desires; they are allowed to do what they wish, and are neither hindered nor aided. In this amorphous setting where no limits are set to group organization, they gradually form a community. Their children move through the public schools and perhaps advance themselves—if not, it may be the grandchildren who do. The children are embarrassed by the poverty and ignorance of the parents. Eventually they, or the grandchildren, learn to accept their origins as they overcome poverty and ignorance. They move into the spheres of American life in which many or all groups meet — the larger economy, politics, social life, education. Eventually many of the institutions created by the immigrants become a hindrance rather than a necessity; some are abandoned, some are changed. American society in the meantime has made a place for and even become dependent on some of these institutions, such as old-age homes and hospitals, adoption services and churches — these survive and perhaps flourish. More and more of these institutions become identified with the religious denomination, rather than the ethnic group as such.

Note one element of this history: demand on government plays a small role; response by government plays a small role. There is one great exception, the labor movement. But even the labor movement, which eventually found support in public law and government administrative structure, began its history as a voluntary organization in the amorphous structure of American society, and achieved its first triumphs without, or even against, government.

Does this history have any meaning for the American Negro? This is the question that Jews and Japanese, Irish and Italians, Poles and Czechs ask themselves. Some new immigrant groups — Puerto Ricans and Mexicans — think it does have a meaning for them. They try to model their institutions on those of earlier immigrant groups. They show the same uncertainties and confusions over what to do with the culture and language they have brought with them. The militant Negro and his white allies passionately deny the relevance or even the truth of this history. It is white history; as white history it is also the history of the exploitation of the Negro, of the creation of privilege on the basis of his unpaid and forced labor. It is not history he can accept as having any meaning for him. His fate, he insists, has been far more drastic and frightful than any other, and neither Irish famines nor Jewish pogroms make the members of these groups his brothers in understanding. The hatred with which he is looked upon by whites, he believes, has nothing in common with the petty prejudices that European immigrant groups have met. And the America of today, in which he makes his great and desperate effort for full equality, he asserts, has little in common with the America of mass immigration.

A subtle intervention of government in every aspect of social life, of economy, of culture, he insists, is necessary now to create justice. Every practice must now be scrutinized anew for its impact on this totally unique and incomparable group in American life. The neighborhood school, the civil service system, the personnel procedures of our corporations, the practices of small business, the scholarship systems of our states, the composition and character of our churches, the structure of neighborhood organization, the practices of unions — all, confronted with this shibboleth, fail. The Negro has not received his due, and the essence of all of them is therefore discrimination and exclusion, and the defense of privilege. It is no wonder that ethnic self-consciousness, after its brief moment of triumph, after its legitimization in American life, now turns upon itself in confusion. After all, it is these voluntary churches, organizations, hospitals, schools, and businesses that have become the pride of ethnic groups, and the seat of whatever distinctiveness they possess. It is by way of this participation that they have become part of the very fabric of American life. But the fabric is now challenged. And looked at from another perspective, the Negro perspective, the same structure that defends some measure of uniqueness by the same token defends some measure of discrimination and exclusion.

It is impossible for the ethnic groups in America, who have already moved through so many protean forms, to be unaffected by the civil rights revolution. For this raises the question of the status of the largest of American minority groups, the one most closely bound up with American history from its very beginnings. Chinese and Japanese, perhaps Puerto Ricans and Mexican Americans can accept the patterns of development and gradual assimilation into American society that are exhibited in the history of the great European immigrant groups. For a while, some of us who studied this history and saw in its variety and flexibility some virtues for a mass, industrial society, which suppresses variety and flexibility in so many areas, hoped that the American Negro, as he entered the more open environments of northern cities, could also move along the paths the European immigrant groups had followed.

We now wonder whether this hope was illusory. Whether it was the infection of Europeans with the virus of American racial prejudice; or the inability to confine the direct and violent conflict in the South; or the impact of slavery and southern experience on the American Negro — it is clear, whatever the causes, that for one of the major groups in American life, the idea of pluralism, which has supported the various developments of other groups, has become a mockery. Whatever concrete definition we give to pluralism, it means a limitation of government power, a relatively free hand for private and voluntary organizations to develop their own patterns of worship, education, social life, residential concentration, and even distinctive economic activity. All of these enhance the life of some groups; from the perspective of the American Negro they are exclusive and discriminatory.

The general ideas that have justified the development of the ethnic group in America have never been too well explicated. We have tended to obscure the inevitable conflicts between individual group interest and national interest, even when they have occurred, rather than set down sharp principles to regulate the ethnic groups. When an ethnic group interest has clashed with a national interest, we have been quite ruthless and even extreme in overriding the group interest. Thus two world wars radically diminished the scale and assertiveness of German American group life. But we have never fully developed what is permitted and what is not. Now a new national interest is becoming defined — the final liquidation of Negro separation, in all areas of our life: the economic, the social, the cultural, the residential. In every area, Negro separation, regardless of its causes, is seen as unbearable by Negroes. Inevitably this must deeply mark the future development of American ethnic groups, whose continuance contributes, in some measure, to this separation. Recently in this country there has been a positive attitude to ethnic distinctiveness. Oscar Handlin and others have argued that it does not divide the nation or weaken it in war; rather it helps integrate the immigrant groups and adds a rich strand of variety to American civilization. Now a new question arises: what is its effect on the Negro?

Perhaps, ironically, the final homogenization of the American people, the creation of a common nationality replacing all other forms of national connection, will now come about because of the need to guarantee the integration of the Negro. But I believe the group character of American life is too strongly established and fits too many individual needs to be so completely suppressed. Is it not more likely that as Negro demands are in varying measure met, the Negro too will accept the virtues of our complex society, in which separation is neither forbidden nor required, but rather tolerated? Perhaps American Negroes will become another ethnic group, accepted by others and accepting themselves.

[1965]

2

Negroes and Jews:

The New Challenge to Pluralism

IF TODAY one rereads the article by Kenneth Clark on Negro-
Jewish relations that was published in *Commentary* almost
nineteen years ago,[1] one will discover that tension between
Negroes and Jews is neither of recent origin nor a product of the
civil rights revolution. In that article Dr. Clark described the
bitter feelings of the masses of northern Negroes toward Jews.
Not that these feelings hampered cooperation between Negro
and Jewish leaders — an effective cooperation which was to play
an important role in the following years in bringing fair-
employment, fair-housing, and fair-education legislation to
many communities, and indeed to most of the large northern
and western states. But whatever the relationships were at the
top, the fact was that down below, the Negro's experience of the
Jew was not as a co-worker or friend or ally, but, in a word, as
an exploiter.

As Dr. Clark wrote: "Some Negro domestics assert that
Jewish houswives who employ them are unreasonably and
brazenly exploitative. A Negro actor states in bitter terms that
he is being flagrantly underpaid by a Jewish producer. A Negro
entertainer is antagonistic to his Jewish agent, who, he is convinced, is exploiting him . . . Antagonism to the 'Jewish
landlord' is so common as to become almost an integral part of
the folk culture of the Northern urban Negro." And, of course,

one would have to add to this catalogue the Jewish merchants in the Negro business districts, believed by their customers to be selling them inferior goods at high prices and on poor credit terms (a charge the merchants might answer by explaining that they were simply covering the greater financial costs of doing business in a Negro area, plus compensation for the physical danger involved).

In any case, long before many of those Negro youths were born who took part in the summer of 1964 in the destruction and looting of Jewish businesses in Harlem and Bedford-Stuyvesant and Philadelphia, Dr. Clark explained clearly enough the basis for the anti-Semitism prevalent in the Negro ghettos. It was, he said, a special variant of antiwhite feeling, encouraged by the more direct and immediate contact that Negroes had with Jews than with other whites, and encouraged as well by the inferior position of Jews in American society, which permitted the Negro to find in the luxury of anti-Jewishness one of his few means of identifying with the American majority. Two years later, also in *Commentary*, the young James Baldwin told ·the same story in one of his first published articles,[2] underlining the point with his elegant acidity: "But just as a society must have a scapegoat, so hatred must have a symbol. Georgia has the Negro and Harlem has the Jew." One still feels the shock of that cold ending: is *that* what the Jew was to Harlem in 1948?

If, however, we knew decades ago that the ironic historic confrontation of Jew (as landlord, merchant, housewife, businessman) with Negro (as tenant, customer, servant, and worker) in the North had produced hatred on the part of many poor and uneducated Negroes, we now have to record two new developments in this confrontation. First, the well of ill-feeling has moved upward to include a substantial part of the Negro leadership, mainly some of the newer leaders thrown up in the North by the civil rights revolution; and second, Jewish feeling toward the Negro has undergone changes of its own.

There is little question that this feeling has never been hatred. It has ranged from passionate advocacy of Negro rights by Jewish liberals (and Communists and Socialists too), through friendly cooperation on the part of Jewish leaders who saw

Negroes as allies in the fight for common goals, to a less effective but fairly widespread good will on the part of ordinary Jews. The hatred of poor Negroes for Jews was not reciprocated by Jews; in the way that Harlem "needed" the Jew, the Lower East Side, Brownsville, and Flatbush perhaps needed the *goy*, but they never needed the Negro. If there was prejudice against Negroes (and, of course, there was), it was part of the standard Jewish ethnocentrism which excluded all outsiders. The businesslike adoption of the norms of behavior of the white world (in refusing to rent to Negroes in New York, or to serve them in department stores in the South) was just that — businesslike rather than reflecting a deeply held prejudice. The Irish had had experiences that had taught many of them to dislike or hate Negroes: their competition with Negroes for the worst jobs in the early days of immigration, their antagonism to a Civil War draft that forced them to fight — as they thought — for Negroes. But the Jews had never come into direct competition with Negroes, in North or South. The tenant or customer might hate the landlord or storekeeper — the feeling was not mutual.

In the North, then, in the late 1940s and the 1950s, well-staffed and well-financed Jewish organizations usually had the support of much more poorly staffed and poorly financed Negro organizations in fighting for legislation that advanced the interests of both groups, even though they stood on very different steps in the economic and occupational ladder. For the same law permitted a Jew to challenge exclusion from a Fifth Avenue cooperative apartment and a Negro to challenge exclusion from a much more modest apartment building.

This situation is now changing. As the Negro masses have become more active and more militant in their own interests, their feelings have forced themselves to the surface; and Jewish leaders — of unions, of defense and civil rights organizations — as well as businessmen, housewives, and homeowners, have been confronted for the first time with demands from Negro organizations that, they find, cannot serve as the basis of a common effort. The new developments feed each other, and it would be impossible to say which came first. The resistance of Jewish organizations and individual Jews to such demands as preferential union membership and preferential hiring, and to the insistence on the primacy of integration over all other educational objectives, breeds antagonism among former Negro allies. The "white liberal," who is attacked as a false friend unwilling to support demands that affect him or his, and as probably prejudiced to boot, is generally (even if this is not spelled out) the white *Jewish* liberal—and it could hardly be otherwise, in view of the predominance of Jews among liberals, particularly in major cities like New York, Chicago, Philadelphia, and Los Angeles. This Jewish resistance, however, is often based not only on the demands themselves, but on a growing awareness of the depths of Negro antagonism to the kind of society in which Jews succeeded and which Jewish liberalism considers desirable.

One important new element in the situation, then, is that the feelings of the Negro masses have become politically relevant and meaningful in a way that they were not in 1935 or 1943. In those years, too, the Negroes of Harlem rioted, and broke the shop windows of the Jewish-owned stores, and looted their contents. But these earlier outbreaks—which in terms of the feelings involved were very similar to the outbreaks of last summer—were not tied up with a great civil rights movement. While the Negro leaders of today could deny all responsibility for such outbreaks, and could point out that this kind of hoodlumism had been endemic in the Negro ghettos since the depression, the growing tendency toward militancy in the civil rights movement meant that the leadership would inevitably be charged with responsibility—as they were not in 1935 and 1943 (except for Communists and race radicals). Moreover, the feelings of the Negro masses were now in greater measure *shared* by middle-class and white-collar and leadership groups. And this is also strikingly new.

For the Negro no longer confronts the Jew only as tenant, servant, customer, worker. The rise of Negro teachers, social workers, and civil servants in considerable numbers means another kind of confrontation. Once again, the accidents of history have put the Jew just ahead of the Negro, and just above him. Now the Negro teacher works under a Jewish principal, the Negro social worker under a Jewish supervisor. When

HARYOU (Harlem Youth Opportunities Unlimited) issued its huge report, *Youth in the Ghetto,* in the summer of 1964, only one of some 800 school principals in the New York system was a Negro, and only four of the 1,200 top-level administrative positions in the system were filled by Negroes! But as significant as these ridiculously tiny percentages is the fact that most of the *other* principalships and administrative positions were filled by Jews who poured into the educational system during the 1930s and are now well advanced within it, while thousands of Negroes, comparative latecomers, have inferior jobs. And what makes the situation even worse is that part of the blame for the poor education of Negro children can be placed on this white (but concretely Jewish) dominance. As the HARYOU report states (though indicating that this is only one possible point of view):

Public school teachers in New York City come largely from the city colleges, which have a dominant pupil population from a culture which prepares the child from birth for competition of a most strenuous type. These students are largely white, middle-class, growing up in segregated white communities where, by and large, their only contact with the Negro finds him in positions of servitude . . . Responsible positions, even within the neighborhood schools, are in the main held by people who perceivably differ from [the Negro pupils]. The dearth of Negro principals, assistants and supervisors is a most glaring deficit and one which leaves a marked, unwholesome effect upon the child's self-image . . . The competitive culture from which the bulk of the teachers come, with the attendant arrogance of intellectual superiority of its members, lends itself readily to the class system within the school . . . which in effect perpetuates the academic preeminence of the dominant group.

This new confrontation of middle-class Negroes, recently arrived at professional status, with middle-class Jews, who got there earlier and hold the superior positions, is most marked in New York, because of its huge Jewish population. It is there that the animus against the white liberal reaches its peak, and where the white liberal tends most often to be a Jew. But the confrontation is only somewhat less sharp in Philadelphia, Detroit,

Chicago, Los Angeles, and other cities with substantial Jewish populations. Perhaps the only place where the term "white liberal" is not used to mean the "Jewish liberal" is in San Francisco. The reason is that radicalism in San Francisco has a peculiarly non-Jewish base in Harry Bridges's International Longshoreman's and Warehouseman's Union; moreover, the Jewish group there contains many early settlers who are closely identified with non-Jewish San Franciscans of the same class and origin. Indeed, in San Francisco, there was never even a Jewish ghetto available to become transformed into a Negro ghetto; yet the fragment of a Jewish ghetto that did exist is now part of a Negro ghetto.

And this brings us to yet another new twist in the historic confrontation between Jew and Negro. I do not know why in so many American cities Negro settlement has concentrated in the very areas that originally harbored Jewish immigrants. There are possibly three reasons. First, Jews have on the whole favored apartment-house living, and apartments provide cheap quarters for newcomers. Second, Jews have been economically and geographically more mobile than other immigrant groups who arrived around the same time (for example, Italians and Poles), and consequently their neighborhoods have opened up to Negroes more rapidly. And finally, Jews have not resorted to violence in resisting the influx of new groups—in any case, most of them were already moving away.

But as Jews kept retreating to the edges of the city and beyond, the Negroes, their numbers and in some measure their income rising, followed—in recent years, as far as the suburbs. This is a problem, of course, for the same reasons that it is a problem for any white property-owner or homeowner: fear of the declining real-estate values that can be occasioned by a flight of panicky white residents; fear of changes in the neighborhood affecting the schools and the homogeneity of the environment. Obviously, Jews are not the only people caught up in such concerns; but since migrating urban groups generally follow radial paths outward (a pattern that is not so marked in New York, broken up as it is by rivers and bays, but that is very clear in inland cities like Detroit, Chicago, Cleveland, and Cincinnati), this new Negro middle class has moved into Jewish areas far more often than statistical probability alone would lead one to expect. Here again, therefore, a novel type of tension — specifically involving middle-class groups and homeowners — has been introduced

In a number of suburbs Jewish homeowners of liberal outlook have banded together in an effort to slow down the outflow of whites and thus create an integrated community (which, of course, also helps to maintain the value of their homes). But to create an integrated community not only means slowing down the outflow of whites; it also means reducing the influx of Negroes. In some cases these good — from the Jewish point of view — intentions (and they usually *are* good) have looked, from the Negro point of view, like just another means of keeping Negroes *out*, but this time using the language of liberalism instead of race prejudice. We are all acquainted with the paranoia of persecuted minorities, and many jokes that used to be told of Jews (for example, the one about the stutterer who could not get a job as a radio announcer because of "anti-Semitism") could now be told of Negroes — and would be just as true.

All this forms part of the background of Negro-Jewish relations today. But in the immediate foreground are the new demands that have come to be made in the North and West by the civil rights movement. Negroes are acutely aware of how few of their young people even now get into the good colleges, and they see as a critical cause of this the small proportion of Negroes in good public elementary and high schools; they are acutely aware that their large-scale entry into the ranks of the clerks and typists of our huge public bureaucracies has not been accompanied by any equivalent entry into the higher positions of the civil service; they know that their new junior executive trainees in the large corporations are matched by hardly any Negroes higher up in these great private bureaucracies. And since political pressure and organized group pressure have been effective in breaching segregation in the South, and in bringing about some of these entries in the North, they see no reason why similar pres-

sures should not be equally effective in making up the deficiencies that continue to be apparent. If whites say, "But first you
must earn your entry—through grades, or examinations," Negroes, with a good deal more knowledge of the realities of American society than foreign immigrants used to have, answer, "But
we know how *you* got ahead—through political power, and
connections, and the like; therefore, we won't accept your pious
argument that merit is the only thing that counts."

There is some truth to this rejoinder; there is, I believe,
much less truth when it is made to Jews. For the Jews have, indeed, put their faith in the abstract measures of individual merit
—marks and examinations. Earlier, before school grades and
civil-service test scores became so important, they depended on
money: it, too, could be measured, and the man who had it
could manage without any ties of blood or deep organic connection to the ruling elite of the land. In addition to this, the reason
merit and money have been the major Jewish weapons in overcoming discrimination, rather than political power and pressure, is that only in exceptional cases (New York City is one of
them) have they had the numbers to make the latter means of
advancement effective. As a result, their political skills are poor
(where are the master Jewish politicians in America?), but their
ability to score the highest grades in examinations and to develop money-getting competence still shows no sign of declining.

The ideologies that have justified the principle of measur-
able individual merit and the logic of the market place, where
one man's money is equal to any other man's, have always appeared to Jews, even more than to other Americans, almost self-
evidently just and right. And the *New York Times*, which most
of the newer Negro leaders dislike intensely, expresses this
liberal ideology in its purest form. The *Times* has never been
tolerant toward the accommodations that others have sometimes seen as necessary in our mixed and complex society—the
balanced ticket, for example, which has nothing to do with the
abstract principles of merit.*

---

*I refer of course to the editorial opinions of the *New York Times* of the early 1960s.

But the liberal principles—the earlier ones arguing the democracy of money, the newer ones arguing the democracy of merit—that have been so congenial to Jews and so much in their interest are being increasingly accepted by everyone else nowadays under the pressures of a technological world. We are moving into a diploma society, where individual merit rather than family and connections and group must be the basis for advancement, recognition, achievement. The reasons have nothing directly to do with the Jews, but no matter—the Jews certainly gain from such a grand historical shift. Thus Jewish interests coincide with the new rational approaches to the distribution of rewards.

It is clear that one cannot say the same about Negro interests. And so the Negroes have come to be opposed to these approaches. But when Negroes challenge—as they do in New York—the systems of testing by which school principals and higher officials in the educational bureaucracy are selected and promoted, they are also challenging the very system under which Jews have done so well. And when they challenge the use of grades as the sole criterion for entry into special high schools and free colleges, they challenge the system which has enabled Jews to dominate these institutions for decades.

But there is another and more subtle side to the shift of Negro demands from abstract equality to group consideration, from color-blind to color-conscious. The Negroes press these new demands because they see that the abstract color-blind policies do not lead rapidly enough to the entry of large numbers of Negroes into good jobs, good neighborhoods, good schools. It is, in other words, a group interest they wish to further. Paradoxically, however, the ultimate basis of the resistance to their demands, I am convinced—certainly among Jews, but not Jews alone—is that they pose a serious threat to the ability of other groups to maintain *their* communities.

In America we have lived under a peculiar social compact. On the one hand, publicly and formally and legally, we recognize only individuals; we do not recognize groups—whether ethnic, racial, or religious. On the other hand, these groups exist in actual social fact. They strongly color the activities and lives of most of our citizens. They in large measure determine an individual's fate through their control of social networks which tend to run along ethnic, racial, and religious lines. Even more subtly, they determine a man's fate by the culture and values they transmit, which affect his chances in the general competition for the abstract signs of merit and money.

This is not an easy situation to grasp. On the one hand (except for the South) there is equality — political equality, equal justice before the law, equal opportunity to get grades, take examinations, qualify for professions, open businesses, make money. This equality penetrates deeper and deeper into the society. The great private colleges now attempt to have nationally representative student bodies, not only geographically, but socially and economically and racially. The great private corporations have reluctantly begun to accept the principle that, like a government civil service, they should open their selection processes and their recruiting procedures so that all may be represented. On the other hand, these uniform processes of selection for advancement, and the pattern of freedom to start a business and make money, operate not on a homogeneous mass of individuals, but on individuals as molded by a range of communities of different degrees of organization and self-consciousness, with different histories and cultures, and with different capacities to take advantage of the opportunities that are truly in large measure open to all.

Here we come to the crux of the Negro anger and the Jewish discomfort. The Negro anger is based on the fact that the system of formal equality produces so little for Negroes. The Jewish discomfort is based on the fact that Jews discover they can no longer support the newest Negro demands, which may be designed from the Negro point of view to produce equality for all, but which are also designed to break down this pattern of communities. We must emphasize again that Jewish money, organizational strength, and political energy have played a major role in most cities and states in getting effective law and effective administration covering the rights to equal opportunity in employment, housing, and education. But all this past cooperation loses its relevance as it dawns on Jews, and others as well, that many Negro leaders are now beginning to expect that the pattern of their advancement in American society will take quite a different form from that of the immigrant ethnic groups. This new form may well be justified by the greater sufferings that have been inflicted on the Negroes by slavery, by the loss of their original culture, by their deliberate exclusion from power and privilege for the past century, by the new circumstances in American society which make the old pattern of advance (through formal equality plus the support of the group) less effective today. But that it *is* a new form, a radically new one, for the integration of a group into American society, we must recognize.

In the past, the established groups in American society came to understand, eventually, that the newer groups would not push their claims for equality to the point where the special institutions of the older groups would no longer be able to maintain their identity. There were certainly delicate moments when it looked as if the strongly pressed and effectively supported Jewish demand for formal equality, combined with Jewish wealth and grades, would challenge the rights of vacation resorts, social clubs, and private schools of the old established white Protestant community to serve as exclusive institutions of that community. But after a time the established Protestant community realized there were limits to the demands of the Jews, as there were limits to the demands of the Catholics. They realized that Jews and Catholics could not demand the complete abolition of lines between the communities because they too wanted to maintain communities of their own. Most Jews wanted to remain members of a distinctive group, and regardless of how consistent they were in battering against the walls of privilege, they always implicitly accepted the argument that various forms of division among people, aside from those based on the abstract criteria of money and achievement, were legitimate in America. Thus, when John Slawson of the American Jewish Committee argued against the discriminatory practices of various social clubs, he did not, I believe, attack the right of a group to maintain distinctive institutions. He argued rather that

Jews in banking or high politics could not conduct their *business* if they were not accepted as members of these clubs. He did not attack social discrimination as such — he attacked it because of its political and economic consequences and suggested it was abetting economic and political discrimination. The grounds he chose for his attack are revealing, for they indicate what he felt were the legitimate claims that one group in American society could raise about the way the other groups conducted their social life.

Now it is my sense of the matter that with the Negro revolution there has been a radical challenge to this pattern of individual advancement within an accepted structure of group distinctiveness. The white community into which the Negro now demands full entrance is not actually a single community — it is a series of communities. And all of them feel threatened by the implications of the new Negro demand for full equality. They did not previously realize how much store they set by their power to control the character of the social setting in which they lived. They did not realize this because their own demands generally did not involve or imply the dissolution of the established groups: they never really wanted to mingle too closely with these established groups. They demanded political representation — which assumed that the group continued. They demanded the right to their own schools, or (like the Catholics today) support for their own schools — which again proceeded from the assumption of group maintenance. They demanded equal rights in employment, in education, in housing. But as a matter of fact many of their jobs were held in business enterprises or in trades controlled by members of their own group. Many of them set up their own educational institutions to create the kind of higher education they thought desirable for their young people. If freedom of housing became an issue on occasion, such freedom was nevertheless used as much to create voluntary new concentrations of the group as to disperse it among other people.

The new Negro demands challenge the right to maintain these subcommunities far more radically than the demands of any other group in American history. As Howard Brotz has pointed out,[3] the exclusion of the Negro from his legitimate place in American society was so extreme, so thoroughgoing, so complete, that all the political energy of the Negro has been directed toward beating down the barriers. The corollary of this exclusive focus is that most Negro leaders do not see the value of separate institutions, residential concentration, or a ban on intermarriage. Or rather, the only thing that might justify such group solidarity is the political struggle itself—the struggle against all barriers. What other groups see as a value, Negroes see as a strategy in the fight for equal rights.

We have become far more sophisticated in our understanding of the meaning of equality, far more subtle in our understanding of the causes of inequality. As a result, political equality alone—which the Negro now enjoys in most parts of the country—is considered of limited importance. The demand for economic equality is now not the demand for equal opportunities for the equally qualified: it is the demand for equality of economic *results*—and it therefore raises such questions as why some businesses succeed and others fail, and how people are selected for advancement in large organizations. When we move into areas like that, we are not asking for abstract tolerance, or a simple desisting from discrimination. We are involving ourselves in the complex relationships between people, and we are examining the kinds of ties and judgments that go to make up our American subcommunities. Or consider the demand for equality in education, which has also become a demand for equality of *results*, of *outcomes*. Suppose one's capacity to gain from education depends on going to school with less than a majority of one's own group? Or suppose it depends on one's home background? Then how do we achieve equality of results? The answers to this question and many similar ones suggest that the deprived group must be inserted into the community of the advantaged. For otherwise there is no equality of outcome.

The force of present-day Negro demands is that the subcommunity, because it either protects privileges or creates inequality, *has no right to exist.* That is why these demands pose a quite new challenge to the Jewish community, or to any sub-community. Using the work of Oscar Handlin and Will Herberg, the Jewish community has come up with a convenient defense of Jewish exclusiveness — namely, that everyone else is doing it, too. The thrust of present-day Negro demands is that everyone should *stop* doing it. I do not interpret Jewish discomfort over this idea as false liberalism — for Jewish liberalism, even if it has never confronted the question directly, has always assumed that the advancement of disadvantaged groups, both Jews and others, would proceed in such a way as to respect the group pattern of American life. But the new Negro leaders believe Negroes cannot advance without a modification of this pattern. The churches, one of the major means by which group identities maintain themselves, are challenged by the insistent Negro demand for entry into every church. And if the Jews, because their church is so special, are for the moment protected against this demand, they are not protected against demands for entry on equal footing into other institutions which are the true seats of Jewish exclusiveness — the Jewish business, for example, the Jewish union, or the Jewish (or largely Jewish) neighborhood and school. Thus Jews find their interests and those of formally less liberal neighbors becoming similar: they both have an interest in maintaining an area restricted to their own kind; an interest in managing the friendship and educational experiences of their children; an interest in passing on advantages in money and skills to them.

The Negro now demands entry into a world, a society, that does not exist, except in ideology. In that world there is only one American community, and in that world, heritage, ethnicity, religion, race are only incidental and accidental personal characteristics. There may be many reasons for such a world to come into existence — among them the fact that it may be necessary in order to provide full equality for the Negroes. But

if we do move in this direction, we will have to create communities very different from the kinds in which most of us who
have already arrived — Protestants, Catholics, Jews — now live.

[1964]

3

E. Franklin Frazier and

the Negro Family

IN HIS PREFACE to E. Franklin Frazier's *The Negro Family in the United States*, on its first publication in 1939, Ernest W. Burgess called it "the most valuable contribution to the literature of the family since the publication, twenty years ago, of *The Polish Peasant in Europe and America*." The passage of twenty-seven years has in no way reduced the stature of this classic work; on the contrary, viewing it now in the new contexts of the Negro revolution and the convulsive response to it of American society and government, we must give Frazier's study even higher praise than Burgess gave it. Written during American sociology's only golden age, it is to my mind one of the most substantial and enduring works of that age. Ironically, many efforts to establish a timeless theoretical framework for sociology and social analysis now appear to us dated and remote. This book, concretely based on the realities of Negro family life, reconstructed eclectically from personal accounts, literature, statistics, and observation and direct experience, has lost nothing in immediacy and relevance.[1]

Indeed, if anything, it has gained. As I write, the *New York Times* reports that the President and his advisers now see the Negro family as a key element in their efforts to wipe out the gap between the social, educational, and economic positions of Negro and white. Conducting a conference on the Negro family in 1965, they will have no better text than Frazier; far from being supplanted, his book has scarcely been supplemented. Its major framework remains solid and structures all our thinking on the Negro family.

Indeed, Frazier's achievement is even greater than that suggested by the remarkable contemporaneity of this book. For in 1932, with the publication of *The Negro Family in Chicago* and *The Free Negro Family*, he had already worked out the main lines of his approach.[2] In these early works, he had to attack the crudities of contemporary sociologists and anthropologists who insisted on finding in the disorganization of the Negro family something primitive, either the "primitive" social structure of Africa or the "primitive" racial characteristics of the Negro. Frazier insisted that the social characteristics of the Negro family were shaped by social conditions, not by race or African survivals. He insisted, too, that one could not indiscriminately take statistics and statistical averages as an index of social disorganization or promiscuity or immorality. While he was more of a puritan in his sexual attitudes than some later anthropologists and sociologists who were more radically influenced by cultural relativism (this was true of W. E. B. DuBois, too), he nevertheless pointed to the great difference between the meaning of illegitimate births in the rural South and in the urban North. Frazier would not justify southern rural Negro family patterns as being simply an aspect of the "culture" of the group, neither better nor worse than the standards and practices of other people; but he insisted that whatever standards existed, whatever behavior we found, could be understood only in terms of the social conditions that had shaped them. The radical condemnation of Negro family life by whites reflected not only ignorance of a variety of patterns, equally well established, but an inability to see the extent to which matriarchy and illegitimacy were adaptations to social and economic conditions, and not necessarily damaging or unhealthy adaptations — though one could make no apology for the social and economic conditions.

In *The Negro Family in the United States*, Frazier displayed the full sequence of social conditions that had shaped the Negro family. Slavery was first. In slavery the African cultural patterns were totally destroyed, and what emerged was a chaos with only fragmentary patterns and structures, easily broken and just enough to ensure the raising of slave children. But even under slavery a stable Negro family, on an American model, was built up by free Negroes and slaves living under favorable conditions. Then there was the crisis of emancipation, with the maintenance and extension of the matriarchy that had emerged under slavery as the one stable element for a good part of Negro family life. After emancipation, too, the father-centered stable families of the free Negroes were extended on the basis of the ownership of property and new occupations. Then there came a third terrible crisis in the cities of the North, the crisis of the impact of urban conditions—crowding, crime, unemployment—with once again the emergence of stability in the form of middle-class Negro families and the families of the new industrial working class. This is the history of the Negro family, as Frazier structured and detailed it, and it has become part of our consciousness and understanding.

Beyond praising Frazier, however, we must place him in the context of the work in the social sciences since he wrote *The Negro Family in the United States*, and ask what additional questions, what further truths, have been suggested by this new work. There are a number of areas in which to my mind significant new material has been developed that we must take into account in considering the Negro family. There is first the development, from psychoanalytically influenced anthropology, of a view of the family in which it is seen as not only the product of social causes but as itself a significant and dynamic element in the creation of culture, social character, and social structure. I refer to the work associated with such names as Abram Kardiner, Erich Fromm, Ruth Benedict, Margaret Mead, David Riesman, and Ralph Linton. Certainly, all these writers agreed, the structure of the family could be seen in terms of causes that were neither racial nor evolutionary. A specific technological and economic background, a specific social order, created a certain kind of family. That family itself, however, was the support of the social structure. Children were socialized into certain values and patterns, and they maintained a society. Sometimes the culture the family supported was sharply structured, sometimes it barely seemed to have any defined structure at all. But behind these varying social forms were family structures, patterns of childrearing.

But the critical point is that this work introduced a complication into the analysis of the family that I think was not present in Frazier's work. Frazier hoped that changes in the Negro family would result from social and economic changes. The free Negro as against the slave, the Negro farmers as against the sharecroppers, the new working class and middle class as against the disorganized lower class: all these had created better family forms, and with further economic progress the weaknesses of the Negro family would be overcome. The newer, psychoanalytically influenced social science, on the other hand, emphasized the tight web of family, personality, culture, and society, and in so doing suggested that change in the family would be enormously difficult.

There is no real contradiction between Frazier's point of view and the point of view of social scientists whose emphasis was on the family as the creator rather than the product of social forms. Yet, it is impossible to overlook the differences in emphasis.

One difference was that from an anthropological orientation, with its strong emphasis on cultural relativism, it became difficult to make the moral judgments (and therefore the judgments concerning social action) that were relatively easy for Frazier to make. The anthropologist saw a variety of family types and cultures. Initially, this variety was explored and brought to our attention by liberal anthropologists, fighting both racism and evolutionary theories and arguing that no culture was "backward" or "primitive" — it was merely different. It is hard for us to see now how an emphasis on the tight and not easily changed web of family life, personality, and culture of a given society could be seen as progressive — for how could one intervene to change such a system? — but the point of the anthropologists was that we were probably culture-bound in emphasizing the need for this system to change in the first place and that this kind of analysis fought the racists by showing that the same racial types had radically different personalities, cultures, and societies, depending on the cultural system into which they were born.

It was not long, however, before it became clear that the potential for progressive social action in this orientation was rather limited. During World War II, the analysis of the relation between culture and personality shifted from harmless New Guinea tribes to the Germans and the Japanese, and after the war, to the Russians. The approach was also used on our own society, by scholars such as Erich Fromm and T. W. Adorno and his coauthors of *The Authoritarian Personality* to analyze the middle classes of Western society and to argue that they had a strong penchant for fascism.[3] At this point, it was clear that national and class antagonism could be bolstered by psychoanalytic and anthropological analyses of differences as well as by racial and evolutionary analyses.

But to return to the Negro family: From this new orientation, one could also argue against Frazier that he was simply being naive, moralistic, and culture-bound in his criticism of the Negro family. The Negro matriarchy, the acceptance of illegitimate children, the more frequent changing of spouses, the more casual discipline could be seen, not as wrong or the product of pathological conditions, but simply as culturally different, producing a different style of personality but one no less valuable. Indeed, if the middle-class child — as suggested by Erich Fromm, T. W. Adorno, and Arnold Green — suffered from some characteristic neuroses and psychopathologies, one could argue that the lower-class family, and the Negro lower-class family, was in some respects superior: it did not produce the complex of anxiety over success, cleanliness, sex, and the like. Thus, in the late 1930s and early 1940s, a good deal of work was done, identified particularly with the names of Allison Davis and R. J. Havighurst, that said something in favor of the lower-class family. It is true that less was claimed for the lower-class Negro family; for whatever degree of cultural relativism and anthropological romanticization existed, there was scarcely an American social scientist from the late 1930s on who was not in favor of radical changes in the political, economic, and social position of the Negroes in the United States. Nevertheless, one must see the dilemmas in the situation: to emphasize only the pathology of Negro life would lead to repulsion perhaps even to justification of the severe patterns of discrimination and suppression. To emphasize that there were virtues in lower-class life might lead to certain gains—for example, less dependence on the I.Q. test as a means of segregating Negro children. Thus, when Allison Davis emphasized that this test was culture-bound, his main objective was to modify the system of segregation by pointing to areas of achievement and fulfilment in which lower-class life might possess advantages over middle-class life. He was not arguing that lower-class Negroes did not need and demand social change. But the dilemma is apparent. If it was so good for them, why should we try to change it?

Frazier I think was more hardheaded, as well as more old-fashioned, as was W. E. B. Du Bois. It was all bad—the abandoned mothers, the roving men, the sexually experienced youth. The only thing that was good was that the mothers, in conditions that should never have existed, did their best by the children. Conditions of economic stability and social equality would change the family. And for Frazier there was no dilemma.

As a matter of fact, the next turn in the development of social research in this area tended to support him. The period of romanticization of lower-class life came to an end under the double impact of change in society and change in social science—and there is no question that the first was more important. The change in society was heralded by the explosion of independence movements in colonial areas after World War II. It became impossible to persuade new nations, impatient to become strong and rich, that their traditional societies had many virtues which they should preserve. Anthropologists might convince colonial administrators that natives should be undisturbed in maintaining their equally valid approach to the organization of social life, but they could not convince the leaders of new nations, who saw in the traditional patterns simply the backwardness that made them weak in international affairs. Thus the cultural relativistic stance in sociology and anthropology went into eclipse. The question now was: How do we get development? And social scientists followed suit, now picking up their leads from Weber as well as Freud and searching for the backgrounds that emphasized ambition, achievement, work, aspiration. In this perspective, of course, the lower-class family came out rather badly — it was studied only as a mine of potential raw materials, some of which might be fashioned into the psychological material useful for achievement. Thus the New England ethnic groups — Italian, Jewish, Yankee, Irish — served as the basis for a series of studies which found that some lower-class groups seemed to take to the achievement pattern better than others (B. C. Rosen, F. L. Strodtbeck). David C. McClelland and his collaborators ransacked the cultures of the world looking for clues to this pattern of achievement.

And, meanwhile, our own colonial problem rose in seriousness to become the major domestic issue in American life. Just as the cultures and psychologies of the peoples of the world were now studied from the point of view of determining how they might be made more equal economically and politically, so we began in a fragmentary way to study the culture and psychology of lower-class Negroes from the same point of view: What obstacles to equality are presented?

Obviously these new questions changed the perspective on the lower-class Negro family. What had been considered warmth and sensual expression and imagery now became emotional inconsistency, inability to defer gratification, and unrealistic fantasy. One presumes that beneath the varying social scientific perspectives was a single reality and that it was the points of view, not the Negro family itself, that were changing as we moved from the forties and fifties into the sixties. And yet it is very likely that the family itself was changing, too. In a situation in which Negroes saw that opportunities for economic and educational advancement were largely blocked, conceivably they adjusted to a low level of incomes in ways that permitted some degree of gratification and satisfaction. As opportunities began to open, satisfaction with the long-established preexisting level declined. Expectations rose faster than opportunities. When an all-embracing social struggle to open up more opportunities developed, engulfing larger and larger parts of the Negro community, then the new political and social situation in which the family found itself may also have changed the family. Its mood may well have changed to one of bitterness and anger.

In the shift from a view of the Negro family influenced by cultural relativism to one influenced by the paramount need for social mobility, the emphasis also shifted from the mother to the father, and in particular the absent father. Thomas F. Pettigrew, in his valuable *Profile of the Negro American*, has summarized the studies that suggest what disorders follow from the absence of fathers in a large percentage of Negro families: the women inevitably take over a masculine role in support and discipline; the children then have difficulty in establishing roles appropriate to their own sexes; the girls become more masculine, the boys more feminine.[4] Even without plunging into the complexities created for psychosocial development, one must observe the problems created by the absence of a male with a stable job that creates a link to some substantial part of society, supplying, in addition to income, knowledge of some part of the work world.

We do not of course find, in this new emphasis in social science on the obstacles to economic and social change, a single unified point of view. Middle-class status is still seen as a morally ambiguous objective. We find less romanticization of lower-class life. But, as James Baldwin has said, "Who wants to be integrated into a burning house?" The middle-class job, the competition, the suburban house with its high mortgage payments, the disciplining of the children to achieve in schools which themselves come under increasing criticism (as does the society these children are being trained to enter): all this is meant by the "burning house." Frazier himself was unhappy with the Negro middle class, as he made clear as early as 1939 in his chapter "The Brown Middle Class," which prefigures his much sharper £242attack on the Negro middle class in *Black Bourgeoisie*.[5] But there is a substantial difference between the perspectives of Frazier and contemporary radical critics of middle-class objectives. Frazier was attacking the Negro middle class for living beyond its means and powers, for aping a life it did not have the political or economic strength actually to achieve. He found nothing wrong with a life that emphasized work, stable family relationships, achievement. He objected to the fact that too many in the Negro middle classes were willing to settle for the shadow of that life, rather than the substance. Radical Negro writers today attack its substance.

Inevitably, in our view of the Negro family, we will be torn between an orientation that finds something positive and unique in its distinctive features, something to be preserved and valued, and an orientation that emphasizes the elements that seem to hold back occupational advance. We find on the one hand the work of Frank Riessman, who in his book on the culturally deprived child describes a special mode of learning that is characteristic of lower-class children, and lower-class Negro children, and to which we should adapt our schools and teachers.[6]   On the other hand, we have the arguments of teachers who insist that learning cannot begin until a child has a vocabulary. For them the lower-class child does not have a different but equal culture: he has a culture deficient in some vital elements for education. There is no question which side Frazier would be on.

Nor is there any question about which side the Negro community and Negro parents are on. They want their children to read and to write and to do arithmetic as well and as early as white children. They may on occasion deny defensively that the failure of Negro children to do so has anything to do with their family background, but their concern is less to defend the cultural particularities of the Negro family—they may appreciate them less than whites—than to insist that the largest possible resources, sensitively and sympathetically deployed, be used to overcome the educational deficiencies of Negro children.

In 1964, during a conference on the Negro family held at the University of California at Berkeley, a leading social analyst and critic pointed out that most of the speakers took it for granted that the model we should attempt to set for all Negro families was the middle-class family. He himself questioned, as so many intellectuals do and for similar reasons, the worth-whileness of this goal. A Negro woman in the audience responded that it was up to Negroes to decide whether the goal was worthwhile or not: "Just give us the tickets; we'll decide where to get off."

This brings us to another striking difference between the situation in which Frazier studied and wrote and the situation in 1965. The difference is that, whatever the causes that produced the Negro family, whatever the consequences for the Negro family, Frazier expected little intervention by government in the attempt to transform the conditions of Negro life and the characteristics of the Negro family. He saw Negro advance — as did the other writers of this time — as dependent largely on Negro self-help. The Negro middle class was the creation of the Negroes themselves; the Negro working class was also based on the spirit of self-help and personal achievement in a society where it was assumed that economic advance was the responsibility of the individual. He writes in chapter 21: "It is in those well-organized workers' families where the entire family is working in order to purchase a home or that their children may obtain an education that one finds a spirit of democracy in family relations and a spirit of self-reliance on the part of the children." Indeed, the entire Chicago school of sociologists — Robert E. Park, Ernest Burgess, and their students, including Frazier — despite its liberalism and progressivism, shared the individualist values of the times, which assumed that government played only limited roles in shaping economic and social life and which therefore viewed social trends and developments as independent, almost natural movements, quite impervious to political influence. Thus the Chicago sociologists could study the transition of neighborhoods as different ethnic and racial groups moved through them and hardly consider whether this was good or bad, desirable or undesirable, and whether political forces should modify such movements in any way. Similarly, Frazier saw the development of the Negro family as in large measure shaped by Negro action (note his applause of a spirit of self-reliance in the passage quoted). Of course government had a role in establishing political equality, in maintaining prosperity, in

establishing sound social and educational services — but did it
have a role when it came to the structure of the Negro family?
Inevitably, reflecting his times, he saw a really very limited role
for government: "The very fact that the Negro has succeeded in
adopting the habits of life that have enabled him to survive in a
civilization based on laissez faire and competition, itself
bespeaks a degree of success in taking on the folkways and
mores of the white race. That the Negro has found within the
patterns of the white man's culture a *purpose in life* and a
significance for his strivings which have involved *sacrifices for
his children* and the *curbing of individual desires and impulses*
indicates that he has become assimilated to a new mode of life"
(italics added).

What a remarkable passage! The Negro is applauded for
surviving in a society based on laissez faire and competition, for
his strivings, for the curbing of individual desires and impulses,
for assimilating a new mode of life. By contrast of course his
failure to strive and to curb his impulses would be seen as *his*
failure rather than society's failure, though society — history —
would certainly have to share a good part of the blame. But
from a position based on the values of striving, competition,
and achievement, what perspective would Frazier have taken to
a White House conference on the Negro family, devoted to the
consideration of measures that would strengthen the family?
Certainly these passages — written in 1939 — did not reflect
Frazier's final view on the role of government in reshaping the
Negro family. But when we put together the terms "government" and "family," when we place in juxtaposition the most
public and formal part of our social life and the most intimate
and concealed part, we obviously must pause and consider
what *are* the relationships, what should be the relationships,
between government and family.

We know how such relationships have developed. Government has taken on responsibility for economic prosperity; it has
taken on responsibility, too, for seeing that every part of society, every group and class, shares in the prosperity. Now then,
if we assume that certain conditions for sharing in that prosperity must be set — the condition of minimal education, of respon-

sibility in work, of the achievement of limited skill — and if we then find that certain familial and social settings are not conducive to the achievement of these minimal conditions, then government becomes responsible in some measure for what goes on in the family.

There is another route by which government becomes related to family, which affects today many more Negro families than this route based on a governmental assumption of responsibility for a generally shared prosperity. Government much earlier took on a responsibility to see that no one who could not earn sufficient income starved; this then required an elaborate system of rules and regulations to determine what was a family, what was insufficient income, what was a minimal standard of living, and so on. In effect, the establishment of a welfare system places today a large proportion of Negro children under the investigative and regulative eye of government and inevitably deeply influences a substantial part of Negro family life.

Through the responsibility for welfare, then, and through the newer responsibility to maintain general prosperity, government is involved with the family. But this is a hazardous involvement. Do we know enough about family life and the significance of any kind of intervention within it to sanction a large effort to restructure or reform the lower-class Negro family? I doubt it. In the nature of the case, this is an area in which not all knowledge can be or should be used for public policy. There are parts of the society that are more legitimately subject to government intervention than the family — the economy, the educational system, the system of police and courts and prisons — and we may hope to influence the family through these institutions. We are now all enamored with the possibilities of social engineering. And yet there are limits to the desirable reach of social engineering.

Daniel P. Moynihan, Assistant Secretary of Labor under Presidents Kennedy and Johnson, once reported to me a meeting of high government officials dealing with the crisis of the low-income Negro in the United States, falling ever behind the better-educated middle class, white and Negro alike. He proposed as one immediate measure that might improve matters restoring two mail deliveries a day—in effect, creating fifty thousand new jobs in the postal service and perhaps fifty thousand new fathers of families for a community where they are too few. I think E. Franklin Frazier would have liked this form of social engineering, which left the structure of the Negro family to each family, but which set conditions that we know produce the opportunity for stability, better education, and higher income. While Frazier wrote his book well before the studies I have outlined that suggest the significance of the independent role of family structure in affecting the large social conditions of peoples and nations, in the end, for policy, it is his approach that is more valuable. We cannot interfere in the intimate spheres of life: we do not have the knowledge, and if we did, we should use it with restraint. We know that the family makes the social conditions. We know too that social conditions make the family. But it is the latter knowledge that is the basis of social policy. Or, as the Negro mother said, "Just give us the tickets; we'll decide where to get off."

[1965]

4

Ethnic Groups and Education:

Toward the Tolerance of Difference

HISTORY AND SOCIAL RESEARCH convince me there are deep and enduring differences between various ethnic groups, in their educational achievement and in the broader cultural characteristics in which these differences are, I believe, rooted; that these differences cannot be simply associated with the immediate conditions under which these groups live, whether we define these conditions as being those of levels of poverty and exploitation, or prejudice and discrimination; and that if we are to have a decent society, we must learn to live with some measure of group difference in educational achievement, to tolerate it, and to accept in some degree the disproportion in the distribution of rewards that may flow from differences in educational achievement.

I am not sure that we can actually do this: that the conflicts between liberty (which inevitably produces differences) and equality (which inevitably means their reduction) which have lain at the heart of American democracy can be compromised (and compromise is all we can hope for, and the best we can hope for) in any permanent and decent way. But at least a first step is to explore this dilemma.

As to the argument that there are deep and enduring differences in the degree to which different ethnic groups achieve educationally: To speak of the differences among groups is to raise incredibly difficult problems. The study of national and ethnic differences, which became popular during World War II and continued for some years after that war, fell into decline during the fifties. The excitement of the work of Ruth Benedict, Margaret Mead, Nathan Leites, Geoffrey Gorer, David Riesman, and others on national culture and values wore off. In part, people lost interest in the work on national differences because of the methodological excesses of some of the practitioners. The explanation of these differences in terms of child-rearing and various kinds of psychoanalytic and psychodynamic models seemed far-fetched. To establish the differences in the first place seemed difficult. To shift the techniques and theories that had been developed in the study of small isolated primitive groups to large, complex, and differentiated societies was questionable. There was also the serious problem of dislike and antagonism between nations that could be fanned when scholars of one nation analyzed the intimate life and resultant character of people of another. Thus, the studies of Germans, Japanese, and Russians in the early postwar period began to look embarrassing a few years later.[1]

I think in the end the attempt to define differences among groups in a global way, to specify the main trends of their culture and character, must always be in large part an exercise in literary and artistic skill and imagination. But this is much less true when we come to specific differences among groups living under similiar historical circumstances. I believe educational achievement represents such a specific area of difference, though still of course enormously complex, and the experience of ethnic groups in America provides a natural laboratory in which to study some of the enduring differences among groups and the specific mechanisms that make them up. The study of such specific areas of difference is in part an outgrowth of an interest in ethnic groups as such. In defining and exploring the differences among groups, certain areas of human experience seem particularly illuminating. One of the most illuminating, for example, is mental health — what symptoms are defined as abnormal, what diseases are recognized, how are they treated and responded to? The beginning of studies of ethnic differences in mental health owes as much to the desire to explore ethnic difference and its significance as such as it owes to the desire to learn something about mental health by looking at its cross-cultural manifestations.[2] Another such area is undoubtedly achievement in education.

There are some striking ethnic differences in educational achievement for which we have good evidence. One of the best documented (though still insufficiently for scholarly purposes) is that of American Jews (specifically Jews of East European origin), who since the turn of the century — that is, a period about midway between the onset of heavy East European immigration in the early 1880s and its end in the early 1920s — have shown a remarkable and disproportionate degree of educational achievement. For example, by the turn of the century East European Jews already dominated the free City College of New York, to which entrance was obtained at that time only by formal educational achievement.[3] Teachers in schools reported to researchers for the Immigration Commission that Jewish children almost uniformly did well in schools.[4] Jews, at a later stage, dominated lists of winners of New York State scholarships. While a simple summary of East European Jewish educational achievement is not easy to provide — since Jews are not identified in census returns — the case for Jewish educational achievement, from various kinds of statistical evidence, is overwhelming and generally taken for granted.

Perhaps even more striking is the achievement of the Japanese Americans. The contrast between these two immigrant groups could not be greater. The pre-immigrant experience of one is urban and small town, the other peasant and agricultural. One defined itself as a priest-people, and placed a high value on formal study of religious classics; the other defined itself as a peasantry of inferior status. In this country, one group settled in New York and other large cities, the other in the California countryside. One showed early evidence of educational achievement, the other was defined as an educational problem. But by 1950 (and this after a period in which the entire Japanese community had been uprooted, lost its property, been sent to concentration camps in the Western desert, suffered intense persecution, all this coming upon the heels of decades of discrimination and persecution), Japanese Americans were already the best-educated racial group in the state of California. Japanese Americans have been represented on the elite University of California campuses in proportions far greater than could be expected by chance.[5]

On the other side, certain ethnic groups have done poorly educationally—the case of the Italian Americans has been studied in some detail by Leonard Covello.[6]

All this is common knowledge. The question is, what does this mean? What do we make of it? One thing it means—and one reason why these differences have been studied—is that it leads us to suspect there must be differences in areas other than educational achievement that help explain educational achievement. If large numbers of Jews and Japanese Americans go to college, we are by that token interested in why this phenomenon arises, what factors in family structure, value teaching, disciplinary practices, goals set before children, the role of voluntary organizations, and so on might explain it, and what thereby we might learn about the *group*. These educational differences help support the argument that there are significant cultural differences among groups. And in order to support the argument of the importance of cultural differences it is important to examine groups that have received no particular support from the general American environment (who have indeed been subjected to various degrees of discrimination, prejudice, and persecution, such as the Japanese and the Jews) because then the argument as to distinctive cultural reasons for high educational achievement becomes all the more powerful.

A second question arises—are these really cultural differences, or are they genetic, racial differences? The study of genetic racial differences went into eclipse, for political as well as scientific reasons, with the rise of Hitler. It has led a shadowy and almost underground existence since. The analysis of genetic differences among groups as a basis for educational achievement has suddenly achieved both new notoriety and a greater measure of scientific respectability as a result of the work of Arthur Jensen.[7] I think we can for the purposes of this chapter avoid such disputed ground, because the differences among ethnic groups, to my mind, need owe nothing to genetic differences. We have a good way to go before we sufficiently expose the cultural and social background of the varying educational achievement of American ethnic groups. Two such valuable works as Mark Zborowski's *Life Is With People*[8] and Leonard Covello's *The Social Background of the Italo-American School Child* assume that cultural differences with no relation to genetic factors can be taken as sufficient explanation. We need more work of this kind. We do not understand well enough how the social and cultural differences that we hypothesize play some role in leading to educational differences actually work. At this stage, to my mind, it is hardly necessary to resort to genetic differences. But I also believe we cannot rule possible genetic factors out of court and refuse to give them any hearing or status. For myself, my interest and concern is with the cultural differences. I feel they are more accessible to study and are more proximate as "causes" that permit us to understand differences in educational achievement. They are attractive on other grounds — they will not raise the fierce passions and the political dangers that we know are inherent in racial, genetic explanation of group difference. On the other hand, we know well enough by now that scholars will not escape political attack even if they restrict themselves to cultural and social differences. At this point in our history, to discuss cultural and social differences among groups opens one to the charge of "racism" almost as much as if one discusses genetic bases of difference. Consider the case of Daniel P. Moynihan.[9]

There is another and somewhat disputed reason why one may prefer to emphasize at this stage social and cultural reasons for differences in educational achievement rather than genetic reasons. If we are interested in raising levels of educational achievement in certain groups it seems reasonable to assume that social and cultural factors that hamper educational achievement may be more accessible to policy intervention than genetic factors. Yet there are problems to this approach. First of all, if we deal with causes that are very intimate, rooted in family culture, for example, it is not easy to see how cultural factors may be any more accessible to intervention than genetic. Secondly, if we deal with such intimate factors in public discussion we inevitably raise a powerful defensive reaction. No one—except perhaps for Jewish novelists—is going to accept coolly or objectively an analysis of his family structure as being damaging and defective in producing some commonly agreed on valuable objective. Either it will be denied that the family is defective in this way, or it will be denied that the hitherto thought-to-be-desirable objective that is hampered by that family structure is indeed desirable.

We have seen both reactions in the case of the question of the Negro family and its relationship to educational and occupational achievement. Nevertheless, despite the political dangers that accompany any discussion of group differences, it has generally been accepted that to emphasize social and cultural factors means to be more "liberal," to be more positive about change and more optimistic that it can occur, than to emphasize genetic factors. This was certainly the understanding of Franz Boas, Ruth Benedict, and other anthropologists when they opposed racial interpretations of cultural differences. And yet, there are ambiguities. The cultural differences analyzed may be so deep-going, so integrated in a complex supportive structure, that it may be scarcely possible to see what policy action might change them. How would one have changed Kwakiutl culture —or Hopi, for that matter? (For further discussion of this point, see Chapter 3). And beyond any political reasons for preferring social and cultural explanations to genetic and racial ones, there remains the question of scientific truth. The fact may be, as Jensen argues, that the social and cultural factors contribute only a small part of the variance or difference. Yet it may also be the part we can get at.

Beyond the "conservative" or "reactionary" racial explanation, and the "liberal" social and cultural explanation, there lies yet another possibility—the economic and political explanation, which is perhaps best called "radical." This would argue that the genetic differences are nonexistent or irrelevant, that the cultural differences are epiphenomenal, that only political and economic differences (in wealth, power, and status) lead to the differences among ethnic groups — and that these can be changed, and not by the subtle measures of social policy whereby liberals might try to modify differences in social structure and cultural orientation. How much guidance science and scholarship can give us in determining which of these interpretations we select is an open question.

A third question arises. What is the importance, after all, of the differences in educational achievement and the presumed differences (let us grant for the sake of the discussion they are social and cultural) on which they are based? The argument as to the importance of educational achievement is too obvious to rehearse. These days it is based on such grounds as the importance of skills and capacities to achieve a decent income and a satisfying occupation and the economic resources for a good life. Somewhat muted today is the argument that skilled manpower is needed for national economic development and military strength. Still further in the past (and yet perhaps to be revived) is the argument that educational achievement is an important part of personal fulfillment, giving one the powers and capacities (and not in this case economic, but cultural and political) to lead the good life as a member of the good society.

But very powerful arguments today attack the notion of educational achievement as a desirable objective, and by extension the presumed desirability of the cultural and personal traits that make it possible. Certainly there is little need to explore the recent devastating criticisms of American national policy — many critics today would consider it desirable that American economic and political power were less than it is. There is a powerful attack, though to my mind less well founded, on the need or desirability of every individual taking up productive economic work in an affluent society. There is even an attack on the idea that schools as now constituted can do anything but thwart the personal fulfillment of a free individual and the creation of a good society.[10]

Since these critical views are so widespread, it is understandable that those traits that presumably lead to educational achievement should also be subjected to searching criticism. Thus the argument that educational achievement is based on some inherent valuable capacity has been attacked. Perhaps, the attackers suggest, it is based on the exaggerated overdevelopment of some capacities and the suppression of other capacities. Suppose educational achievement is based not on differences of intellectual capacity but on differences in motivation, in ambition, in work habits. Suppose it is based on differential ability to adapt to the environment of schools and to the desired expectations of teachers — which are various and only one of which is intellectual capacity and creativity.

Educational achievement might then relate less to intellectual capacity than to the ability to make use of schools and what they have to offer so as to achieve various desired ends — money, position, prestige, and so on. Or perhaps we have yet another kind of relationship between personal traits and educational achievement, one in which educational achievement comes as the consequence of certain uncontrollable or unconscious trends of character, for example, docility, the desire to please, the preference for passive sitting as against active physical movement, and so on.

Obviously educational achievement can be seen in a variety of ways, and one will judge the ethnic differences that seem to be related to it differently as one judges educational achievement. If one sees it as the consequence of an ability to tolerate a repressive and authoritarian environment, one will have one point of view. If one sees it as the ability to make use of a variety of environments of varied qualities for instrumental ends, one will have another point of view — depending on how one judges the ends. If one considers it the simple consequence of abilities and talents, one will have yet another point of view. There are other possibilities.

While I share in some degree all three of these interpretations, I lean most strongly to the last — capacity determines achievement; and next to the second — a strong desire for the things educational achievement can give determines achievement; and least to the first — uncontrollable traits of character determine achievement. And while I see some virtue in such arguments as those of Robert Theobald and others that the puritan ethic or work ethic as taught in the schools unfits people for the society they are entering, I think this a rather exaggerated and distorted argument.[11] I believe what most people want from their lives (and legitimately want) requires, for as long as we can look ahead, a society in which there are more opportunities in the form of useful and satisfying work than there are people to fill them. I think of these wants not only in terms of gross consumer needs that are now attacked by young radicals in such countries as Germany and France, as well as in the United States, but in terms of needs for education, for cultural activity, for knowledge, for health, for recreation — all of which demand enormous numbers of trained people. Even the desires for consumer goods are hardly as gross as radical critics think they are. French workers, many of whom lived without indoor baths and toilets, were mystified by the student radicals' attack on "the consumer society." American workers, who might still look forward to a better house or to a hunting camp or a motorboat, might still be mystified. The demands for work in society are not determined only by the desire to minister to our pleasures but by the needs of a still overwhelmingly poor world, and by more than that, the simple satisfaction that men take in productive labor, something that one would hesitate to see go. Men who can avoid work often choose to define a work life for themselves — even if that consists of politics, charity, philanthropy, sports, or art collecting.

The fact that one can define humanly valuable and humanly satisfying work does not mean that most work men do today is of that kind; or that educational achievement is the best test for sorting out people for various kinds of higher education and work; or that the qualities needed for educational achievement in the kind of school system we have, which has been so devastatingly described by Edgar Friedenberg and others, are themselves more humanly valuable or desirable than their opposites. These are all serious questions, and to answer them involves serious and extended effort. And yet, to make a brief answer, I think that educational achievement in our schools reflects qualities that can be put to various valued uses, in varied settings. Thus, for example, those groups — to return to the ethnic problem — that do well in school do well in a variety of schools, for example, conservative and progressive, in a variety of educational systems. Now perhaps all existing schools tap only a narrow range of possible talents. It is still impressive that those groups that do well in one school system will very likely do well in another; that in effect they have talents that can be displayed in a range of settings. For example, take the case of East European Jews again—helpful not because they are the only group that shows high school achievement (I have pointed to the Japanese; there are also the Chinese, the Armenians, Asian Indians, and others), but because they live in a wide range of social settings. We will find that Jews do well in Soviet Russia, not only in the United States. Now the differences between the contemporary Russian school system and the American school system are fairly large, if not as large as those between either of them and the kinds of schools Paul Goodman and Edgar Friedenberg would like. In other words, if a group shows high achievement in a school system that some of us may consider unduly repressive and destructive of decent human traits, and gains an advantage in taking up work in a society some of us consider the same, this does not mean the same group will not show high achievement in a revolutionized school system, in a revolutionized society. Indeed, it probably means it will—because we have good evidence of the enduring character of differences in educational achievement under varied school systems and social systems.

It is this enduring quality to which I turn, and which is our most serious problem. If we believed—if we could believe—that educational achievement was fully a matter of concrete economic opportunities, concrete characteristics of the home, or if we believed that home differences in occupation or income could be compensated for fully by remedial measures in school, then we would not find differences in educational achievement among ethnic groups such a serious matter. We would find such differences; but we would believe that, if our measures for social reform succeeded in narrowing the gaps in occupation and income and style of life, as they have done to some extent, this would be a problem we could solve. The fact is that while there are correlations between occupation and income—class, in a word — and educational achievement (and these are terribly important correlations), class factors are not the only ones that affect school achievement. It is not because of the class characteristic of an ethnic group that it shows a certain distinct level of educational achievement. Ethnic factors play an independent role. When we say ethnic factors, we say cultural factors. We know by now something of what makes up the cultural factors relevant to educational achievement — language styles in the home, interaction between mother and child, the degree of encouragement and stimulation provided the child, expectations for him, and so on. These form a complex that is to some degree subject to intervention, but forceful intervention — perhaps of the kind that is being undertaken in Cuba and China, and was undertaken in Russia early in the revolution — would certainly conflict with other values we possess, values that favor individual privacy, familial integrity, and even the desirability of maintaining cultural styles and characteristics that may directly hurt educational achievement. Who, for example, was to determine that the tight South Italian family culture and peer group, which we know had negative consequences for educational achievement, was to be broken up in order to increase educational achievement?

One of the most impressive demonstrations of the distinctive character of ethnic styles as they affect capacity for educational achievement is in the work of Susan Stodolsky and Gerald Lesser.[12] By inference, their work also demonstrates how enduring these styles are. They have studied, using various tests, children of four New York ethnic groups — Chinese, Jews, Negroes, and Puerto Ricans — of two class levels. They find a distinctive pattern of mental ability (as defined by scores on their tests of reasoning, verbal ability, number ability, space conceptualization) for each group. The striking thing is that the profile is the same for lower-class and middle-class children in each group, although the level of performance is higher for middle-class children in each group. Since working-class children show the same pattern of performance as middle-class children of the same group, we can assume that when most Jewish children were working class rather than middle class (let us say forty years ago), they would have shown the same pattern of performance too.

A great deal of imaginative work is now under way on changing levels of achievement: for example, directly through new types of curricular materials, teaching approaches, changing school environments and administrative patterns, by going into the home, working with parents, working with children, and so on. It is scarcely possible to summarize all this. It is possible to take the position that differences in levels of ethnic achievement will crumble under the impact of such changes in education, if the changes are sufficiently extensive and sustained. But it is also possible, and this is the position the evidence to date leads me to, that these differences, which have endured under such varying social circumstances in the past (conditions of deprivation and of affluence, of prejudice and its absence, of rigid schools and permissive schools, of strict patterns of childrearing and loose patterns) will continue into the future, even if reduced.

The question that troubles me most is what attitude we are to take to these differences. Are we to view them as the consequences of ill will — that of teacher, administrator, the society in general? How elaborate are we to make our efforts to wipe them out, and how successful can we hope to be no matter how elaborate our efforts are? Are our measures to equalize to include the restriction of the opportunities of those groups that seem to find school achievement easy? Or are we to develop a set of values that accepts some measure of difference as desirable and expectable, and tries to mitigate the negative consequences that society imposes for such differences? These are hard questions, and they are questions to which we do not have answers. Nor are they questions for the United States alone. In every ethnically diverse society in which some groups show distinct patterns of educational achievement, whether in Malaya, Nigeria, Indonesia, India, or what have you, all these questions are real and live.

They are questions that can destroy a society, and we are already halfway there. We need not only to press our research on these differences, their origins, their extent, their causes, the measures that reduce them, but also to develop and strengthen a political and social philosophy that permits a society to accept them, to live with them, and to be stronger because of them.

[1969]

5

Blacks and Ethnic Groups:

The Difference and the Political

Difference It Makes

Do BLACKS in this country suffer from a unique prejudice and discrimination that we can sum up under the general heading "racism"? Or do the prejudice and discrimination they suffer form part of a common pattern that has also affected white ethnic groups— a general ethnocentrism? Or is it part of a quite different complex, a general racism directed toward all non-white races but not toward white immigrant and ethnic groups? Or does the pattern include not *all* other nonwhite races but only peoples colonized by Americans: American Indians, Mexicans, Puerto Ricans, Filipinos, Samoans, perhaps, and others?

When we consider black deprivation in this country, we are presented with a variety of models from which to interpret and understand it. I have suggested four. There undoubtedly are others. The issue is not one for interpretation and understanding alone, for it is clear that the interpretation one selects will affect one's political stance and one's involvement in practical measures. There is a range of possibilities, which can be placed along one continuum. At one extreme, we can see black experience as unique, shaped by the historical experience of African slaves and free men in this country. At the other extreme, we can see blacks as one of a number of groups that have suffered from the prejudice and discrimination that have affected in some measure every distinct ethnic and racial group in this country. Other interpretations are in the middle of the continuum: there are those linking the fate of blacks in this country to that of other racial groups; and there are those linking it to that of other groups, whether of different races or not, that have had a colonial relationship to the United States.

On the reasons for black deprivation scholarly opinion is divided, and popular opinion, white and black, is also divided. Members of white ethnic groups say, "We worked hard and suffered from discrimination, and we made it. Why don't they?" And blacks retort, "You came after us and were nevertheless favored above us and given all the breaks, both when we were in slavery and since." It is a question that cannot be asked without arousing emotions so strong that one wonders just how far scholarship will be allowed to go on this issue. In this chapter I would like first to discuss some of the implications for policy and politics of the different views one can take on this issue and second to address the issue directly.

POLITICAL IMPLICATIONS

The political significance of black deprivation can be quite easily and simply set forth. There has been a process of what is variously called assimilation or integration of ethnic groups into this country. Without trying to elaborate definitions of these slippery terms, I may say that both suggest that a group once considered in some measure *outside* the polity, economy, and society is now considered *inside* the polity, economy, and society. For some time, most Negro leaders saw Negroes as outside and worked to get them inside. This formerly fairly uniform position of most prominent Negro organizations and spokesmen has been transformed since about 1965. Now, it is argued, to get inside, the way white ethnic groups have done, is either inconceivable, because of white opposition, or undesirable, because of black internal development. But if the path of assimilation or integration is rejected, difficult questions arise: What

will be the character of the resulting separatism? What will be its
legal status? What will be its relationship to land? What will be
its relationship to those who do not want to take on the status?
How will it affect relationships with the white majority?
Separatism can mean anything from a separate state to various
kinds of minority status or ethnic status. Thus the crucial nature
of the argument.

It is an argument of peculiar complexity, because relevant to
it are not only the history and social status of black Americans;
equally relevant are the history and status of white Americans
of different groups. Thus, whether we believe that blacks share
in some measure a position similar to that of white Americans
or whether we believe they do not, we must have in mind some
conception of what the status of white ethnic groups has been, is
now, and will be in our society. We cannot carry through a
comparison in which one term is left murky. I believe some of
the difficulty in dealing with black and white ethnic group comparisons is that we are not clear about ethnic status in this country. There are a number of points on which opinion diverges
sharply. Four are particularly important for this discussion: (1)
What is the *time scale* in which we view ethnic status? Is it temporary or enduring? If enduring, how long does it endure? (2)
What are the differences among white ethnic groups in political
power, in economic power, in social characteristics? Are these
differences important or minor? (3) If ethnic groups endure, in
some manifestation, with substantial differences in political and
economic power and in social characteristics, do they endure
and maintain these differences because of prejudice and discrimination, because of social, economic, and cultural characteristics which precede entry upon the American scene, or
because of characteristics which have in some degree emerged
on the American scene and which must be reckoned, in some
measure, as owing to choice? (4) What is the role of race in this
discussion? Does race change all the terms of the discussion so
that an ethnic group of a nonwhite race faces, for that reason
alone, a completely different situation and history?

One can settle these matters neither by fiat nor by reference
to authoritative studies and settled positions. Let me simply

summarize my own position.[1] Ethnic status may be enduring — more enduring than expected and more enduring for some
groups than for others. The status of English-speaking Canadians will merge rapidly into that of white Americans of English
origin; that of Italians will last longer; that of Jews, if history is
any guide, will last as long as any social identity. Ethnic groups
differ in political power, in economic power, in social characteristics. There is no common history for white ethnic groups, no
common status, though there are processes that in some degree
may be found in many groups. These differences are not simply
the result of differences in prejudice and discrimination alone,
though these play a role. They are the result, too, of cultural
differences created in other settings and of new differences that
arise in this country because of the complex interaction between
the pre-existing cultural characteristics, various degrees of prejudice and discrimination, the economic and political skills
characteristic of each group, the political and economic situation of the country and relevant parts of the country at the time
of arrival, and other elements. The line between white ethnic
groups and ethnic groups of other races does not determine their
fate. Racial identities can change their meaning. Italians and
Jews, considered "racially" different by Americans at the turn of
the century, are not so considered today. Southern Italians,
who were considered "racially" different from Northern Italians
fifty years ago, are not so considered today.[2] Neither in
America nor elsewhere are race and ethnicity categories so different that the processes that affect the assimilation and integration of ethnic groups change completely when groups of a different race are involved. Brazilians of African origin seem less
black as they rise in the social scale, and whites seem darker as
they go down the social scale. Moreover, groups physically un-
differentiable from the larger population may be singled out for
all the obloquy that has descended on members of the African
race in the United States. Thus, in Hitler's Germany, Germans
with one Jewish grandparent became subject to the status of
Jews — including, eventually, extermination — and in Japan, the
descendants of the old lower caste, the *eta* (now called the
burakumin), are subject to ostracism and severe social penalties

if their descent is discovered.[3] Thus one possible position on ethnicity and race, and the one I hold, is that they form part of a single family of social identities — a family which, in addition to races and ethnic groups, includes religions (in the Netherlands) and language groups (in Belgium and India). All these categories can be included in the most general term "ethnic groups," groups sharing a common history and experience and defined by descent, real or mythical.

At the other end of the spectrum from the position that sees similarities between the status of blacks and that of other groups are those positions which emphasize the differences. There, two approaches are possible. One is to emphasize the racial differences between blacks and whites, and perhaps between blacks and all other races. The other is to emphasize the significance of the colonized status, the status of slaves (in the case of Africans) or of derivation from subordinate colonized areas (in the case of some other groups). The latter approach has become increasingly popular in the last few years and encourages a perception of common interest (based on common status) among black Americans, Mexican Americans, Puerto Ricans, and American Indians.

The debate has grown. A key point in the history of the debate was the Kerner Commission's report, which devoted a chapter to the question of why the situation of blacks is different from that of white ethnic groups.[4] And since the publication of that report, the question has moved further into the arena of public debate and common consciousness. The recent flood of articles on and discussions of what are variously called the "white ethnic groups," the "working class and lower middle class," "the forgotten Americans," and "the other other America" indicates clearly that the comparison of experience, status, power, poverty, and affluence among different groups in American society is no longer a matter only for sociologists and persons with theoretical and scholarly concerns. It is a matter about which millions of Americans, drawing on their own experience — even if that experience is unrepresentative or distorted and misinterpreted in their minds — are coming to their own conclusions, conclusions sufficiently strongly felt that they affect elections and public policies. In 1968 I wrote, "We must consider the present crisis of the ghetto in the light of the experience of the groups that have gone before because the power to respond to Negro demands, to the problem of the ghetto, is in large measure in the hands of groups who themselves have had and can recall ghetto and slum experience."[5] This is still true.

THE SOCIAL SCIENTIST'S DILEMMA

The debate proceeds on a scholarly and popular level, among sociologists and other social scientists, and among all of us, white and black, engaged simply in living in America, and there are subtle and complex relationships between the two levels. Scholars are people, and people are in some measure scholars trying to find guidance in understanding their lives, their places in society, their groups, and their groups' places in society, from discussions, newspapers, magazine articles, books. As a result, the political consequences of the debate are important and have already deeply affected the way the debate is conducted among scholars. None of us, I hope, is so much a purist as to believe that scholarly work must be carried on in complete disregard of political consequences; in any case, I am not. The study of race and ethnic relations is perhaps the first field where a sober and judicious sense of what can be said and how it should be said must restrain scholars.

Let me bring to the fore the implications of this debate for political action. The most common position is this: If it is generally believed that there has been a radical break between white immigrant experience and black experience, people will be impelled to adopt new and unprecedented measures to achieve for blacks the measure of status that white immigrant groups reached without such measures. If people are convinced that because blacks have been subjected to the varied consequences of three hundred years of American racism, there is indeed no connection between white immigrant experience and black experience, and that all those who have benefited in some measure from American society, as immigrants have, must bear some responsibility for its crimes and derelictions, then we might expect a greater measure of support for radical policies designed to change the position of blacks. It is also possible that if the two experiences are seen as totally disparate one response might be to conclude that American society cannot adopt measures necessary to achieve a reasonably satisfactory position for Negroes and thus that revolution is necessary. On the other hand, if people believe there is a substantial degree of similarity between the experience of white ethnic groups and black experience, arguments for unique and extreme measures to end black deprivation will be undermined. If the last-mentioned point of view is valid, the social scientist who believes that there is considerable continuity in the experience and position of blacks and other ethnic groups but who also believes that strong and well-directed state action is necessary in many areas to improve the position of black and other minority groups is in a dilemma indeed.

However, I do not believe that we can draw the political consequences of the two positions in only one way. Political consequences quite different from those suggested might flow from seeing continuity or discontinuity between the experience of white ethnic groups and that of blacks. If one sees continuity, then one may take an optimistic view of the future of American blacks: not only "If we made it, why don't they?" but "If we made it, so will they." This is the position that Irving Kristol argued in his article "The Negro Today Is Like the Immigrant of Yesterday."[6] And on the other side, one consequence of seeing radical discontinuity may be a pessimistic outlook: whatever it is the white ethnic groups have achieved, one may decide, blacks cannot achieve it, because the society is now different, they are different, or the society is different for them. Thus emphasis on the differences may not lead to a great effort to institute new kinds of political, social, and economic action or, even further, to the demand for revolution; it may simply lead to despair and to the feeling that nothing can be done.

Of course, it is rather too simple to assume that the scholars in this field are affected only by the political consequences of their scientific work. As a matter of fact, the relationships run the other way too; their scientific work is affected by their initial political considerations. (I do not exclude myself from this general observation.)

If one initially takes a pessimistic view of American society, one will tend to discount the possibility of a satisfactory situation for blacks without drastic and revolutionary social change and will emphasize the uniqueness of the black position. If one initially takes an optimistic view of American society, one will tend to emphasize improvements in the situation of blacks, the ways in which the relatively successful integration of white ethnic groups is being duplicated for nonwhite groups. And these views will have further dynamic consequences, altering the views of other parts of the American social structure. For example, those who are pessimistic about blacks sometimes argue not that their situation is unlike that of the immigrant ethnic groups but that the immigrant groups are *also* badly off. Thus, whereas until a short time ago most observers thought there had been a rapid decline in the discrimination toward Chinese and Japanese and a rapid rise in their economic and social position, some supporters of Third World ideology now argue that they are badly off too, that they too suffer from racism. And if one were to suggest that Poles are not that well off either, as a way of moderating the view of the black position as unique, Third World supporters would answer. "Quite true. Poles too should join the revolution." The point is that the commitment may be to revolution, whatever the facts.

One hopes that whatever their political commitment, scholars will act as scholars: that they will search out the facts, suppress none, give greater attention to those who dispute their political preconceptions than to those who support them, argue with other scholars on the basis of data and reasoned argument. Just as we must be aware that scholarly positions have political consequences, so we must be aware that political positions affect the way one views the data.

Thus scholarly investigation has consequences for policies, but what those consequences will be is not immediately and simply predictable. The human mind operates in strange ways, and along with scholarly investigation there is the reality of social change, which has great influence on public opinion. The very unpredictability of the impact of scholarly views on public opinion gives the scholar a certain degree of freedom — though not absolute freedom. He pursues his investigation and analysis, and while he may judge that certain findings will tend to strengthen certain political views, he also knows that many other things affect political views and that human reasoning travels surprising paths. Consider the political effect of rioting in the ghettos. It was widely believed — and certainly social scientists shared the belief — that riots would lead to backlash and repression. There has been a good deal of both, but we have seen a good number of cases now in which the backlash, instead of effecting the election of law-and-order men, has supported black and liberal candidates, on the reasoning that blacks and liberals have credibility with the black population and are able to prevent riots.

Not only are the political conclusions people draw from their beliefs unpredictable; in addition, and also helping to give the social scientist some measure of freedom, popular opinion on matters on which people feel they can come to their own conclusions is in large measure independent of the outcome of research. It can draw upon memory, even if distorted, and experience, even if limited; and it will certainly be influenced by people's present position and interests. Members of white ethnic groups may forget how much they suffered and how angry they were at even moderate discrimination, and their desire to maintain whatever position and property and power they possess will encourage them to believe that there is nothing special in the situation of blacks. And blacks may refuse to recognize elements of similarity between their position and the position of white ethnic groups — the presence of discrimination and prejudice, the effects of language and dialect in restricting opportunity, the effects of poor education and different cultural attitudes, the reality of increases in political and economic power over time, and the diminution over time of discrimination and prejudice.

To sum up: Scholarly opinion does not dictate what people believe, but it will have consequences for what they believe.

Scholarly opinion is not completely free of popular opinion. Scholars are affected by the outlook, experiences, and prejudices of their groups, whether ethnic, social or scholarly. When one examines a question such as the relationship between immigrant and black experience, one should exercise great care in the discussion and in the presentation of data and position (as one should in all scientific discussion), but one must be true to one's role as a scientist.

THE ARGUMENT FOR INTERNAL COLONIALISM

The most influential scholarly statement to date of the belief that there is a radical discontinuity between white immigrant and black experience in America is that by Robert Blauner, and I would like to examine, and set against the evidence, his argument that blacks, as against white ethnics, are internally colonized:

Of course many ethnic groups in America have lived in ghettoes. What makes the black ghettoes an expression of colonized status are three special features. First, the ethnic ghettoes arose more from voluntary choice, both in the sense of the choice to immigrate to America and the decision to live among one's fellow ethnics. Second, the immigrant ghettoes tended to be a one and two generation phenomenon; they were actually way-stations in the process of acculturation and assimilation. Where they continue to persist, as in the case of San Francisco's Chinatown, it is because they are big business for the ethnics themselves and there is a new stream of immigrants. The Black Ghetto on the other hand has been a more permanent phenomenon, although some individuals do escape it. But most relevant is the third point. European ethnic groups like Poles, Italians, and Jews generally only experienced a brief period, often less than a generation, during which their residential buildings, commercial stores, and other enterprises were owned by outsiders . . . Afro-Americans are distinct in the extent to which their segregated communities have remained controlled economically, politically and administratively from the outside . . . The educators, policemen, social workers, politicians and others who administer the affairs of ghetto residents are typically whites who live outside the Black Community.[7]

All three elements of difference can be supported. But the differences are smaller and the similarities greater than this passage suggests.

First, there is the question of the voluntary character of the ghetto. Blauner argues that the black ghettos are involuntary, the ethnic ghettos more voluntary. The voluntary character has two sources: one the voluntary character of the migration itself, the other the voluntary choice to live among fellow ethnics. The nature of their migration is by far the most substantial difference between blacks and white ethnic groups, but it is not an absolute difference. A significant number of the blacks in New York City, for example, are immigrants from the West Indies who came by choice. (Their original migration to the West Indies was as slaves, but their arrival in this country constituted an act of choice not very different from that of white immigrants motivated principally by the pressure of economic deprivation.) In 1930, Ira De Augustine Reid pointed out, 17 percent of black New Yorkers were foreign-born.[8] In addition, the migration of blacks from the South to the North and West has much of the quality of the migration of European and Asian immigrants from Europe and Asia to America. It meant moving into a very different social world, as memoirists and novelists make clear. It was a move from a situation of dire deprivation and persecution to one of some opportunity and a much more moderate degree of discrimination and prejudice.

Nor, if we consider the decision to live among one's fellows, will we find the distinction as sharp as Blauner suggests. First, there is the simple economic limitation set by low income, a limitation that characterizes black and white immigrant groups alike.[9] Second, there are the positive attractions of a community of people of common descent and culture, one that plays probably as strong a role among blacks as among white ethnic groups. Most blacks do not want to live only among blacks. Recent surveys make this clear. Nor do most want to live only among whites. This is not very different from immigrant ethnic patterns.

The degree to which residential concentration of black and immigrant ethnic groups occurs and the degree to which it can be ascribed to economic factors or to other factors (which must include both discrimination and positive attachment to a community of one's fellows, two factors that cannot be easily sectioned out) have recently been subject to empirical research. What the research suggests is that the degree of segregation among white ethnic groups is still extensive and not rapidly declining. Nathan Kantrowitz has analyzed the degree of segregation among white ethnic groups and concludes the decline has been quite small:

The segregation index between Norwegians and Swedes [in New York City], 45.4 [immigrants and their children only], indicates a separation between two Protestant Scandinavian populations which have partially intermarried and even have at least one community in common . . . If Swedes and Norwegians are not highly integrated with each other, it is likely they are even less integrated with other ethnic populations. The index of segregation between various white ethnic groups that are more distant from each other than Norwegians and Swedes runs much higher — thus, the index of segregation between Swedes and natives of the U.S.S.R. and their children (primarily Jews) is 70.7. That is not very far from the higher indexes of segregation that characterize Negroes.[10]

These indexes are about 80. The segregation indexes for Puerto Ricans are the same. Thus the degree of segregation of blacks in New York City, while high, seems to be at one end of a continuum, one shared by Puerto Ricans, rather than radically different from white ethnic segregation. Kantrowitz also demonstrates that New York City is not unique in this respect.

Kantrowitz's detailed analysis suggests that the assertion that white ethnic groups' segregation is voluntary and nonwhite segregation is involuntary must be reexamined. The segregation of the two kinds of groups has many features in common, and while the evidence I have referred to leaves inconclusive the degree to which segregation is voluntary or forced, or, if forced, whether it is based on economic or discriminatory factors, our other knowledge of these communities suggests that voluntary motives play a large part, even if they are different in their importance for the two kinds of communities.

Blauner's second point is that the immigrant ghettos are a one-generation and two-generation phenomenon, while the black ghetto is more permanent. Once again, we can exaggerate this difference. Erich Rosenthal has documented the move of Jews in Chicago from Lawndale to the northern suburbs and their reconcentration there.[11] These are second-generation and third-generation immigrant Jews. The concentration of Jews in some communities that are by now largely of the second and third generation, and similiar concentrations of Italians and other ethnic groups, suggest that the ghetto, or something like the ghetto, has a relatively long life for some groups, even though it may change its physical location. Black ghettos have also moved; the original Lower West Side ghetto of blacks in New York City is no more. The population of Harlem is already in decline; and were it not for the placement of permanent low-income housing projects in black ghettos, we would see some of them disintegrate more rapidly before the pressure of other uses. We already see the rise of middle-class, second- and third-generation (if measured by generations in the North) black areas in the major northern cities. These are not so different from the concentrations established by white ethnic groups. Thus, against Blauner's second point I would argue that it underestimates the longevity of white ghettos and the mobility of black ghettos.

The ghettos of the "older immigrants" (Irish and German) have indeed largely disappeared, but their history began with heavy immigration one hundred and thirty years ago. We do not know what the state of black ghettos in northern cities will be after such an expanse of time. While it is true there have been blacks in northern cities from their founding; the rise of large black populations in the North came *after* the major immigration of the Eastern European and Southern European ethnic groups — Italians, Jews, Poles. Indeed, one of the weaknesses of various comparisons of blacks and white ethnic groups is the choice of time spans used for comparison. From the national point of view, blacks are among the oldest components of the American population, and a very large component. But in the northern and western cities, as a mass element, they are relative latecomers. Thus, for example, in New York City in 1900, blacks formed only 2 percent of the population — a minor group indeed, statistically — while the Germans and Irish and their children formed 20 percent each, Russians and their children (an index to the Jewish group, though it understates the size) 7 percent, and Italians and their children 6 percent. Twenty years later, Russians and their children formed 18 percent of the population, Italians and their children 14 percent, and blacks formed only 3 percent. Not until 1940 did blacks form as large a part of the population of New York City as the Italians and their children had formed in 1900.[12] Using a national measure, blacks are first-comers and unquestionably deprived in light of their three-hundred-year history in the United States. In the northern urban perspective, they are latecomers, and this perspective makes a good deal of sense to many people in the northern city.

Economic and Political Power

Blauner's final point is that while European ethnic groups rapidly gained economic and political control over their ghettos, blacks did not. This is perhaps the key point in his argument in support of the thesis of internal colonialism. And yet it is remarkably difficult to support with empirical evidence on the ghettos of the northern and western cities that are Blauner's main concern in his article. Any responsible discussion of this problem must begin with some consideration of the problem of relevant time spans for comparison. If the issue is "rate" of acquisition of economic and political power in a new setting, then this rate must relate to a period of time. If the period of time is the three-hundred-year span of black experience in this country, compared with approximately two hundred years of German history, one hundred and fifty years of Irish history, and one hundred years of Italian history in this country, then Blauner is right. But if we stay within the context of northern cities, then blacks — who settled in the North in large numbers at a time when Protestants exercised major economic power, Germans were already a solidly established middle class, the Irish exercised political power, and Jews and Italians were prominent in small business — are latecomers.

From the national point of view and the point of view of national responsibility for the black condition — a responsibility in which all share, even immigrants who came here long after the end of slavery — blacks are far behind. If we look at the northern and western cities and consider the history of groups within them in terms of generations spent in those urban areas (as did, for example, W. Lloyd Warner and Leo Srole in their pioneering work, *The Social Systems of American Ethnic Groups*), then the situation is quite different.[13] Blacks are still behind, but not as far behind.

There is a second point to be made about the problem of "rate." If we use as our model "white immigrant experience," not further differentiated, then blacks are far behind. But if we look at the experience of individual ethnic groups, the matter is quite different. The Irish have shown remarkable political success, the Jews remarkable organizational and economic success, and the Japanese remarkable educational success; but Poles and Italians, for example, are not distinguished in these areas. There was a *range* of experience. Within this range, my judgment on the basis of scanty data is that blacks fall near the bottom, but not on all scales, not uniformly, and not so radically that we must set up a new model called "internal colonialism" to explain their position in the northern and western city.

Unfortunately, neatly arranged data that prove this point are simply not available. We do not, for example, have good studies of the economic and educational status of Polish Americans and other Slavic groups by generation and length of residence. If we did, I would think that there would be similarity in many respects between such immigrants and blacks; one would find that, at comparable times, these immigrant groups also exhibited a rising and substantial degree of homeownership, a substantial body of unskilled and semiskilled workers, and considerable social disorganization and family breakup because of cultural change and economic distress. One would not find any economic power wielded by such groups outside the ghetto, except perhaps labor power.

The European immigrants' major economic differences from blacks seem twofold. First, they opened more retail stores. Was this owing to "internal colonialism"? Eugene Foley has made a detailed examination of black small business and other small business, and he finds no major difference between them in, for example, access to credit from banks.[14] The weakness of business among blacks is owing, first, to a tradition in which business and its practices are not widely dispersed and well known (and this may well be traced to slavery); second, to inadequacy of patronage by the black group itself because of a number of factors. Thus, because blacks used English, language did not serve as a protective barrier for the black ghetto businessman. Interestingly enough, the Irish, another group that spoke English, also did poorly in establishing small retail businesses. The argument that racism destroyed black business in pre-immigrant American cities and prevented the rise of new black businesses has a good deal of merit but cannot be an exclusive explanation. Chinese and Japanese also met vicious racism; Jews faced a more moderate prejudice. A variety of factors were relevant.[15]

There was struggle, of course, over jobs and political power. In this struggle, racism — prejudice and discrimination — played a major role. These same weapons were used against other groups. In their struggle the small settled black communities of northern cities lost, badly. But was this a matter of "internal colonialism" or did the fight go against blacks for many reasons?[16]

The same issue is relevant for the second major difference — though I have no good statistics and know of no systematic comparison — between black and immigrant ethnic communities, namely, the degree of unemployment and social disorganization among blacks. I am not referring to comparisons made at this time. Today blacks do show much more unemployment and social disorganization than do other groups; but do they show more than, let us say, Poles showed in the 1920s and 1930s in the northern city? And are these problems matters of formal or informal racial disqualification — colonialism — or the result of many factors: level of skill, cultural change, conflict with better-organized groups?[17] The history of every ethnic group reveals how little was simply given, how much achieved by conflict. Consider the history of the labor movement, which is largely a history of immigrant ethnic groups. And the history of the labor movement seems to me a record of almost uniform defeat for the immigrant groups throughout their first hundred years in this country.

We have better evidence for the rate of acquisition of political power, and it is hard to see any major difference between the black experience and the white immigrant experience except for the phenomenal political success of the Irish. White ethnic areas generally managed to elect members of their own group to represent them when they had a majority. So did black areas. This was not done without struggle — often very fierce struggle.[18] The same was true for black sections in Chicago, in New York City, and in other cities. Blacks are now being elected mayors, councilmen, state legislators, and congressmen, largely on the basis of statistical predominance, but not always. (Note the election in 1970 of three black congressmen from areas with black minorities.)

But just as in the case of economic power, a slow rate of acquisition of political power is not proof of "internal colonialism." Other factors prevent blacks in northern cities from gaining political power proportionate to their numbers.

Arthur Klebanoff has made a close analysis of black political power in Brooklyn, measured by the number of black assemblymen and senators in the state legislature.[19] He shows that the increase in their numbers has not matched the increase in the black population. He also demonstrates that this is owing to two features: ingenious redistricting influenced by powerful Jewish and Italian state legislators in order to maintain their seats in the face of increasing black and Puerto Rican population, and a low rate of registration among blacks and Puerto Ricans. I do not see any support for the colonial analogy here. Gerrymandering against new groups was not invented to keep blacks underrepresented; rates of registration, just like rates of taking out citizenship and of voting, have varied for a long time among groups for various and complex reasons. The enormous differences among immigrant groups with regard to their interest in taking out citizenship and their participation in formal electoral politics were documented in the first decade of this century by the Immigration Commisssion. Only 4 percent of immigrant Greeks became citizens, as against 58 percent of the Armenians![20] And this was documented again in the 1920's.[21] Studies have been made of the voting rates of ethnic groups in New York City. One survey shows that Puerto Ricans vote least (32.5 percent); blacks next (43.4 percent); foreign-born Italians and their children do somewhat better (56.2 percent); white Protestants are next (64 percent); the Irish and their children show a much higher rate of voting (73.9 percent); and native-born Jews show the highest (78.9 percent). Clearly rates of voting play a role in ethnic political representation. Yet how can internal colonialism explain this difference in rates between groups, today as sixty years ago? [22]

Blauner says, and many agree with him, that "the educators, policemen, social workers, politicians and others who administer the affairs of ghetto residents are typically whites who live outside the Black Community." I have suggested that blacks have more power than Blauner's third point asserts; I would also argue that white ethnic groups had less power than he implies. They too did not staff — certainly not for the first generation — the schools, police forces, social work agencies, and political positions. The evidence on this is clear. Humbert Nelli records for the Italians of Chicago their small numbers in the police force and the school system.[23] Almost every ethnic group was initially educated, policed, and administered by persons of other ethnic groups, earlier arrivals. I am talking about rates. In some areas the rates of change have been slowed down by civil service laws. But it can hardly be argued that these reforms were instituted to maintain colonialism or with any thought that they would eventually serve to reduce the rates at which blacks took over government jobs in areas that affected them.

My point is *not* that there are no major differences between the large immigrant ethnic groups and blacks. Rather, the question is the character and scale of the differences, and whether they justify considering the experience of immigrant ethnic groups as one that leads to some degree of acculturation and assimilation, while considering the experience of blacks (and perhaps some other groups) to be colonial or quasi-colonial and of the sort that does not lead to integration — or more precisely to that measure of integration that is characteristic of immigrant ethnic groups — but rather to separation and, if we push the colonial analogy far enough, to "independence."

NORTH AND SOUTH

Chapter 9 of the Kerner Commission's report gives another and to my mind a more balanced view of the differences between the experience of immigrant ethnic groups and that of American blacks. There the differences are grouped into five categories. The first is the change in the economy between the time of major European ethnic migration and that of major black migration to northern cities — in particular, the decline of opportunities for unskilled labor. Second, the high visibility of race itself: racial discrimination is far more pervasive and severe than the moderate discrimination that some white ethnic groups faced. Third is the change in the political system and in particular the decline of ward-based politics and the rise of civil service. Fourth are the differing cultural orientations of white ethnic groups and black migrants — the first, the report asserts, were ready to accept poorly paid and low-status labor, had stronger families more able to pool resources and sponsor members' mobility, and had needs that required distinctive stores and services. Obviously this is a mixed bag, but an important one. And fifth, Chapter 9 refers to the "vital element of time." There, in a manner similar to my critique of Blauner, the report argues that ethnic groups did take a long time to reach whatever degree of economic affluence and political power they now possess and that blacks are moving faster than many believe.

I would disagree with only one of the commission's points — that the economic situation blacks face in northern cities is harsher than that faced by white ethnic migrants. Admittedly there is less need for unskilled labor now than in the periods of peak European migration. But this cannot be translated into the conclusion that there are fewer *jobs* available. For while the number of unskilled jobs has declined, the number of those who are capable of filling only unskilled jobs has also declined. Black migrants have a higher level of education than European immigrants of the beginning of the century and are consequently not as restricted in the kinds of jobs they can fill. The fact that many jobs for the unskilled are not filled shows that there has not been a substantial decline in the ratio of jobs to applicants. Two other things have happened, however. There are now more alternatives to unskilled work. There are social programs, and consequently fewer people are driven to unpleasant and low-paying jobs by the need to feed their families. Secondly, there is a change in attitudes toward unskilled and low-paying work. It is less commonly seen as a suitable or acceptable lifelong activity for men. Expectations have changed, and fewer blacks or whites today will accept a life at menial labor with no hope for advancement, as their fathers and older brothers did and as European immigrants did.

One reason the Kerner Commission's report could emphasize as much as it did the degree of continuity between the immigrant and the black experience is that the commision concentrated on the northern urban experience. If it had taken a national view (more than half of all black Americans still live in the South; perhaps three-quarters were raised in the South and almost all have been in some way shaped by the searing experience of southern racism), it would not have found many elements of continuity — there are almost none between the experience of the black slave in the South and the free immigrant worker in the North. But if one concentrates, as the commission did, on northern blacks and on the cities in the North, there is a substantial degree of continuity between the experience of immigrant workers and that of black migrants.

If one takes the national view, the view that includes black enslavement, the legally inferior position of blacks set forth in the Constitution and in state and local law for centuries, the disfranchisement of blacks after the Civil War, and the heroic and not yet completed struggle to achieve full legal equality in the South, then it is indeed enraging to be answered with the ethnic comparison. The conservative and optimistic bias of this comparison underestimates what has been and still is necessary to achieve full equality for blacks.

But if one concentrates on the northern urban experience, then the elements of continuity are important. There the blacks arrive as migrants. There they arrive in a position in which, despite severe discrimination and prejudice, civil equality is protected in law. They are the worst off of the groups — but worst off because they face the most severe prejudice and discrimination on a scale of discrimination applied to almost every immigrant (one on which Chinese and Japanese probably fared as badly), because they come with the poorest job and community skills, and because they are also the latest of the arrivals. As in the case of the other groups, this is not an unchanging situation: prejudice and discrimination decline (in part because of the struggles of the group itself and its growing power), skills improve, and time passes.

The northern view emphasizes continuity because it is aware that there is a great range in the experience of the white ethnic groups. They vary in time of arrival, skills at time of arrival, character of the cities into which they came, character of their cultural attributes, and degree of discrimination and prejudice they faced; thus they have a wide range of different experiences. In this range, the gap between the experience of the worst off of the white ethnic groups and the blacks is one of degree rather than kind. Indeed, in some respects blacks in some places are better off than some other groups. They have more political power than Puerto Ricans in New York City, a somewhat higher income, a substantially higher proportion of professionals and experienced persons able to take leadership positions. If one takes all ethnic groups and lumps them together, blacks are far below. If one views them in a more realistic manner — as groups — then the blacks are worse off than most yet in some respects perhaps better off than some. Blacks probably have more college graduates than Polish Americans, more political muscle than Mexican Americans, more clout in the mass media than Italian Americans. It is the comparison of "blacks" against "whites" that shows such a radical distinction between black and white (and this is made even sharper in national figures by putting together North and South), but this is not so if we compare blacks against the whole range of white ethnic groups.

There is another point to be made about the consequences of taking the northern view. From the point of view of the North, the differences in power and wealth of the varied groups that make up the northern city are somewhat understandable. There is a sequence of arrival. There is a sequence of prestige. Some groups are considered superior, some for a time inferior. This inferiority is resented and fought. It was fought by the Irish, the Jews, the Italians. But it does not become a basic cause for divorce from society. The reason it does not is that there is an underground and grudging acknowledgment that those who were here first, who "started" the country, understandably and with some justice have greater wealth and power in the North. In the South, no such acknowledgment can be made. The blacks were brought as slaves, and at the same time, they also built the country; they should have full and equal position, and the subtle and half-grudgingly accepted order of precedence of the ethnic groups in the North plays no part in their experience in the South.

Perhaps the tragedy of this country is that it did not become two nations, because the two sections have developed such a radically different orientation to the facts of ethnic diversity. I believe the main reason the argument that there is a radical discontinuity between ethnic experience and black experience is so powerful is the South — because there it is true, and because southern attitudes have not been limited to the South. They have been brought North, physically, by blacks and whites; they have become an integral part of this country's history through the often disproportionate power of the white South as reflected in national policy; and models have been available — through the history of colonialism — that made it possible for intellectuals, social scientists, blacks, and others to apply the southern model to the whole country.

How one views society is never a consequence simply of social reality (assuming that it is accessible); it is also a matter of how one wills to see society. I believe it is possible to see the position of blacks in northern cities in ethnic terms, that is, to see them as the last of the major groups, badly off at present, but due to rise in time to larger shares of wealth and power and influence. This is a possibility in harmony with as many facts as any other. However, there are credible alternatives. It is also possible — and equally true — to see the present plight of blacks as the consequence of the special crime and burden of American society. In this view, blacks will not become part of American society without radical, almost superhuman efforts in every area of life. Without these efforts only separation is possible — hard as it is to imagine. These are alternatives both in social reality — where there is evidence for both — and in political reality. One can choose either, and one's actions can make one or the other dominant.

The ethnic analogy is losing among black youth. Some alternative — pluralism? separatism? a separate nation? — is winning out. It can take the relatively mild form of ethnic pluralism, in which case it is quite conformable to the experience of other ethnic groups, white and nonwhite. Or it can take — and among many of the youth it does take — a more radical form, one that cannot be realized within the present political structure of American society. If it takes the mild form, then we can see it as a stage in a process to fuller integration and a larger measure of power and wealth in American society. Such a stage — withdrawal in order to gather strength — is not a new pattern. But if it takes the more radical form of a demand for political restructuring to formally acknowledge the position of blacks as a permanently separate group, then we will have certainly entered a new and hazardous period in national development. For such a demand must have repercussions on other groups — Mexican Americans, Puerto Ricans, American Indians. It will affect even the relatively prosperous Oriental communities. And it may begin to affect the white ethnic groups, to lead them to reflect on their experiences and position in American society and perhaps to decide that they too are subject to insupportable deprivation and that the American ethnic system has failed. The political consequence of the position that there is no relationship between black and white immigrant ethnic group experience might well be to divide the country, to the disadvantage of all groups. And if this is one potential political possibility, should it not be taken into account in the debate?

[1971]

II

CULTURAL PLURALISM

AND BILINGUALISM

6

The Problem of Ethnic Studies

"CULTURAL PLURALISM" seems to have won out, at least temporarily, as the preferred model for responding to the reality of a multiracial and multiethnic society. Now that it has won, however, we do not appear to be very sure of what it means. It denotes a broad middle ground, stretching between the extremes of "assimilation" and "acculturation" at one end, and "separatism" at the other end.

In each sphere of life it may mean something entirely different, however. We are not sure of its political implications, of its social and economic implications, or even of its implications in the sphere where its impact has been greatest — education. This is true in spite of an endless array of proposals, programs, and even laws and judicial decisions that are available to guide or confuse us. As we know, cultural pluralism is now not only an academic model for education in a multiethnic society, but also a matter for federal, state, and municipal legislation and for determination by the ever more intrusive courts, spurred by public legal advocates who seem convinced that the most complex problems will submit to judicial determinations. The U.S. federal system makes no simple description possible of any development, in view of the variety that may (and does) exist in our thousands of semi-independent units. One thing is possible, however, and that is a clarification of our thinking about cultural pluralism, particularly in the light of the conception we have of a desirable social order for our very distinctive nation, made up of many ethnic strands.

Certainly we have to begin with the terms that define the parameters of cultural pluralism. At one end, as I have suggested, there are "assimilation" and "acculturation," to which we may add as a third, "Americanization." These terms defined at one level the aim of almost all those involved in the discussion of the multinational aspect of the United States from 1900 to 1940. There were two writers, now well known among the students of cultural pluralism, who spoke out against the prevailing trend — Randolph Bourne and Horace M. Kallen.[1] But dominant power rested with those in favor of assimilation, acculturation, and Americanization. These policies are now presented to us as a form of domestic imperialism or colonialism. We are told that instead of colonizing foreign peoples in their homelands the United States imported them and then subjected them to colonial conditions. These conditions involved an arrogant dismissal of any possible virtues of their native cultures and an insistence that they recast themselves as Americans. At the same time, argues the prevailing critique of the assimilationism of the early part of the century, the Americans had no intention of accepting the members of the new groups as equals, even if stripped of their original cultures by these policies of assimilation. They were to be left nothing of their own to stand with against Anglo-American culture, but they were not to be allowed entry into American society on fully equal terms.

This is certainly a severe criticism of policies of Americanization, but there is enough to support it. On the one hand the new immigrants were attacked for their foreignness; their inability to speak English; their presumed high crime rates (never proven); their crowding in slums, which was an inevitable consequence, after all, of their poverty; their continued attachment to their homelands, particularly if these homelands were, like Germany, enemies of the United States in war; their susceptibility to the city political machines; their uncertain knowledge of democracy; and their tendency to adopt socialist, anarchist, and communist doctrines. These arguments against them were used to exclude immigrants almost completely, from the early 1920s on. Once here, they were to be "Americanized." In the meantime Jews and Catholics and, even more, blacks, Orientals, and Mexican Americans suffered from various forms of prejudice and discrimination, and it was not at all clear that their "Americanization" would lead to the reduction of such prejudice and discrimination. The only hope held out was that a full assimilation would indeed end the prejudice and discrimination directed against them, since at that point they would exist, not as individuals with some given inheritance, but as individuals who could not be identified as being different from other Americans. "Acculturation" was a stage on the way to "assimilation."

This criticism of policies of assimilation is familiar enough, but the problem with it is that assimilation was not the objective only of the reactionary, conservative, and ethnocentric forces in American life, but also the objective of liberal forces. It was not the objective only of the old American element, but also that of the new immigrants. We have long been familiar with the fact that it was possible both to be populist and progressive and also to oppose immigration on the grounds of the presumed unassimilability of the new immigrants. This was the point of view of John R. Commons, Edward Allsworth Ross, Henry Pratt Fairchild, and others.

However, there was a stronger current in American sociology that was not so strongly populist and more basically liberal, which was identified with Robert E. Park, whose career included a long stretch as secretary and close associate of Booker T. Washington, and who founded a school of sociology at the University of Chicago that reflected sympathy with, concern for, and curiosity about the various races and streams of immigration that were making up the American population. This was a severely empirical school and was ethnographic in its emphasis. However, insofar as it had a direction, that is, a proposal for the American multiethnic society, that direction was also assimilationist. The paradigm of race and ethnic relations that Park suggested ran from contact to conflict to accommodation to assimilation.

We sociologists, in our search for "theory," have made more

of this simple scheme than it warrants, but as a matter of fact it did reflect the values, perhaps insufficiently thought through, of Park and his leading students. Louis Wirth, who was the chief successor to Park, made clear in *The Ghetto* that his preference was for assimilation: the Jew continued to exist only because of prejudice and discrimination; all the reactions of the Jew to this antagonism were humanly limiting; and assimilation, which to be sure required lowering the barriers to assimilation, was the desirable end result of the interaction of Jews and non-Jews in contemporary society.

The major works of E. Franklin Frazier on the black family went in the same direction. Insofar as the black family was stable and puritanical it was good — that was unquestioned. There was no hint, or scarcely any, that any distinctive cultural feature should survive as specifically Negro or black, or that there should be any effort to seek for such features.

This was not cultural arrogance or imperialism; instead, it was the point of view of the best-informed, most liberal, and most sympathetic analysts of the ethnic and racial scene. Assimilation was a desirable consequence of the reduction of prejudice and discrimination, while acculturation, that is, becoming more like the majority, would contribute to the reduction of discrimination and prejudice. This was the dominant liberal view until at least the 1950s.

It was also the view, insofar as a view could be discerned, of the representatives of racial and ethnic groups. The NAACP and the Urban League were clearly "assimilationist." Although it was clear that blacks could never because of race be indistinguishable from whites, it was desirable that they become culturally, socially, economically, and politically assimilated, that they be simply Americans with dark skins. All public agencies, including the government and the schools, and all private agencies that affected individual circumstances, including banks, businessess, housing producers, and renters, were to be "color blind." In the 1950s the only legitimate form of differentiation proposed for American life was religious. The distinction of Catholic, Protestant, and Jew (Jew in religion) was acceptable, but racial differences of any significance were to disappear through fair treatment, while ethnic differences were to remain, if at all, only in religious form. It was Will Herberg who held that the religious differences were also disappearing, in a common "American" religion. They existed, to his mind, only to maintain surviving ethnic differences.

Admittedly, in each group there were the maintainers and upholders of the ethnic conscience and consciousness, including schools, churches, philanthropic and civic organizations, networks of insurance societies, and social groups, but except by those whose direct interest was in maintaining them and the jobs they offered, these were regarded as survivals, fated to fall away as acculturation and assimilation progressed.

Acculturation and assimilation, if not the cruder "Americanization," were thus not simply the positions of the old Americans who were antagonistic to new immigrants and nonwhite races; they were also the positions of those who were most sympathetic to these groups and who understood them best, and even of the representatives of these groups.

Why was there such blindness to the possibility that these groups or elements within them would not want to acculturate and assimilate but would want to preserve their corporate characters and distinctiveness even if prejudice and discrimination disappeared? One reason seems to explain it: The focus of concern was with the immediate position of these groups, with the problem of prejudice and discrimination, and with their low economic and social position. How could they make the transition to a better position? First by becoming more like other Americans, and then by persuading other Americans to abandon prejudice and discrimination on the grounds that the ethnic groups and different races were really just like them anyway. The main aim of propaganda for tolerance in the 1930s and 1940s, a propaganda the need for which was heightened by the rise of Hitler and the greater salience of anti-Semitism and racist propaganda and feeling, was that the groups that were objects of hostility were really just like other Americans: there was nothing different about them.

This strategy seemed to be reasonable, but as time went on it created a confusion between the point of view within liberalism that argues, "They are just like everyone else, so they should not be objects of prejudice and discrimination," and the one that asserts, "They are different and have a right to be different, and this difference does not justify any antagonism."

The development of attitudes toward cultural pluralism was also deeply affected by the two world wars. In World War I the United States went through a period of hysterical affirmation of Americanism and oneness. The teaching of German was briefly driven out of the schools, the use of German words or terms was banned, any form of dual loyalty that threatened a total commitment to the United States and its allies was viewed with fierce suspicion, the foreign-language press was closely monitored for disloyalty. After the war the great suspicion continued, now directed against Bolshevism rather than Germanism. Immigrants from Eastern Europe who showed any attachment to socialism, anarchism, or communism came under severe attack; many were deported; socialists elected to office were denied their seats.

This is an old story, often told. In this environment, to take account of the cultural differences of schoolchildren — which would mean for the public schools to acknowledge the distinctive background of Germans, Hungarians, Jews, Czechs, Russians, and the like — seemed out of the question. It is true that the major founding statements of cultural pluralism — by Horace Kallen and, of lesser significance but great interest, Randolph Bourne — came out of the dispute over hyphenated Americanism during the war. These statements, in their hope for an America that would be an orchestra of many nations and cultures, were before their time.

Ethnic loyalty was considered a drawback to a full national effort to fight World War I, for our enemies were Germany and multiethnic Austria-Hungary; and, soon after our entry, multiethnic Russia exited from the war under Bolshevik rule to become what seemed like an ally of our enemies. (The ethnic loyalties of the Americans of English origin did not seem to be ethnic, but simply American.) Even in World War I there were, of course, ethnic loyalties that could have been drawn upon to assist the allied cause in America — Czechs had no attachment to the Austro-Hungarian Empire, Italians were on the allied side, and so on. It was ideology as well as practical considerations that led to the criticism of "hyphenated Americanism" and dual loyalties. The war had come in the full flood of immigration, and the problem of forging common loyalties, a common American nation, was inevitably seen as a severe one. No political leader was inclined to encourage ethnic loyalties during World War I.

After the war, a public commitment to ethnic pluralism seemed an equally vain hope. This was the age of the Red Scare and the Ku Klux Klan. Nor did matters improve with the sudden collapse of the Klan and the apparent weakening of antiforeign prejudices as a major force in American politics with the onset of the Great Depression, when other issues seized public attention and when the working man and the middle classes were concerned with more important things than the maintenance of cultural and linguistic heritages.

The rise of Hitler and the coming of World War II again made the relationship of the various foreign stocks paramount to American life and national interests. But this time ethnic loyalties seemed for the most part something that could support our allies and our own national interests, rather than something to be viewed with suspicion. Americans of German, Italian, and Japanese origin could again be seen as potential enemies. But Germans had been chastened by the experience of World War I; the Italians were not seen as very political; the Japanese were circumspect — though that did not save them from forced relocation. Almost every other ethnic strand seemed to have good reasons for opposing Hitler and Nazism. The voluminous writings of the Yugoslav immigrant Louis Adamic best symbolize the coinciding in World War II of a reawakening of pride and commitment to ethnic heritage with the great national effort of the war.[2]

Nazism and World War II gave rise to curricular innovation in what was then called "intercultural education." There were two themes in intercultural education: the first was that one should not be ashamed of one's heritage; the second and more important was that all should be tolerant of racial, religious, and cultural differences. In effect, intercultural education was America's answer to Hitler's preaching of group hatred. The second theme, that of tolerance, outweighed the first, that of the celebration of heritage and diversity.

Whereas the first founding statements of cultural pluralism of World War I had no impact on the schools, the second wave of interest created organizations, publications, new curricula, and extensive discussion. There existed during this period a Center for Intergroup Education in Cooperating Schools of the American Council on Education, a Service Bureau of Intercultural Education, a Common Council for American Unity, a newsletter, *Intercultural Education News*, edited by William Heard Kilpatrick, and other journals presenting material on intercultural education.[3]

The content of intercultural education was rather thin. It should be seen as a response to the frightfully dangerous upsurge of racism that the rapid explosion of Nazi power stimulated all over the world — and in the United States, too, though our own domestic roots of racism were strong enough. One of the chief keynotes of intercultural education was tolerance, enlisted in the fight against prejudice. Intercultural education concentrated on the processes that might counter current intolerance of other peoples and cultures; what end it envisaged for a diverse America was less clear. One suspects that to advocates of intercultural education the picture of a decent America consisted of one in which Americans of whatever origin were really very much alike, and were not discriminated against for their origins, religion, or vestigial cultural differences. Certainly there was no notion that it was the task of the public schools to present or preserve a full-bodied version of ethnic cultures. It was enough to teach tolerance of whatever existed.

Thus, the intercultural education version of cultural pluralism would seem very weak to us today. Indeed, the notion of cultural pluralism itself was rejected in one influential formulation of intercultural education — as, on the other extreme, was assimilation. The new middle path was labeled "cultural democracy." William E. Vickery and Stewart G. Cole, whose presentatation of intercultural education I am following, present three fundamental propositions to define their approach:

1. That there are certain essential democratic loyalties and beliefs, as well as practices which have been established for the general welfare, which all Americans should have in common . . .

2. That the dominant majority group can rightly require individuals and minorities neither to isolate themselves from the community and nation as a whole, nor to cling to ways of living which are incongruent with democratic practice.

The majority, however, is called upon to be careful in distinguishing between undemocratic beliefs and practices and

those which are only different . . . The latter the majority is required to honor, though not necessarily to adopt. Nor can the majority justly make conformity to the dominant culture pattern or membership in the dominant race a requirement for full and equal participation . . .

3. That individuals . . . should be free to practice and perpetuate such of their group's traditional values, folkways and customs as do not conflict with essential democratic principles; or to repudiate their ancestral ways of living and thus to lose themselves in the population as a whole.[4]

Goodenow gives a somewhat similar evaluation of the intercultural education movement:

In part, however, intercultural programs suffered from the progressive spirit of the times. Their endeavors were only partly successful because they were highly committed to an ideology of national unity, democracy, and tolerance that would resist authoritarianism at home and abroad and defend America's national interests. Attacking anti-Semitism and other forms of intolerance the interculturalists focused upon international and cross-cultural aspects of racism and noted the "commonness" of all men to the point where they blurred the differences between ethnic groups. Drawing on anthropological and biological research they often failed to consider the structural and institutional nature of racism in the United States. Indeed, by placing considerable stress upon the past cultural contributions of ethnics and others to American life, pluralism was portrayed as a static phenomenon. Virtually no attempt was made to suggest that these groups could themselves shape the nature of American society.[5]

Goodenow's article is particularly valuable for describing the attitudes of the intercultural education movement toward the problems of blacks. Blacks had been ignored in earlier writings on cultural pluralism; these came out of the experiences of European immigrants, and particularly Jews. John Higham writes of Horace Kallen:

He liked to describe the American ensemble as an orchestra; but there was a fatal elision when he wrote that America could become "an orchestration of mankind" by perfecting "the cooperative harmonies of European civilization." Nothing in Kallen's writings gave away the magnitude of that elision. In the fullest statement of his argument there was only a single, obscure footnote on the point. "I do not discuss the influence of the negro," Kallen confessed in fine print. "This is at once too considerable and too recondite in its processes for casual mention. It requires separate analysis." The pluralist thesis from the outset was encapsulated in white ethnocentrism.[6]

There was considerably more interest in other (Asian) racial minority groups among the intercultural educators. But a good part of even this interest was stimulated by a European event, the rise of Nazi racism, which evoked a defense of racial equality and tolerance in the United States.

National loyalty came first; there was no great virtue to sticking to group customs and practices, even though they should be tolerated. Clearly, a good deal was going to change in the next upsurge of commitment to ethnic heritage in the later 1960s. In this stage there is little talk of striking a middle path between "assimilation" and "cultural pluralism." Cultural pluralism itself is the correct path, and presumably if one wants to protect one's reputation for moderation, one must create another extreme pole that one can reject, one we could label "separatism." It is interesting to contrast the Cole-Vickery principles I have just quoted with a document of the 1970s, a statement by the American Association of Colleges of Teacher Education. Note first that the term "intercultural education," with its variant of "intergroup education," is now a thing of the past. The issue is no longer to teach tolerance for other groups (though that is not totally ignored); the new term is multicultural or bicultural education. Consider now the language of the early 1970s:

Multicultural education rejects the view that schools should seek to melt away cultural differences or the view that schools should merely tolerate cultural pluralism . . . Cultural pluralism is a concept that aims toward a heightened sense of being and a wholeness of the entire society based on the unique strengths of each of its parts . . . Schools and colleges must assure that their total educational process and educational content reflect a commitment to cultural pluralism.[7]

Consider also another authoritative statement on multiethnic education, "Curriculum Guidelines for Multiethnic Education," of the National Council for Social Studies (1976). The four major principles upon which this statement is based are:

1. Ethnic diversity should be recognized and respected at individual, group, and societal levels.

2. Ethnic diversity provides a basis for societal cohesiveness and survival.

3. Equality of opportunity should be afforded to members of all ethnic groups.

4. Ethnic identification should be optional for individuals.

Four major differences should be noted in contrasting the new multiethnic education with the intercultural education of thirty years ago. First, the new development has emerged directly out of the demands of minority groups for recognition. There was the explosive impact of the "black power" slogan and all it carried in its train — the demands of Mexican Americans and Puerto Ricans, of Asian Americans, of American Indians, and then the "new pluralism" of the white ethnic groups with their demands for equal time and equal recognition. In contrast, there was little in the way of demands by racial and ethnic groups themselves in the inspiration for intercultural education. Or, if any one group was involved, it was the Jewish group, frightened at the rise of anti-Semitism. Undoubtedly blacks were worse off than Jews, but they did not face in the 1940s and 1950s any marked increase of antiblack prejudice and discrimination. Jewish defense agencies played a substantial role in launching and supporting intercultural education. And in sponsoring major research on anti-Semitism, on ethnocentrism generally, and on authoritarian and prejudiced attitudes, they provided much of the intellectual base and many of the concepts that were behind intercultural education. But we should not exaggerate the Jewish role: academic anthropologists and social psychologists were perhaps rather more important in providing this intellectual and conceptual base.

The point to be noted is that the intercultural education movement of the 1940s was in large measure something devised by elites — academic scholars, liberal church organizations, intergroup relations organizations — for a mass that they believed was imminently available for prejudiced and antidemocratic social movements. The movement of the later 1960s and early 1970s, on the other hand, grew directly from the demands of group leaders — leaders of black and other minority groups. The academic and religious leaders and intergroup relations agencies were dragged into the train of these new demands, and they themselves did not initiate the movement for multicultural education.

A second major difference, and the major reason for the new multiethnic education, is the poor achievement in education of certain groups, a record which is then used to deny entitlement to further education, jobs, promotions, and, in short, a better life. This issue played no role in the cultural pluralism proposed by Kallen (Kallen was also a Jew and a Zionist, and poor educational achievement is clearly not a Jewish problem), nor did it play any role in intercultural education; in that movement there was no suggestion that what was being proposed would generally improve the educational achievement of minority groups.

A third major difference is that the issue of tolerance as such has almost disappeared. Attitudes and prejudice are no longer the center of attention: the demand now is for "recognition" and "respect," which are somewhat different from mere tolerance. A number of new elements have supplanted tolerance as central foci in multicultural education. First, there is an emphasis on individual and group wholeness, health, identity; a "heightened sense of being," "respect," "cohesiveness and survival." Ethnic identity, the ethnic group, is good; it should not be merely tolerated. Second, there is an emphasis on an expanded equality of opportunity—which in the present moment is translated to mean an equality of achievement, of result, of entitlement, and an intolerance of substantial difference in the credits derived from education and used as the basis for higher occupation, income, and prestige. This is an inevitable corollary from the second point of difference: that multicultural education derives from a concern with the educational deficiency of minority groups.

And finally the fourth major difference: the state is now actively involved in the new multicultural education. It pays for much of it, requires a good deal of it, and surrounds it with state regulation and enforcement. This is a new twist indeed.

I will consider the significance of state action for cultural pluralism at length in Chapter 7. My concern here is with the justification for what might be called "strong" cultural pluralism. The purpose of the "weak" cultural pluralism that emerged as a response to Hitler and World War II, let us recall, was not to maintain differences but to create the kind of situation in which differences could disappear. It reflected a period of accommodation on the part of the ethnic and minority groups. Of course, they said, our intention is to acculturate and Americanize and perhaps assimilate; but meanwhile our need is for toleration, and this can be assisted by an understanding of something of our background and culture.

Strong cultural pluralism comes out of quite another perspective, one in which the ethnic groups and minorities, with the assistance of liberal allies, are on the offensive. Strong cultural pluralism derives from a different perspective on U.S. history, one in which the dominant note is exploitation and in which the extremes of this exploitation are described as cultural or physical genocide. It is this strong cultural pluralism that we must subject to some analysis in the light of the actual history of ethnic and minority groups, of their needs today, and of the social future we envision for our multiethnic society.

The new cultural pluralism is not based on the desire for a transitional period of tolerance to ease the way to full acculturation and assimilation. Instead it is based on the assumption or expectation that separate groups in the United States will continue to exist, that they have value, and that there are both pragmatic and moral reasons why the government should provide some assistance to their maintenance.

"Weak" cultural pluralism had the problem of justifying itself against a demand for acculturation, assimilation, and Americanization; "strong" cultural pluralism emerged from the black pride and black power movement of the later 1960s, was rapidly taken up by other minority groups, and arose from a situation in which the challenge to an integrated and multiethnic society came not from the integrationists but from the separatists. Separatism, of course, has many meanings. For one brief moment, there were voices raised in black and other minority groups that demanded specific territorial areas under the control of each group. Only a few black nationalists and Mexican American nationalists ever made this claim seriously. For American Indians there were of course already separate territories identified as the domains of certain tribes, and the issue that has arisen in recent years is what political powers come along with this territorial area.

I need not spend much time on the possibilities of political separatism, which were extremely slight; however, there was one thread in the argument for separatism that was rather more important than the demand for political separation. This argument was broadly accepted, even though political separation was not. It was based on a definition of the situation of blacks,

Mexican Americans, and Puerto Ricans as colonial peoples. This definition found broad acceptance among social scientists. The colonial imagery began with the blacks and spread rapidly to other groups.

To define the status of a nationality as colonial has very different implications from the assertion that it is being subjected to discrimination and prejudice. In the latter case the course to be followed is clear: ban the discrimination and overcome the prejudice. The implication is that a group is being prevented from becoming part of a larger group by prejudice and discrimination and thus that the process of assimilation will be aided by eliminating prejudice and discrimination. If a group is defined as "colonized," however, a different course of action is envisaged to overcome the deficiency. In the modern world colonies are expected to be freed, not for the purpose of permitting the colonized groups to become like the peoples of the mother countries but for the purpose of permitting them to find their own distinctive courses of political, economic, and cultural development.

Clearly if the proper image for the relationship of ethnic groups to American society is that of colonies, we have a powerful political justification for cultural pluralism in a strong form. For instance, this view would imply that ethnic groups should be granted control of institutions or parts of institutions that deal with subjects of interest to the group in question. It would also foster a demand that special forms of education strengthening individual attachment and allegiance to the group be instituted.

This was, I believe, the first and major justification for the rapid development of black studies programs, Mexican American studies programs, Puerto Rican studies programs, Oriental American studies programs, and Native American studies programs. The wave has spread, in reduced form, to Italian, Jewish, Polish, and other groups. This was only one motivation for the growth of distinctive ethnic studies programs, but it was a powerful one. It will be argued that this is an extreme and tendentious view of the explosion of ethnic studies programs, since there were clearly two other strong justifications. One justification was scholarly: the contribution of these groups to American life had indeed been ignored, and a fair handling of the information required that the lives and cultures and problems of these groups be introduced into the curricula of colleges and indeed of high schools. A second argument was pragmatic: this was necessary to make possible the effective education of the groups in question.

In order to illustrate the degree to which ideology, truth, and practical necessity have contributed to the establishment of ethnic studies programs, I must describe a few of their characteristics. First, it was taken for granted, and in fact it was generally a key demand, that these programs be taught by members of the groups that were being studied. Blacks should teach black studies, Oriental Americans should teach Oriental studies, and so on. Leaving aside the fact that this contradicted one of the key elements of the consensus of the Civil Rights Act of 1964, it should be pointed out how remarkable a demand this was. In American universities there had been, of course, studies of the great cultures of the world aside from Western culture. China, Japan, Latin America, and Africa had been subjects of research and teaching by historians, anthropologists, sociologists, political scientists, literary scholars, art historians, and others. The new demand was that these studies were now to be taught only by members of the groups studied, on the theory that only they could understand them. A George Foote Moore would no longer be permitted to teach about Judaism or a Melville Herskovits to teach about Afro-Americans: membership and allegiance were now set forth as a prerequisite.

Second, it was demanded that the major focus must not be on the study of great cultural areas but on the problems and contributions of the immigrant groups that had come to the United States from these areas. This was a legitimate scholarly demand. It is always possible that a neglected subject can be added to the curriculum, but there are mechanisms within higher education for determining when a new subject should be given independent existence, and instruction in it expanded. However, as a matter of fact, the determination for, let us say, a program of black studies was rarely settled on scholarly grounds: instead these programs were instituted on political grounds.

Third, there was a strong implication that the new programs were intended only for the members of the group that was being studied. In many cases, others interested in learning about a group and its culture felt uncomfortable when they appeared to take the new courses; they were told, by signs or directly, that they were not welcome. This was a truly surprising development in U.S. higher education. All kinds of extracurricular activities had existed for a distinctive ethnic or racial group, but it was unheard of for a racial or ethnic test to be set for a given academic course.

Fourth, these programs, it was assumed and intended, were to advocate instead of analyzing, exploring, considering. What they were designed to advocate was commitment to the group as well as a distinctive view of its history and problems. Thus, for example, it was generally the colonial view of the group's history in the United States that was presented; assimilation and acculturation were attacked as surrender to the colonial power; and commitment to the more militant elements of the group was encouraged. This description may be considered somewhat heightened, but I believe it describes the earlier years of the history of the new strong cultural pluralism, even though there have been some modifications. It is still true that these are the only areas of the colleges and universities and, insofar as they exist, of the high schools, in which racial and ethnic tests for employment are taken for granted and are not as yet challenged by the Equal Employment Opportunity Commission; the Office of Civil Rights of the Department of Health, Education and Welfare; the Civil Rights Commision; the Department of Justice; or any of the state agencies the duty of which is to prevent discrimination on account of race, religion, or national origin. Insofar as persons not of the groups are involved in this form of education, they too are generally advocates rather than scholars or teachers because advocacy has become the predominant tone of these programs.

Thus we had the rise of programs taught by members of groups, devoted to the problems of the members of the groups in this country, taught to members of the groups, and advocating a distinctive point of view about their pasts, problems, and futures, all under public auspices.

There were of course also important legitimate educational reasons for bringing the study of these groups into the curriculum. Along with the older groups, they are part of the United States. They have contributed significantly to the history of the country, and they have been part of its culture, economy, and society. They had also been neglected in the curriculum.

As a student of ethnic issues for thirty years now, I am fully aware of the important place of ethnic studies in American life, and I would agree that they have not been given their full due. Nevertheless, it is hard to think of any area of American life that, from the point of view of those studying it, has received full and sufficient recognition by granting agencies, university and college administrations, textbook writers, students, or fellow scholars. I myself do not think the study of the racial groups in American life has been much neglected. A better case can be made for the neglect of the history of some white ethnic groups. The best case can be made for the neglect of the integration of our knowledge of these areas into the general curriculum. There was a scholarly case, and there still is a scholarly case; but there is no good argument why only members of these groups must teach about the groups or why only members of the groups need to learn about them.

Finally, let us consider the pragmatic argument. This, too, has a good deal of legitimacy. It asserted that the members of different racial and ethnic groups either could not learn well or learned to be ashamed of their heritage when it played no role in the awesome institution of the public school and the college. There are of course limits to this pragmatic argument, even if we grant, as I do, that there is a solid basis to it. There is still the common knowledge of humanity to be transmitted — skills in reading and calculation and the knowledge of science and history. The pragmatic argument comes up against the pragmatic need to set some limit to the kind of teaching and learning the purpose of which is to give people a good opinion of themselves and to convince them they are accepted, in order to allow for the kind that is simply valuable and necessary for them and for all people. The pragmatic argument has been carried to extremes, as when special schools were set up in Berkeley, under the auspices of the public school system, for Mexican Americans and for blacks. Perhaps they could be justified as experiments, and they *were* basically experimental, but I can scarcely accept the argument that for some groups learning can go on only in separate enclaves. On some college campuses something perilously close to this was instituted at the height of this movement.

I have defined a weak cultural pluralism, which was basically a kind of tolerance on the way to an expected acculturation and assimilation, and a strong cultural pluralism, which was based primarily on an ideological view of the position of racial and ethnic groups in American life, one that emphasizes their colonial status and the repression of their cultures by Anglo-Americans. These may be seen as two extremes in cultural pluralism. We can define something that stands between these two extremes, and here "integration," another ambiguous term, will be helpful. Integration implies, on the one hand, an organic relationship: just as a personality may be integrated, so may a society. On the other hand it implies that there is still a clear articulation of the parts, that is, some degree of identifiability of each part. I wish to divorce the word from its most current usage, as in an integrated school or an integrated organization, but even there the meanings I want to emphasize are apparent, as indicated by the fact that we differentiate desegregated, which means numerically distributed, from integrated, which is assumed to imply some organic connection between the races.

The form of cultural pluralism that to my mind would be in the interests of both individual groups and the entire nation is one in which the emphasis on distinctive histories and cultures is integrated into a larger sense of American history and the American experience.

To show how this integration may be achieved, I shall emphasize the situation in the elementary and secondary schools rather than in the colleges and universities. In the latter, all points of view could properly have a role, as long as they are presented by teachers committed basically to the search for truth, in a situation in which students are not presented with a single exclusive view. The colleges and universities, because they are committed to a search for truth, paradoxically may tolerate a greater degree of extremism and error. We assume, even though the facts often do not support this assumption, that we deal with mature, if young, people and that if extreme positions are presented — I am speaking of positions supported by evidence, presented according to the canons of science rather than propaganda — the students will be able to determine for themselves what position they want to take.

The situation in lower schools, I believe, is really quite different. In these schools we are engaged in the introduction of basic skills. Although there may be arguments about how to teach reading or writing or calculating skills or foreign languages or the large structure of historical events, there can be no argument about what the end product of such a process must be, even when we deal with the most ambiguous of these elements, such as history. It is important that students should know, for example, that the New World became known to Europeans as a result of the voyages of southern and western European navigators in the late fifteenth and the sixteenth centuries and that Spaniards and Englishmen were the first significant European settlers of North America, rather than that they should believe, for example, that the New World was really settled by the ten tribes of Israel, or by black people from Africa, or by travelers from outer space.

We are also engaged in a process of socialization. We want to teach the students to work on their own and in groups, to respect the common rules of any social order, to regard achievement through their own efforts as possible and rewarding, to understand that blaming others for their own failings is self-defeating and frustrating, and to comprehend all the other things that make for a good and satisfying society.

Finally, we are still engaged in the process of making a nation, a distinctive nation that is based on the primacy of no single ethnic group, but still one with a defined history, character, and ideals. In other words, in the schools we are involved in the making of Americans, since this is still a country of mass immigration with large populations still imperfectly integrated into a common nation, for reasons of both past prejudice and discrimination and current parochialism.

These objectives, the teaching of skills, socialization, and the making of Americans, are crucial to elementary and secondary education, and they must be held in mind when we talk about truth in education. There are many levels of truth, and we must judge what we teach by what we want to attain. We could emphasize in our teaching that a dominant ethnic group, the Anglo-Americans, enslaved, suppressed, and carried out genocide, physical or cultural, against all other groups. We could emphasize that these other groups attained equality through organization, force, and violence. We could emphasize that it is a betrayal of manhood and authenticity to surrender to Anglo-American cultural values and that the values of each group are good for it and must forever be maintained. We could concentrate on every gap in education, income, or political influence among the groups and ascribe that gap fully to prejudice and discrimination. I could continue the litany. Some evidence can be found for each of these views, though all distort some other kind of evidence.

We do exercise selection in our teaching of history and current problems; but our selection and choice in history, economics, and sociology must be guided not only by truth, a difficult enterprise in itself because scholars disagree, but also by our conception of a desirable society, of the relationship between what we select to teach and the ability of people to achieve such a society and live together in it. In other words, our view of the future, the future we want, must in some sense determine our teaching about the past and present.

Thus, after World War II there was a great concern in Europe with the way history should be taught, because it was believed that the kind of teaching done might encourage nationalism and antagonism toward other nations, or the opposite. I would make the same argument about cultural pluralism in American schools: we must decide whether we will teach separatism, antagonism to the formerly dominant ethnic elements; or whether we will emphasize the contribution of each group to the United States, the maintenance of its culture in as full a form as possible, and perhaps criticism of members of the group who prefer acculturation and assimilation; or whether we will emphasize the opposing assimilationist views. It is my impression that those who want to teach loyalty to a single nation that has virtues are intimidated and demoralized by the events of 1965–1975 and the way these have been interpreted in the dominant media and in many scholarly circles. Thus the problem is not that minority groups will be crushed by American culture but that, quite the opposite, they will be taught an unrealistic and unrewarding emphasis on the independence and separate virtue of each group, and the necessity for it to defend itself from the basically corrupt Anglo-American dominated society.

The argument is sometimes made that at least for some groups a stronger culturally pluralist emphasis is both politically justified and socially necessary. Many in the black and Spanish-speaking groups feel that their need for an education that recognizes special needs and a special cultural distinctiveness, and that raises their group's consciousness, is much greater than that of the white ethnic groups, and that their right to it is more solidly established. They point out that statistically and otherwise they are truly deprived, especially in income and jobs. The blacks point out that the extermination of their cultural traits was almost total, while the white immigrants could, if they wished, maintain their cultures in churches, afternoon schools, and parochial schools. The Spanish-speaking point out that they have a distinctive language situation. Both blacks and the Spanish-speaking point to a distinctive political situation: the blacks were brought as slaves, and the Mexicans and Puerto Ricans were conquered. The American Indians were also conquered. The white ethnic groups, however, came as free immigrants. Thus the blacks, the Spanish-speaking groups, the American Indians, and perhaps some other groups can make stronger claims for public support of their distinctive cultures than can European groups.

I think there is a good deal of weight in the argument that the distinctive cultural differences of blacks, the Spanish-speaking, and American Indians give them a larger moral claim on American society than European ethnic groups possess. However, we should not exaggerate the weight of this argument. After all, many blacks are also "free immigrants" from the West Indies and elsewhere. Most Mexican Americans are free immigrants or the descendants of free immigrants, and the Puerto Ricans choose voluntarily to enter an English-speaking environment. If the argument is that the black and Spanish-speaking immigrants were forced to migrate for economic reasons, why, so did the immigrant ancestors of the present-day European ethnic groups.

The fact is, we cannot separate ethnic and racial groups into two classes: those that have suffered, economically and culturally, in American society and therefore deserve redress; and those that have not. Perhaps at the extremes we might make such a distinction, but the history of each group is so unique that a broad separation does not make sense. Consider the Asian Americans, the Chinese and Japanese, who have been among the most successful in introducing special programs devoted to their heritage in the colleges. They did not come as slaves, and they were not conquered, but they did suffer racial prejudice and, in the case of the Japanese Americans, confiscation of their property and incarceration. Nevertheless, they do well in school and well economically. Therefore the question arises: Does deprivation give special rights to ethnic programs?

Another powerful argument gives special weight to the claims of black and Spanish-speaking groups as against those of white immigrant groups. This is the pragmatic argument that as a matter of fact the blacks do poorly in school, and so do the members of the major Spanish-speaking groups, and for that reason alone some special attention to ethnic studies programs is required. The first claim is made on the basis of a past deprivation, and the second on the basis of a present deprivation; but since this is a pragmatic argument, there are pragmatic questions. Do ethnic studies actually raise the scholastic achievements of the students? There are many reasons why an ethnic studies emphasis might improve the achievement of blacks or of the Spanish-speaking, but the arguments are quite different and we do not know how much weight to give them. One argument is that the present dominant curriculum is alien to members of certain groups; there is no way for the black or Mexican American or Puerto Rican child to relate to a middle-class curriculum based on Dick and Mary. In other words, the argument is that relatedness is necessary, and that this must be a relatedness the objective of which is to bring the black or Spanish-speaking child to competence in what we may call the general curriculum, which is sometimes and improperly called the "white" or "middle class" curriculum—I say improperly because the ability to read and calculate is a general human need, not based on class or color. Whether this ethnically related curriculum is more effective, I do not know. It may be. We should find out.

There is a second and quite different pragmatic argument for ethnic studies, which is not so much that they directly serve to make the curriculum more attractive and meaningful but that they give a greater sense of self-respect to the child of a minority group and in so doing make the child a more competent and self-assured learner. Discovering that blacks and Mexican Americans and Puerto Ricans have played a major role in the United States, according to this argument, the child will display greater self-confidence in his or her studies.

The first pragmatic argument asserts that the child will do better in his or her studies if their content relates directly to the child's actual, concrete life. The second argument says the child will do better if his or her group or members of that group are visibly reflected in the curriculum, because that will raise the child's pride and self-confidence, the sense that he or she is part of the educational enterprise rather than an outsider in it. Yet a third pragmatic argument is that ethnic studies will of course bring more blacks and Spanish-surnamed teachers into the school and that this will increase the number of role models and will again lead the child to achieve more.

All this may well be true; yet it is also true that Chinese, Japanese, Armenians, Greeks, Jews, and some other groups learned well when nothing about their ways of life or about their groups was in the curriculum, and when none of the people of these groups served as teachers or administrators in the schools. However, there are many ways of learning, and perhaps the direct contact through the curriculum with their actual ways of life, with the histories of their ethnic groups, and with individuals from their groups is needed by the children of some groups or by some children in all groups. Ethnic groups are not as alike as peas in a pod. Not only are they concretely different, but their differences may result in very different educational needs; for this reason some groups may need ethnic studies while other groups do not.

When we contrast Chinese, Japanese, Armenian, and Jewish students with black, Mexican American, and Puerto Rican students, we are contrasting groups that have seemed to achieve academically even in the total absence of any public recognition of their cultures and group lives with groups that have done poorly and might be benefited by a recognition of their cultures and group lives. However, we have left out a host of groups in the middle: Polish, other East European, Irish, and German, the achievements of which have been neither remarkable for speedy progress in the face of adverse circumstances nor for backwardness. Would the children of these groups be helped academically if recognition were to be given to their group characters and their cultural backgrounds? This is not at all clear. In some cases the descendants of these groups have only a distant and vague sense of their group characters. In any case, their demands for the recognition of their group characters are not based on either a deprived political condition (conquest or slavery) or any particular backwardness in academic or economic achievement. Instead they are based on the demand that all cultures be recognized, that all group heritages be of equal significance, and that all be given roles in education and in the curriculum.

The claims of truth, of the pragmatic educational necessities of certain groups, and of what I would call the nation as a whole may thus give different answers about the place of cultural pluralism in American life and in the school curriculum. I have suggested the word "integration" as the key by which we can evaluate the place of cultural pluralism. We reject in this term the absolute demands of assimilationists on the one hand and of cultural separatists on the other. I don't believe that either of these rejected positions is dominant; the issue is the definition of the middle ground. There we have many problems. Even a small amount of cultural pluralism begins by raising troubling questions. Should ethnic studies be only for the children of the group having that heritage, or should ethnic studies be for all? Should ethnic studies be required for members of the groups to which they pertain, or should they be offered as electives? Should ethnic studies be a separate enclave in the curriculum, or should they be diffused through and affect the entire curriculum? Should ethnic studies be taught only by persons who belong to the groups they teach about, or is the teaching of ethnic studies available to all, from any background? Should ethnic studies be seen as advocacy — "belong to the group, have pride in it, study its language " — or should they point out the varied positions that individuals in the United States have taken in relation to their heritages?

These are all enormously difficult questions, and the talisman of "integration" does not give all the answers; nevertheless, it suggests, for example, that we should not limit enrollment in ethnic studies to those of a given heritage, though it is understandable that those of a given heritage will be more interested. The model here should be the teaching of foreign languages in the high schools. They are all considered of value and are made available because they are of value; yet it is understandable that one will find Italian taught more commonly where there are many students of Italian background. The achievements of a group should be taught insofar as they play a part in American history. Understandably, blacks have a much larger share in American history, and thus should take a larger place in the curriculum, than, let us say, Polish Americans. However, in areas where there are many Polish Americans, additional attention should be given to their contribution.

The teaching of ethnic studies must not be the teaching of resentment and antagonism. Here the argument is the same as that which leads us to reject a chauvinistic emphasis in history in general.

Teaching must be open to all on the basis of their real qualifications. Real qualification will very often mean that members of the group in question are much better qualified than anyone else, since they have more background and motivation.

Ethnic studies should be integrated into those parts of the curriculum where they have a place: into history, first of all, but also into economics, sociology, social science, and literature. In each case distortion must be avoided, both for the sake of truth in education and for the sake of the country. I think a black literature of resentment and anger has played a larger role in teaching in recent years than can be justified by any large view of American and English literature.

My view of cultural pluralism in the schools and in the society is that we should not support the creation of sharp differences, with the children of an ethnic background, neatly labeled and numbered, automatically taking special courses in that background. That is not the reality of U.S. society, for here all groups are to some variable extent acculturated and assimilated. Not all black children should be taught as if black English were their language, nor all Chinese as if they were deficient in English. We should think of teaching about a subgroup in American society as a focus of interest and subject of relevance; primarily it will turn out to be most useful for members of that group, but not exclusively for them. A focus of interest and a subject of relevance is not a means of mobilization. Indeed, education in general should not be a means of mobilization of any sort.

This general picture of cultural pluralism in the schools is based on my view of ethnic groups in their relationship to the general society: ideally, this place is also not defined by sharp differences. The society should be open to those who have no interest in a background defined by their descent and have no desire to maintain it or make claims for it; but it should also be open to those who do take an interest in their background and wish to maintain it and instill it in their children. The public agencies should take a position toward ethnic inheritance that I would describe as benign neutrality. We are not interested in a situation such as that of the Soviet Union, in which every person must carry his nationality on his identity card and may not change it even if he has no interest in it. Subnations and subgroups have no legal identity in this country, and should have none. They are protected against discrimination and prejudice, and they are given the liberty, as all individuals and groups are, to maintain whatever part of an ethnic heritage or a distinct identity they wish, as long as that does not transgress on the rights of others. I do not think, however, that it is the place of public agencies to go beyond a benign neutrality toward ethnicity, whether to suppress it or to strengthen it.

We want a truthful account of our past and our present, and this involves considerably more attention to race and ethnicity than it has received in the curriculum. We want effective teaching in common skills and knowledge, and this pragmatically may involve paying attention to the fact that many children do not know English or that they need role models or need material that relates to their interests. This is a pragmatic concern, however, and I do not think most of the American people, including most of the people who are defined or see themselves as members of distinctive subgroups, want the government to maintain an interest in their survival as distinctive group. This would raise the problem of how the government should deal with the claims of many subgroups, which are poorly defined, and with the varying relations among those who may be considered their members. There are mechanisms for going beyond what the public and the common agencies of government and education can or should do to maintain distinct groups; these mechanisms are the independent churches, schools, and organizations. The definition and survival of a fuller and more robust subculture for those groups who find a need for it should be the function of these institutions and not that of the government and the public school.

We should still engage in the work of the creation of a single, distinct, and unique nation, and this requires that our main attention be centered on the common culture. Cultural pluralism describes a supplement to the emerging common interests and common ideals that bind all groups in the society; it does not, and should not, describe the whole.

[1977]

7

American Pluralism:

Voluntarism or State Action?

IN 1964 there was as yet almost no acknowledgment of a public responsibility to provide any assistance to groups to help them in maintaining their cultures or corporate characters. Indeed, in 1964 legislation was passed that seemed at the time to mark the full triumph of the color-blind and thus, in a sense, the assimilationist position. The language of the Civil Rights Act asserted that no place of public accommodation could limit its patronage "on the ground of race, color, religion, or national origin"; that no public facility could deny the right to equal protection of the laws "on account of . . . race, color, religion, or national origin"; that the Attorney General would intervene if there were a complaint that any public school or college were denying admission "by reason of race, color, religion, or national origin"; that no employer could practice discrimination "because of . . . race, color, religion, . . . or national origin"; and most sweepingly, that "no person in the United States shall, on the ground of race, color, or national origin, be excluded from participation in, be denied the benefits of, or be subjected to discrimination under any program or activity receiving Federal financial assistance." At about the same time, all racial and national origin references were expunged from the immigration laws. Justice Harlan's dissent in *Plessy v. Ferguson*, that "our constitution is color-blind," had now apparently been written, sweepingly and with no possible restriction, into law.

Although this development meant that government, and a good deal of private activity with a public character, could not in any way make distinctions that would harm anyone because of ethnicity, by implication it would appear that the same institutions were also enjoined from making distinctions that would aid anyone because of ethnicity.

This did not mean that cultural pluralism was dead, however, since the entire private realm available for the maintenance of distinctive cultures still existed. Private religion existed for the maintenance of religious distinction and, if desired, of ethnic distinction. The entire realm of education existed, under Constitutional protection, for the maintenance of ethnic cultures. The Constitutional protection of speech, publication, and assembly protected the thinking, writing, orating, and disseminating of any image or argument or information that enhanced the survival of any ethnic group and culture. It was as if the United States had been struggling since its birth to define some coherent relationship between the universalistic sentiments of the Declaration of Independence and the Constitution, which seemed to establish or call for a nation based on principles rather than on race or ethnicity — on rational exposition rather than on primitive sentiment — and the reality of a nation in which one major ethnic stock, the original settlers, dominated and others faced discrimination and prejudice and even, in various degrees, denial of the rights guaranteed to all. The relationship between law and reality could become coherent only if the original principles were abandoned and one stock was raised to dominance by law, or if they prevailed and no stock was given any recognition by law. The Civil Rights Act of 1964 and the Immigration Act of 1965 determined that the initial principles should prevail over any lingering attachment to the English or Anglo-Saxon or Protestant or English-speaking original founders of the republic. However, the same principles also guaranteed a wide range of freedom for the voluntary maintenance of whatever ethnic distinctiveness anyone wanted to maintain. The limit of protection, it appeared, was tax exemption for religious, educational, and philanthropic organizations. The rest was up to each individual and each group.

Under these circumstances, the range of alternatives that had been selected by various groups was extensive. Undoubtedly the fullest network of independent organization of any ethnic group was that of the Jews. This elaborate network was encouraged, first, by the fact that in the case of the Jews ethnicity and religion largely coincided and the institutions of religion and ethnicity were established to serve the same group, sometimes in cooperation, sometimes in antagonism, and sometimes in such a way that one institution, such as the local synagogue or temple, seemed to serve the interests of both in equal measure; and second, because the special situation of Israel, a unique homeland in a uniquely dangerous situation, encouraged the strongest measure of ethnic attachment.

Religion was mixed in with the maintenance of ethnic attachment in the case of most other groups, too. Religious institutions were the main form in which some knowledge of the ethnic groups and their cultures and characters were handed on, and some effort was made to maintain this attachment, though in many groups political, philanthropic, and religiously neutral educational institutions contributed to the task. Aside from any institutional network, and perhaps more important than it, were the informal networks of family connection, neighborhood, and friendship.

This was, to my mind, the emerging and distinctive ethnic pattern of America in the mid-1960s; indeed, it could be argued that a consensus about the proper arrangement of a multiethnic society in the United States had been emerging over some time: the consensus called for public neutrality and private freedom. Admittedly, the movement in this direction had been marred by many aberrations, including public denigration of and discrimination against some groups (blacks, Mexican Americans, American Indians, and Orientals). And public schools were scarcely aware that they were favoring white Protestant America when they sanctioned Bible-reading and Christmas celebrations in the schools and used history textbooks in which only Anglo-Americans appeared. However, opinion and law steadily moved toward public neutrality and the elimination of restrictions on private efforts to maintain group distinctiveness.

Public neutrality did not mean there was no public recognition of diversity, but much of this recognition was ceremonial. Ministers representing all major religions and groups would open sessions of Congress and political conventions. Distinctive group festivals, holidays, might evoke a public declaration. A history week for a group would be proclaimed. More significant was the informal recognition of group reality by party leaders, who would propose for election a balanced ticket representing major groups, and the arrangements in some cities to balance appointed bodies for religious and ethnic representation: Thus, outside of any formal requirement, the school boards of New York and San Francisco were balanced by religion and later by race.

All these arrangements were to change in the period of heightened expectations and demands of minority groups of the later 1960s and 1970s: the state was now called upon directly to assist in the maintenance of group loyalty, native language, original culture. When we shift from voluntary action to state action in these areas, however, some very serious problems arise, and they are the subject of this chapter.

The cultural pluralists of World War I wanted little enough from the state: they wanted it to stop imposing forceful assimilation. The intercultural educators of the 1940s wanted a bit more: it was the responsibility of the state to assist in education for tolerance of other groups; after all, intolerance was one of the chief weapons of the enemy, and weakened the common war effort. The new multicultural education of the late 1960s and 1970s emerged at a time when the state role generally was far more extensive and assumed much greater power than in the past. The minority groups that began the demand for an education to support cultural difference were, to begin with, poor and without an organization that would permit them to launch extensive programs of after-school and weekend education, as had some other groups. The state in any case engrossed far more resources in the later 1960s than it had in the 1940s or the 1920s, and it was generally expected that if there was something good to be done, one should get the state to do it.

The role of voluntary groups, it would appear, had shrunk to the function of putting pressure on the state so that it provided the money. But of course if the state provides money something new enters the situation: the state, disposing of state power, must carefully define what it is that it is supporting, what it expects from it, who is eligible for it, and who is required to do it. This is not to say that the state cannot do what voluntary private organizations can do. It can support research, curricular innovation, experiment. But there is a quid pro quo for state support. And this must inevitably shape the concrete reality of multiethnic education.

The multiethnic education of the later 1960s and 1970s was based on a heightened self-consciousness and militancy of ethnic groups; it was strongly motivated by a sense of failure to achieve in the educational system; it emphasized the value of group identity for mental health, group cohesion, and individual achievement; and it demanded and received state support for multiethnic education, both by means of legislation and administrative rulings that required local school systems to do something, and by means of budgetary support provided from state and federal sources for the purpose.

And because the state is now deeply involved, what we have today is not simply another phase in a series of explosions of interest in relating to ethnic heritage or maintaining it: once government enters, as it has today, it is clear we have a tendency in education that is firmly fixed. Government does not easily withdraw from a field once it has entered upon it. In the past, cultural pluralism and intercultural education were the concern of groups of intellectuals, of leaders of voluntary organizations, of organized elements within ethnic groups. Programs had to be developed and advocated without government assistance. Voluntary budgets have to be raised anew each year. But government budgets, once established, possess a dynamic of their own. In the past, when individuals and group leaders lost interest in ethnic education, then activity generally declined: there was no one to keep up the pressure. Once a program is incorporated in legislation and budgets, however, one can expect the program to keep going even if the intensity of lobbying activity for it declines: there are now, after all, paid agents of government who have developed an interest in the program and are there to see that it does not die.

Multiethnic education is, of course, no fixed matter; in the nature of the case it could not be. We have already moved through a number of phases in the years since the black power and black pride explosion once again placed ethnic concerns on the educational agenda. We have seen a number of excesses and false turnings. One wonders, for example, whether there are many courses in Swahili still being given; this was advocated on the assumption that it was an equivalent of the advocacy of the teaching of Italian and of Hebrew by Italian and Jewish groups in New York State, but there is, as a matter of fact, no single African language that can play the role Italian did for Italians, Hebrew for Jews. Since the history of these past fifteen hectic years has to be reconstructed from raw materials, one can give no clear description of the phases through which the multiethnic education movement has gone, but a few overlapping phases can be discerned.

The first phase, beginning in the late 1960s and early 1970s, emphasized advocacy of group pride by the minority groups that most strongly felt their oppression. In this phase, the only minority groups that counted were blacks, Mexican Americans and Puerto Ricans, and Asian Americans. In this phase, America was scourged for its racism; self-deprecation and self-hatred were in the air, for it was the period of the Vietnam war and the black urban riots. In the second phase, it was argued that learning about America's iniquitous treatment of minority groups was something that everyone needed, majority groups as well as minority groups. History books were criticized, and new texts were created. English curricula were overhauled, and works of minority authors describing minority experience were added to the required readings. In the third phase, the issue of language was raised, particularly for the Spanish-speaking students; a bilingual education act was passed as early as 1968, strengthened in 1974. In the fourth phase, white ethnic groups also entered the scene; they, too, wanted their ethnic experience to be noted. Just as the bilingual thrust was marked by federal legislation, so too was the white ethnic thrust: an Ethnic Heritage Studies Program was first proposed in 1970, passed in 1972, funded in 1973, and implemented in 1974.

We have thus moved from minority studies for the most oppressed; to minority studies, integrated into the curriculum, for all; to bilingual studies; to ethnic studies for all. What has emerged sharply is a national commitment to facilitating the maintenance of the ethnic heritage and, rather more significantly, a commitment that *requires* that school authorities take into account ethnic and linguistic difference in education. It may seem too strong to assert that we have moved from *facilitating* to *requiring*, but if we look at the history of bilingual education requirements, I believe we will see that this is not an inaccurate characterization of what has happened.

THE EVOLUTION OF BILINGUAL REQUIREMENTS

The story, like much in the strange history of policy affecting racial and ethnic groups in the United States in the last decade, begins with the Civil Rights Act of 1964, Title VI: "No person in the United States shall, on grounds of race, color, or national origin, be excluded from participation in, be denied the benefits of, or be subjected to discrimination under any program or activity receiving Federal financial assistance." The next year the Elementary and Secondary Education Act of 1965 gave teeth to this general prohibition of discrimination by providing for the first time substantial federal financial aid to school districts. Next, concern over the poor education of Spanish-speaking minority groups led to the passage of the Bilingual Education Act in 1968, offering funds for new educational approaches to meet the needs of children of limited English-speaking ability; these funds were to be used in school systems with high concentrations of children from low-income families. The sums involved were at first not large: $118 million were spent between 1969 and 1973.

While bilingual education thus developed as an effort to im-

prove the education of children of foreign-language background, simultaneously new requirements were imposed on
school districts on the basis of the Civil Rights Act of 1964. In
May 1970 an "interpretative memorandum" from the Director
for Civil Rights of the Department of Health, Education, and
Welfare (HEW) asserted that "compliance reviews" undertaken
to enforce the ban on discrimination in Title VI of the Civil
Rights Act of 1964 had revealed, in school districts with large
Spanish-surnamed populations, "a number of practices which
have the effect of denying equality of educational opportunity
to Spanish-surnamed pupils. Similar practices which have the
effect of discrimination on the ground of national origin exist in
other locations with respect to disadvantaged pupils from other
national origin–minority groups, for example, Chinese and Portuguese." The HEW office described its major areas of concern.
The first was that "where inability to speak and understand the
English language excludes national origin–minority group
children from effective participation in the educational program . . . the district must take affirmative steps to rectify the
language deficiency in order to open the instructional program
to these students." School districts must not assign these students "to classes for the mentally retarded on the basis of criteria
which essentially measure or evaluate English language skills."
They must not deny them access to college preparatory classes
for the same reason. Grouping or tracking to deal with language
problems should not become permanent tracks. School districts
are responsible for proper notification of parents, a notification
which may have to be provided in languages other than English.

In the *Lau* case (1974), the Supreme Court entered the fray
as to what was required: Where a student could not get advantage from an English-language program because he understood
only Chinese, some "appropriate relief" should be furnished.
The HEW Office of Civil Rights (OCR), having seen its earlier,
moderate statement as to what was required quoted approv-
ingly by the Supreme Court, proceeded further:

In order to facilitate efforts by both State Education Agencies and this
Office to secure voluntary compliance with current Title VI require-

ments [after *Lau*], this Office designated a Task Force to develop an outline of those educational approaches which would constitute appropriate "affirmative steps" to be taken by a non-complying school district "to open its instructional program" to students foreclosed currently from effective participation therein.

The outline was attached, and it supplies a further expansion of what the law requires. Culture now enters the scene. A school district, having determined which language or languages students speak and how well, must then determine the students' educational needs,

and then prescribe an education program utilizing the most effective teaching style to satisfy diagnosed educational needs. The determination of which teaching style(s) are to be used will be based on the cognitive and affective domains and should include an assessment of the responsiveness of students to different types of cognitive learning styles and incentive motivational styles—e.g., competitive v. cooperative learning patterns. The diagnostic measures must include diagnoses of problems related to areas or subjects required of other students in the school program *and* prescriptive measures must serve to bring the linguistically/culturally different students(s) to the educational performance level that is expected by the Local Education Agency (LEA) and State nonminority students.

The issue is no longer merely one of language use; we now have a problem of differential responsiveness by students of different cultures to various teaching styles. Schools should be responsive to cultural differences as well as differences in language facility among students. Simply bringing the student up to adequate facility in English has become only one of a number of possible approaches a school district may implement. In addition to "transitional bilingual education," it may undertake a "Bilingual/Bicultural Program" or a "Multilingual/Multicultural Program." While it is not mandated, one acceptable affirmative response to the presence of students of different language backgrounds is education in the language "and culture" of the individual student. "The end product is a student who can function, totally, in both languages and cultures."

In 1974, finally, the Bilingual Education Act of that year, "recognizing (1) that there are large numbers of children of limited English-speaking ability; (2) that many such children have a cultural heritage which differs from that of English-speaking; (3) that a primary means by which a child learns is through the use of such child's language and cultural heritage," and so on, declared it to be the policy of the United States "to encourage the establishment and operation, where appropriate, of educational programs using bilingual educational practices and techniques."[1]

And so Congress itself in 1974 capped a movement that had begun with its own Civil Rights Act ten years earlier, and which had seemed then to be directed only against discrimination in federal programs. This became defined (or redefined, since no one in 1964, one may assume, realized that nondiscrimination meant educational programs adapted to the presumed cultural differences of students in this multicultural nation) by both the Office of Civil Rights and the courts as taking into account cultural as well as language differences.

What we see in these documents that establish the law is a pulling and hauling between a number of different concepts of bilingual and bicultural education. One concept, which begins to emerge in the OCR document of 1970, is that education should be appropriate to a student's needs: if a student cannot speak English, some adaptation must be made so that the student gets something from the educational process. Here we see bilingualism as a means to an effective education. We see the same reasoning in the Supreme Court's *Lau* decision. But by 1974 and 1975 a second concept has entered the scene. Language inability is a rather clear notion. Now we deal with "culture" as a barrier to educational achievement, and educational programs must not only be in a language that can reach the child but in a cultural mode that can reach the child.

A third concept sees bilingual and bicultural education as no longer simply a means to a common educational achievement; there is at least the implication that educational programs should maintain distinctive cultures, along with their distinctive languages. The Ethnic Heritage Studies Program Act of 1972 proposes a mild version of this in its Section 901, Title IX:[2]

In recognition of the heterogeneous composition of the nation and of the fact that in a multiethnic society a greater understanding of the contributions of one's own heritage and those of one's fellow citizens can contribute to a more harmonious, patriotic, and committed populace, and in recognition of the principle that all persons in the educational institutions of the Nation should have an opportunity to learn about the differing and unique contributions to the national heritage made by each ethnic group, it is the purpose of this title to provide assistance designed to afford to students opportunities to learn about the nature of their own cultural heritage, and to study the contributions of the cultural heritages of the other ethnic groups of the Nation.

No one in this version is *required* to study his or her ethnic heritage; no school system is *required* to provide Ethnic studies. A school system is only assisted insofar as it wishes to do something, within the limits of the small sums that have been made available for this program.

But a fourth concept does carry with it some element of compulsion: this is the concept of bilingual-bicultural education as something that it is the *right* of students to get, and the obligation of school systems to provide — rights and obligations deriving not from legislation dealing with bilingualism and ethnic heritage, but from interpretations of what non-discrimination requires under the Civil Rights Act of 1964. It is only in the multicultural education that derives from authority under this act that we can see compulsion employed. It should be made clear that the compulsion is imposed on states and school systems, not on individual students. These must be counted and their language facility tested to see if a program adapted to their language capacities and cultural mode of learning should be developed; once a minimal figure of students who may need bilingual-bicultural education is reached and a program is triggered, a school system *must* provide a program; there is no requirement that a student *must* enroll in it. (And yet, why does one count the students?)

The States Move In

In describing the course of federal legislation dealing with multicultural education, I have been dealing with only one body of law and regulation. There are fifty states, and parallel changes in law have occurred there. Many of these require some kind of education to take account of cultural heritage. The strongest laws are those which mandate some kind of multicultural education. According to Judith Herman:

Those states where legislation mandates the teaching of ethnic material vary in their inclusiveness. New Jersey requires that Black history be a part of the two-year American history curriculum; Illinois, on the other hand, says that " . . . the teaching of history shall include a study of the role and contribution of American Negroes and other ethnic groups including but not restricted to Polish, Lithuanian, German, Hungarian, Irish, Bohemian, Russian, Albanian, Italian, Czechoslovakian, French, Scots, etc."

This Illinois law was passed in 1967 but almost no action was taken until 1972, when the State Superintendent of Public Instruction, Michael Bakalis, established the Office of Ethnic Studies . . .

. . . In Pennsylvania . . . the regulations of the State Board of Education require that schools' instructional program include intergroup concepts to improve students' understanding and relationships around sex differences, race, national origin, religion, and socioeconomic background . . .

In Hawaii, perhaps the state most conscious and least shy about its diversity, the Legislature called in 1972 for a "more comprehensive program of ethnic studies," listed some of the specific groups to be included (Hawaiian, Chinese, Japanese, Filipino, Samoan, Portuguese, and Caucasian-American), and urged a concentration on their differences and problems as well as their similarities. The Legislature also asked for curriculum to include the pros and cons of the ethnic groups' assimilation into the dominant culture, to focus on the interrelationships among the groups, and to deal with the relationship between ethnicity and the state's labor movement.

California's mandate goes one step further and includes sex along with class and ethnicity. The State law requires "correct portrayal" of ethnic contributions (Blacks, Mexican-Americans, Indians, and Orientals are listed but "other ethnic groups" are included). It also demands that textbooks "correctly portray" the role and contributions of the entrepreneur and of labor; and, further, that men and women be characterized in textbooks in all types of professional, vocational, and executive roles.[3]

But there are many other laws, too, dealing with textbook selection, teacher training, and the like. The states also have their own bilingual-bicultural programs. In 1971 no state had requirements for school districts to conduct bilingual education. Twenty-two required teaching in English only, except for foreign-language courses. Over the next few years many of these statutes were repealed, so that in 1976 only eleven states still had such a requirement. Ten states had enacted statutes that required bilingual programs under varying circumstances. According to the National Advisory Council on Bilingual Education:

In Massachusetts, Michigan, New Jersey and Rhode Island, bilingual education is compulsory when twenty children of the same non-English language are found in a school district. In Texas, the program is required if there are twenty children in a given grade throughout the district. Illinois requires the program for each school which enrolls twenty children of a single non-English language.[4]

It is clear the situation is still in flux. We have a mixed set of programs required, suggested, aided, proposed, with authority and funds flowing from federal, state, and local levels, and divided among legislatures, courts, and education authorities, operating by means of law, order, and regulation. We have in addition a host of voluntary organizations representing distinctive ethnic groups, local alliances of ethnic groups, groups of educators, each proposing programs, developing curricula, bringing pressure on textbook publishers and local school systems. In short, we have a distinctively American buzzing confusion, and it is not easy to describe concretely and realistically what is going on. We have the orders of courts and regulatory agencies which sound severe and sweeping, but we do not know to what extent they are actually carried out, or indeed to what extent they can be carried out with limited school resources. (Federal funds for bilingual education amounted in

1976 to about $100 million, state funds in 1974-1975 to $38 million, local funds to $44 million; but it would be impossible to determine how much was spent for multicultural education generally, since so much of it is incorporated into social studies, English, and civics courses.[5])

Voluntary choices, local options, and federal and state requirements are all in play, with what result it would be impossible to say as yet — except for the large result we have already indicated: that some sort of distinctive education for any group of non-English background has become a right, and that bilingual education is the preferred response.

A HAPPY ENDING?

A happy ending to a long story of forced assimilation? Perhaps. But there are still some troubling issues, as there always are when the regularities of state requirement enter a subtle and complex area of education, one that must be suited to individual and group needs. There is something ironic about the government's mandating responsiveness to individual and group needs — and then issuing rigid guidelines as to how this is to be achieved. Thus, government specifies how students should be counted, what groups must be counted, the threshold number of students that will trigger a program, and so on. (As I pointed out, these "must" requirements derive from the extension of the notion of nondiscrimination, as provided in Title VI of the Civil Rights Act of 1964, by regulation and court rulings; the federal Bilingual Education Act only provides opportunities and does not mandate programs. But state programs may be mandatory.) The fact that these groups are as various as Navajo Indians and Greek immigrant children, or lower-class Puerto Ricans moving to and fro between island and mainland and middle-class Cubans committed to making a life in the United States, cannot be taken into account in government regulations, and one wonders whether it is taken into account by government compliance-review agents.

Ethnicity and race are subtle and complex matters; one doubts there are enough people in the country responsive to this complexity and to the variety of needs of different groups to do more than check whether pro forma requirements—some less than any group needs, some more than a group requires or desires—are being met in the over three hundred school districts investigated for compliance in 1975–1976. This number is up from seventy-four in 1973–1974, and even so is a small fraction of those districts with more than 5 percent linguistic minority children which must provide bilingual-bicultural programs according to the regulations.

In some communities—for example, one with a substantial Greek-origin population in Chicago—there has been resistance to the institution of a bilingual-bicultural program; these parents want their children educated in English. One notes that in Quebec there is severe resistance among immigrants, even among those speaking related languages such as Italian, to a requirement that their children must be educated in French rather than in English. In any group there will be division: there will be assimilationists, those who demand linguistic competence, those who want only maintenance of cultural attachment, those who insist on full education in language and culture. It is hard to see how school districts operating under governmental regulations will satisfy such a variety of interests.

Purely voluntary educational activities, conducted in private schools under only limited public authority, might respond to this variety of needs. In the case of Jewish education, for example, we have seen schools that are religious and secular, Orthodox (of several varieties), Conservative, and Reform, all-day, afternoon, and Sunday, variously emphasizing Hebrew, Yiddish, or English, reflecting a history of political tendencies including Zionism, diaspora nationalism, territorialism, anarchism, socialism, and communism. One wonders, after this history, what kind of bilingual-bicultural education established under public auspices and common central rules can possibly satisfy or be relevant to—to take one example—the children of Hebrew-speaking Israeli immigrants who are now coming to this country in substantial numbers. Or, to take another recent immigrant group, those from India and Pakistan; they speak a dozen languages, are in religion divided among Moslems, Hindus, Sikhs, Jains, and others, and reflect a variety of cultures. Will it now be up to school districts in which their numbers are substantial to provide a program? And even though their parents probably insist their education be in English, fully and completely?

The large question that multicultural education has not dealt with as yet is how very different are the desires and requirements of different groups in the area of bicultural and bilingual education. It is not possible for the state to legislate for each group separately, according to its needs and desires. That would run afoul of the state's need for general legislation, legislation that provides the "equal protection of the laws." Yet blacks, Mexican Americans, Puerto Ricans, American Indians, Cubans, Portuguese from the islands and the mainland, French-speaking Canadians and Louisiana Cajuns, Jews, Chinese, Japanese, Poles, Italians, and so on need and want very different things. Some of these groups are concerned primarily with poor educational achievement: they want anything that will work, and if that means multicultural education and black English, so be it, but if it means the exact reverse, they will choose that. Some of these groups have only a transitional language problem and have no desire to maintain in a public school setting education in ancestral languages. Some want only to be recognized: if anything is to be done for any other groups, they want education in their own group's heritage, "equal time," but they may not even be sure they want their children to spend time taking it. And I have simplified the complexity, for in each group there are people with very different demands and needs.

Whether it is possible under state auspices to meet all these needs and requirements is a serious question. What tends to happen is that one model is created to deal with the most urgent needs—let us say, black studies for blacks to build up self-respect, and some teaching in Spanish to help bridge the transition to English. But then these initial model programs become models for others, too. They become the most extreme demands for some in each group who bargain for whatever any other group has, even if most people in the group do not recognize the need. The problem with state programs is that they must prescribe the same for everyone, even though the very essence of this situation is that each individual and each group has a rather different set of needs and wants something quite different from multicultural education.

The reason for this complexity derives directly from the American ethnic pattern. It is not a pattern of sharp lines of division between groups. If it were, if each individual were unambiguously a member of one group or another, then perhaps the same program could be prescribed for each. Some people want to see America this way, the way the early cultural pluralists saw it. Indeed, in this perspective, everyone is a member of an ethnic group, including those of Anglo-Saxon origin, and so we have proposals of ethnic studies for those who do not want them and do not need them simply because of someone's ideological commitment to the notion that every American must be a member of an ethnic group and must need the same things. So we have the outlandish discussions in educational journals of "white studies"—if we have black, brown, yellow, and red studies, why not white studies? But in fact some groups in this country are sharply distinguished by color and culture; others are not. Even so, many members of each of the sharply disinguished groups, through cultural change and intermarriage, move toward the boundaries of their group, and perhaps out of their group. And the overall hope for this country—a hope shaken in recent years—is that ultimately no group boundary will be important, that everyone will have the right to accept whatever he or she wants of ancestral culture and ethnic identity, and that this will be a private choice in which government will play no role, whether to encourage it or to discourage it. And it is still, I believe, part of the general expectation that a general American culture will prevail as the dominant one in our country, and one that does create national identity, loyalty, and commitment.

John Higham has given to my mind the best characterization of what ideally we should hope for in the way of a relationship between the distinctive ethnic cultures and the general American culture. As against "cultural pluralism" or "assimilation," he proposes "pluralistic integration":

Even to consider this possibility will require a conception, clearer than we have yet formulated, of what a system of pluralistic integration might be. In contrast to the integrationist model, it will not eliminate ethnic boundaries. But neither will it maintain them intact. It will uphold the validity of a common culture, to which all individuals have access, while sustaining the efforts of minorities to preserve and enhance their own integrity. In principle this dual commitment can be met by distinguishing between boundaries and nucleus. No ethnic group under these terms may have the support of the general community in strengthening its boundaries. All boundaries are understood to be permeable. Ethnic nuclei, on the other hand, are respected as enduring centers of social action. If self-preservation requires, they may claim exemption from certain universal rules, as the Amish now do from the school laws in some states. Both integration and ethnic cohesion are recognized as worthy goals, which different individuals will accept in different degrees. Ethnicity varies enormously in intensity from one person to another. It will have some meaning for the great majority of Americans, but intense meaning for relatively few. Only minorities of minorities, so to speak, will find in ethnic identity an exclusive loyalty.[6]

The virtues of this approach are first, that it reflects existing social reality, at least as I understand it — this is what ethnic groups want, and it is all they want — and second, that it does not propose the dismantling of what is after all a great, integrating, culture which, whatever iniquities we may charge it with, has brought within its boundaries more varied groups from more varied origins than any other great culture.

But how does this subtle understanding of the relationship between the American center, ethnic boundaries, and ethnic nuclei get realized through state action? It is not easily done. For state action does not recognize gradations. One either does or does not have the right to bilingual education or to ethnic heritage education. One must get either so much more or so much less, measured in money or time. The fact that many of us want none of it, many a lot of it, many want it for someone else, does not easily get incorporated into state action, though we are trying.

Certainly one easy solution was to create one system for

all — the public system — and to let anyone who wanted something special or distinctive find a means for paying for it through private education. We have by now moved far from this model. We have incorporated into our public education so many elements responding to needs of distinctive groups that it is not likely that this neat model, distinguishing between the general and the particular, can be restored. We will have to find new models that respond to the varied needs and desires of various groups, and to the distinctive tastes and desires of the individual within those groups. One approach is state education vouchers, on the basis of which individual students and their parents can choose whatever type of education and whatever supplement to general education they feel best suits them. Presumably there are other ways of bringing together American pluralism in all its variety with our commitment to a common culture. But it will take a lot of hard work and clear thinking about the nature of American pluralism and the directions in which we would prefer to see it move.

[1977]

8

Bilingualism: Will It Work?

WE HAVE INSTITUTIONALIZED, through law and practice, bilingual-bicultural education; to what extent and with what effectiveness is unknown. There are several reasons for this institutionalization. One is the desire to improve the educational achievement of children of foreign-language background. A second, the hope of maintaining the cultures and languages of immigrant groups, is not formally the objective of either legislation or judicial decrees, but it *is* the objective of those who push for legislation and institute court cases. These two objectives are clearly discernible. A third is somewhat less clear. It is to enhance respect for immigrant cultures among the children who bear them and others, which it is hoped will both contribute to better educational achievement by immigrant children — by way of the greater self-respect induced in the child — and help maintain the culture.

That is the present situation. One hears a good deal of grumbling by congressmen and columnists and writers on occasion, but bilingual-bicultural education seems to be well established, and it is hard to see any development that will reduce its present scale, and more likely it will be expanded.

What reason do we have to be skeptical about these programs? First, bilingual-bicultural education does not do anything for, and is not likely to do anything for, one of the problems it was meant to deal with and the one of greatest concern to Congress, namely, poor educational achievement. Admittedly this argument — does it work? — is always trotted out to show that some innovation, whether Head Start, or progressive education, or increased drill, is not the answer to problems of low educational achievement; and bilingual-bicultural education is no exception. It is also true that research findings never seem to affect the fate of such programs much, and in view of how complicated it is to show the positive effect of any one variable on educational achievement, maybe they should not.

But there are more serious reasons for doubting the effects of bilingual-bicultural education on educational achievement. These are historical reasons. It was not necessary to spur the on-the-average higher academic achievement of Jews, Japanese, and other high-achieving immigrant groups, nor was facility in English relevant to explaining the more modest educational achievements of an English-speaking immigrant group, the Irish. In short, historically, bilingual-bicultural education does not seem to have mattered, one way or another. Its absence did not seem to affect differential achievement. And that suggests that its presence will not either.

It is not only history that leads us to doubt the significance of bilingual-bicultural education for educational achievement; it is contemporary experience (not research). In 1979 the *New York Times* reported that Houston faced the loss of two million dollars in federal funds because it could not find fifteen teachers who spoke Vietnamese, whom the Office of Civil Rights insisted it had to employ to teach the 417 Vietnamese pupils in the Houston schools.[1] Does anyone who knows anything about these matters believe for a minute that Vietnamese bilingual-bicultural education in the public schools will matter for the educational achievement of Vietnamese children? Other reports indicate that they already surpass American-born children in mathematics. There are good grounds for believing their class background and the excellent education in some respects — especially in mathematics — of the schools they attended in Vietnam to be the decisive elements in affecting their educational progress.

Or consider a newspaper account of a class of children of foreign-language background in New York City:

"But soft! What light through yonder window breaks? It is the East, and Juliet is the sun!"

With that familiar Shakespearean pronouncement, Wook Nae Kim, nine years old, bounded to the center of the fourth-grade classroom and spread his arms dramatically.

"O Romeo, Romeo! Wherefore art thou, Romeo?" responded Catalina Martin, a native of Ecuador. "Deny thy father and refuse thy name!" At the end of the exchange, the class applauded.

When Wook Nae came here from Korea last September, he did not speak English. Neither did most of the children in Andrea Gilmore's "NES" (non-English-speaking) class in Public School 89.

Standing up in turn, each child introduced himself to a visitor and noted his country of origin. There were thirteen children from Korea, four from Taiwan, three from the Philippines and Hong Kong, and one each from Colombia, Haiti, Vietnam, Ecuador, Bangladesh, Honduras, India, Guyana, and the Dominican Republic.

And where was Miss Gilmore from? "California!" the children shouted in unison.

"The plane lands every day on the roof," Cleonice LoSecco, principal of the elementary school, said, tongue in cheek. Enrollment increased to 1,600 from 1,353 in 1975, which forced the sending of kindergarten and sixth-grade pupils to other schools . . .

The elementary pupils are divided into fifty-one classes, including fourteen bilingual Spanish classes and a bilingual Korean class of first- and second-graders, the first such class in the city. In addition, there are two so-called "TESL" classes (teaching English as a second language).

Although she taught Spanish-speaking youngsters in another school last year, Miss Gilmore had no formal training in dealing with a plethora of languages.

"I'm required to teach the usual fourth-grade curriculum," she said, "the Monroe Doctrine, the amendments to the Constitution, even though they don't know English."

As a result, she has relied on inventiveness and imagination to prod her shy students into grappling with English. One day she took them to see the Zeffirelli movie of "Romeo and Juliet." After that, nearly everybody wanted to try the speeches in class.

For Ferdoushi Haguelo of Bangladesh, growing bean sprouts in paper cups broke the language barrier. She had not said a word for weeks until Miss Gilmore put moistened towels and the seeds into a cup. "You're doing it wrong!" said Ferdoushi. Miss Gilmore was thrilled.[2]

How important is a formal program of bilingual-bicultural education, whether mandated by a court or the Office of Civil Rights, to the educational achievement of these children? Of course, not all children will be blessed with a Miss Gilmore. But is the element of bilingual-bicultural education, in itself, crucial for the educational process for these children?

Am I being cavalier in dismissing the significance of bilingual-bicultural education to educational achievement on the basis of these crude references to history and to current experience? Perhaps. Certainly the experience of having to attend school in a foreign language with unsympathetic and prejudiced teachers is bad for children. But I would think it is the lack of sympathy and the prejudice that are the problem, in which case mandating bilingual-bicultural education may not be the answer. In any case, it will take a very long time to find the conditions under which bilingual-bicultural education contributes to educational achievement.

Even if the educational achievement argument will not hold, what about the respect argument? Was it not a bad thing that immigrant children were Americanized, forced to give up their parental culture, told to forget ancestral languages in favor of English? Did it not make them less than full persons, did it not make them people with a void, ignorant of their true roots, of who they were? We have heard much of this argument in recent years, from Michael Novak and others.

First, let us recall that there was and is a mechanism for maintaining outside the public schools a consciousness of people and culture. The largest private school system in America was established by the Roman Catholic church, to protect children from the Protestant (or nonreligious) influences of the public school but also to transmit ethnic culture. It did this best for the Irish (of course, as in any culture, there are many traditions that can be labeled "Irish," and the parochial schools selected only some of these), but there were also parochial schools for children from French-speaking families, from Polish-speaking families, and from other ethnic groups. There was a problem in that the Irish-dominated church was often unsympathetic to the desires of non-Irish Catholics for an ethnic component in their parochial school education, but the opportunity nevertheless existed for parents to maintain knowledge and consciousness of people and culture outside the public school system. In addition to the parochial schools, Roman Catholic and other, there were afternoon schools maintained by many groups, and Sunday Schools.

A second caution in accepting this argument that public schools imposed the English language and American culture on children whose parents wanted the maintenance of ethnic language and culture is that most American parents liked what the public schools were offering. Most had come to this country not to maintain a foreign language and culture but with the intention, in the days when the trip to the United States was long and expensive, to become Americanized as fast as possible, and this meant English language and American culture. They sought the induction to a new language and culture that the public schools provided — as do many present-day immigrants, too — and while they often found, as time went, on, that they regretted what they and their children had lost, this was *their* choice, rather than an imposed choice. And every choice involves regret for the path not taken.

Third, the fact was that, whatever immigrant hopes and intentions, the American environment turned out to be enormously attractive to their children (and often to them). American culture assimilates because it sets its face against the maintenance of foreign language and culture and makes this difficult, and it assimilates because it is itself a new culture, adapted to new immigrants, which makes their transported culture seem less attractive. After all, American culture, or at least certain aspects of it, is very attractive even to youth who do not live in America and do not intend to. How can one fight rock and jeans, or their equivalents in earlier decades?

Finally, there were the simple pragmatic advantages to accepting education in English, and in American culture. The public schools had the money and prestige, and they controlled access to whatever further higher education could give; one did not get very far by being very good in Chinese or Hebrew afternoon school, and these schools suffered from being cut off from the larger culture.

But does one fool children about all this by bringing bilingual-bicultural education into the schools? Do children thereby gain an appreciation of their past culture as being equal in importance and significance in affecting their fate to the culture of an English-speaking America? I doubt it. The school is only one thing. Outside, television is still in English, as are movies and major league sports and big-time politics. English is what the President speaks, and the congressman, even if he has a Spanish name. There has been, in other words, an inevitability, once the process of *permanent* migration has taken place, to the relative lesser importance, in reality, of ancestral language and culture, and nothing much can change that. One will never do as well in the United States living in Spanish, or French, or Yiddish, or Chinese, as one will do living learning, and working in English.

And if bringing the languages and cultures into the public schools will not do much for their relative status and importance, it also will not do much to change other people's minds as to their relative status or importance. I think it is therefore a naive argument to say that putting bilingual-bicultural education into the public school curriculum will make a significant difference in affecting the general respect in which a given culture and language are held.

Neither the educational achievement argument nor the maintenance of culture argument is persuasive to me. It is not clear what, if anything, bilingual-bicultural education will do for educational achievement; and it is hardly likely we will ever find out, in view of how various will be the kinds of bilingual-bicultural education provided, and how complex its interaction with other factors.[3] Nor is it clear that there is either a strong demand for the public schools to help maintain immigrant and non-English languages and cultures (some are not immigrant, of course, as in the case of the American Indians and many of the Spanish-speaking), or that bilingual-bicultural education will help meet this demand in the face of the assimilating power of American culture and the advantages it offers.

There are other arguments for bilingual-bicultural education, of course. For example, bilingual-bicultural education is one way to bring into the teaching force persons of a given culture and background who are poorly represented within it and who are important to relate to children of that language and culture. This seems a better argument than the two I have given, but even this is not completely convincing. After all, we have seen huge transitions in the ethnic composition of the teaching force without bilingual-bicultural education. In New York City, Protestant teachers were replaced by Catholics, and Catholics by Jews, and Jews are now being replaced by blacks and Puerto Ricans. The relative rates of change raise some questions. Also it is true that transitions in the past have generally occurred *after* the composition of the students had changed, and there was no necessary close statistical correspondence between the ethnic composition of the student body and the teachers. But need there be? Nevertheless, it is worth pointing out that whatever the general soundness of this argument, the push for jobs for persons from given groups is probably the strongest force leading to more bilingual-bicultural education; and the resistance to giving these jobs to members of these groups is one of the strongest forces in opposition to bilingual-bicultural education.

But probably the most powerful source of opposition to bilingual-bicultural education is the fear that it will hamper the assimilation of new immigrant groups, and delay the acquisition of a common culture and a common loyalty. Behind this fear is the feeling that it was a good thing for this country that people of many stocks were molded here into a nation speaking a common language, and that we would have been worse off had this not happened. This is the concern that carries the most weight with me.

I have asked myself why, and I can give some pragmatic reasons, starting with the assumption that had previous immigrants been less assimilated and Americanized we might have been more badly divided than we were in two world wars. In answer, one can say that the maintenance of language facility and cultural loyalties does not necessarily undermine an overarching loyalty to the federal republic. Patriotism in Switzerland does not seem to be lessened by its four official languages. Furthermore, it is hardly likely that we will want, for a long time to come and, it is hoped, ever, to test the loyalty of our new immigrant groups in hostilities with their countries of origin.

It would seem the pragmatic arguments for a common language and culture and an educational system that imposes them do not stand up very well. One cannot avoid issues of value, which are hard to justify pragmatically. Those of us from the immigration that was Americanized in language and culture think Americanization was a good thing, and we simply prefer that kind of country. And with our skepticism we are telling the newer elements, principally Spanish in language, that we think our path — the path of the immigration that ended in the 1920s — is better than that of the current immigration, even as we recognize that the newer immigrants (their leaders, at least) are pressing for bilingualism clearly not for pragmatic reasons, either, but for reasons of the values they hold.

How does one resolve such a conflict? The degree to which it is a conflict is revealed in a 5–4 Supreme Court decision in 1979 on whether public school teachers have to be citizens.[4] Any 5–4 decision reveals a deep value conflict; it could have been 5–4 the other way. Here are pragmatism and emotional, irrational value commitments lined up on one side, represented by the teachers who will not give up foreign citizenship but who are clearly good teachers; and here is another set of values (also emotional, irrational, if you will) on the other side, claiming that teachers induct into citizenship, and that students have to be educated to values as well as to skills.

I realize this is a different situation from one in which bilingual-bicultural education is required, where the issue is language in the public schools, not citizenship. But at bottom the issue is the same. The demand for bilingual-bicultural education is not purely linguistic or pragmatic. It is not only for educational achievement and jobs. It is also a demand made out of an alternate loyalty, loyalty to a culture and language that must inevitably be linked to foreign countries.

And yet, the 1980s *are* different from the 1920s; there may be good reasons for a change in educational practice.

The groups for whom bilingual-bicultural education is being instituted, and who are most active in demanding it, are different from the old immigrants from Europe in a number of important respects. First, many among these groups are not immigrants — they are American Indians, Puerto Ricans, and Mexican Americans resident for many generations in this country. Without untangling all aspects of their complex political status, we know them to have full rights as American citizens; the requirement, still part of American naturalization law, that naturalized citizens should know English, does not apply to them. Indeed, we have decreed by law that for all those of Spanish origin, for American Indians, and for Chinese and Japanese, inability in English should be no bar to full participation in the American political system. The Voting Rights Act now requires that those who speak these languages and are unable to exercise their voting rights in English must be given assistance, written and oral, in their native languages. Thus their status is already rather different from that of the European immigrant, who had no right to assistance in his language in exercising his political rights, even though this might have been given as a matter of convenience rather than of law.

A second respect in which these groups who are the main claimants for bilingual-bicultural education differ from the older immigrants is that many have only an uncertain and fleeting attachment to this country. These are the "undocumented aliens," who may or may not have decided they want to stay here permanently. It may be understandable that for them the Americanizing experience of the public school is something they might find repugnant or to which they would be indifferent. A useful comparison here is with the foreign guestworkers of Germany, whose children must be educated; it is fair question, in view of their legal status as only temporary German residents, whether it would not be wiser to educate them in Turkish or Serbo-Croatian or Greek than in German, since most of them are expected to return to their home countries. (Fewer and fewer informed Germans, it should be noted, now expect this to happen.)

Further, the country at large differs in a substantial way from the United States of the old immigration: it is less unambiguously patriotic or chauvinistic. There is, first, an embarrassment (at least among intellectuals) over how American power has been exercised in the world, and a strong sense that we are not better than most other countries. Why then should we impose some view of the virtues of American loyalty on new immigrants, when old settlers only partially accept it and are themselves doubtful of whether this loyalty is a good thing?

We seem in our culture today to be in a situation in which no single course receives unambiguous and universal acceptance, and thus it is hardly likely that we will roll back bilingual-bicultural education so as to reinstate a single-minded loyalty to American culture, society, and polity, with universal emphasis on learning English. And I would be the last, despite my criticism of the arguments for bilingual-bicultural education, to urge such a roll-back, because I see the reasons why we have changed, and I see that it is unrealistic to expect new immigrants to be like old (though many are), or persons of non-English language and non-American culture who are not immigrants to behave like immigrants. I see, too, that the country is different now and that Americans no longer want to direct a single-minded energy into the creation of a common people and common culture.

But given this situation, it is still possible to urge a looser and more tentative approach to development of bilingual-bicultural education policies. Unfortunately, this is not easy, because we have developed these policies not pragmatically, not even in the give and take of political debate, but through court order and agency regulation, and they are thus given a rigidity and a presumed sacrosanct base in Constitutional right that does not favor tentative and experimental steps. This does make for problems, because it treats all alike although they are not. To require the same for all is properly bureaucratic. But I wonder who raised the question of the need for Vietnamese-speaking teachers in order to fulfill Office of Civil Rights regulations in Houston. I doubt that it was the Vietnamese themselves, because it is my impression that they are very much like the old immigrants, want to learn English fast, and prefer to maintain their religion and culture and language outside school, through the family, their churches, or their voluntary organizations. I would guess that many other substantial streams of immigrants are of the same mind, over all. Do Koreans want a public school commitment to bilingual-bicultural education? Do Indians and Pakistanis? Do many of the immigrants of Latin America, leaving aside Mexican Americans? We do suffer from the fact that these policies are being developed and imposed by national bureaucracies, applying their own rules, and by federal courts, and that important distinctions among groups and what they think is best for them will be ignored.

A second point: One way of taking into account the differences among groups and within groups is to make these programs, in greater measure than they are, voluntary. In the case of the New York City consent judgment under which New York is obligated to provide education in Spanish to those of Hispanic background, there was an unsettling dispute in which the plaintiff's lawyers wanted to *require* students deemed after testing to need bilingual education to take it, even in the face of the opposition of their parents. Fortunately Judge Marvin Frankel rejected this demand. A true voluntarism will permit each child or its parents to select what they think is best.

Finally, we should consider to what extent we want to have these programs in the public schools, as against providing assistance to parents and ethnic groups to develop programs outside the public schools. The reason to explore this is that *within* each group we will find considerable differences as to what they want to teach in the way of culture, and this undoubtedly affects what they want to teach in the way of language. Most of these programs are, or are supposed to be, transitional, but the tendency is for children to stay in them for a number of years and to take subject-matter courses in those languages. Thus there is an issue as to what kind of emphases the public schools will present in their bilingual-bicultural education. Will they teach that we robbed Mexico of its territories — in which case there will be conflict with patriotic school boards? Will they teach that Puerto Rico should be independent — in which case there will be conflict with those Puerto Ricans who want Puerto Rico to become a state or maintain its commonwealth status?

Some groups are strongly divided over their history, over the role of the church, over the role of the socialist or communist movements.

Consider, as an example, if the public schools had had to teach Jewish immigrants something of their language and culture. There would have been disputes over whether they should teach Hebrew or Yiddish (or Ladino), Zionism or anti-Zionism, Orthodoxy or Reform, as the "true" language, culture, and religion of the Jewish people. In any event, of course, hardly anything was done in the public schools. When Jewish children formed one-third of the children in the New York City public schools there was no reference to Jewish history in the textbooks, no reference to Jewish religion, hardly any reference to any Jew. It was only in the 1930s that some modest opportunity to study Hebrew as a language in the high schools was offered, and that, I am sure, was in part because Hebrew is one of the classical languages that, in early colonial days, had been required or taught in our rudimentary colleges.

I do not argue that what happened in the past was for the best. I only draw from it the example that groups of non-English language and culture may be so divided that the public schools would have to provide a bland pap acceptable to all and satisfying to none. Under these circumstances, might we not experiment with providing education vouchers so that parents can find the kind of bilingual-bicultural education they prefer?

Whatever course we develop, I would urge the virtues of tentativeness and experimentation, and what they lead to is voluntarism in the choice of programs, the provision of a variety of programs, and consideration of whether we should not encourage efforts to provide the programs outside the rather rigid frame of the public schools.

[1980]

III

THE AFFIRMATIVE

ACTION DEBATE

9

Affirmative Discrimination:

For and Against

In the late 1960s and early 1970s the United States entered a new phase in the long fight against racial and ethnic discrimination. It is difficult to find the proper term to characterize the new phase, because so many terms have had their meanings distorted or become slogans. One might say that we shifted from being color-blind to becoming color-conscious. Thus, the Civil Rights Act of 1964, the Voting Rights Act of 1965, the Immigration Act of 1965, the Fair Housing Act of 1968 referred to no specific groups as victims of discrimination and beneficiaries of nondiscrimination. These pieces of legislation, following the liberal orientation of the period, were color-blind: discrimination against *anyone* on grounds of race, color, religion, or national origin was banned. The Voting Rights Act of 1965 even found a color-blind formula to overcome Southern resistance to blacks registering and voting: in any jurisdiction where those registering or voting fell to less than 50 percent of those eligible on the basis of age and citizenship, its stringent provisions came into effect.

The first indications of color consciousness raised little opposition. Thus, one of the first acts of the Equal Employment Opportunity Commission (EEOC), created by the Civil Rights Act of 1964, was to require employers to report the numbers of Negroes, Orientals, Spanish Americans, and American Indians employed in different job categories on an EEO-1 form. This degree of color consciousness required only that employers be aware of the racial-ethnic affiliations of those who applied for jobs, took tests, were hired, or were promoted. Even this raised certain difficulties, for during the color-blind phase of the fight against discrimination the keeping of racial-ethnic records was forbidden in many jurisdictions. (Similarly, as we moved into the color-conscious phase of school desegregation in the 1960s, many school districts in the North and West did not have racial-ethnic records of how many students of each group attended which school, and the position against racial record-keeping which had been adopted to fight discrimination came under attack as preventing further action against discrimination.)

Color consciousness meant initially finding out where few minority members were employed, in what occupations they were absent. The general picture was of course known. Color consciousness meant zeroing in on which employers or which institutions had a "problem." Color consciousness meant, in a term just beginning to come into use in the middle 1960s, "affirmative action"—doing more than just stopping discrimination. Did blacks and other minorities know that an employer did not discriminate? Seeing few of their kind among his employees, did they pass him by in their search for employment? Did he recruit in high schools, colleges, neighborhoods where there were few blacks and other minorities? Did he advertise in media they did not see or hear? Did he make any effort to recruit them into training programs? The employer, the institution were expected to try harder, and there were government programs making it incumbent on both to try harder.

AFFIRMATIVE ACTION VERSUS AFFIRMATIVE DISCRIMINATION

Having made this first move from color blindness to color consciousness, we moved on to another stage, still called "affirmative action" but very different from that of only trying harder. Now the government required that statistical goals be set for each specific minority group, in every type of employment, by each employer.[1] When color consciousness became a matter of setting statistical goals for employment, many involved in the fight against discrimination began to realize that something quite radical had happened. For they believed that the objective of fighting discrimination was the achievement of a society in which racial and ethnic affiliation did not affect important individual decisions (whom to employ, to rent or sell a house to, and the like) or public decisions. Statistical goals began to emerge in the late 1960s and early 1970s, and that seemed to many a very different matter from banning discrimination. Those who attack statistical goals are often asserted to be *against* "affirmative action." This is inaccurate and unfortunate. The error arises because the term "affirmative action" covers both color-conscious policies and statistical goal-achievement policies.

Both the programs that emphasize reaching out and those that set statistical goals are required by "affirmative action" plans. We need a term that describes the new departure, because it is that which has split the supporters of civil rights and created sharp conflict. It is called by some "reverse discrimination," because the point of setting a goal is that one will hire more of one group, less of another, simply because individuals are members of one group or another. Accurate as it is, it is considered a "code word," designed to arouse antagonism. For this reason, I titled a book I wrote in which I analyzed the rise of this kind of policy *Affirmative Discrimination*. The point of the title was to emphasize that those elements of affirmative action which did *not* involve discrimination on ground of race, color, and national origin were *not* in question. Only those elements of affirmative action that required discrimination on grounds of race, color, or national origin were in dispute. Admittedly, if one seeks to recruit members of a minority group and creates special training opportunities, one is also "discriminating" in their favor. But this is considerably less serious than the kind of discrimination which says in effect, "no whites or males need apply" — and we have had many examples of just such discrimination.

I will designate as "affirmative discrimination" the programs that set statistical goals by ethnic group. Whatever we call it, the new policy clearly is a departure from the general understanding of what was necessary or desirable to fight discrimination that prevailed until at least the middle 1960s; it clearly also has created a serious split among social and political organizations that earlier had worked together to combat discrimination. What is less clear — and disputed — is whether it is leading to a society in which a person's race, color, or national origin becomes crucial in affecting his opportunity to attain education, to gain a livelihood, and to advance in a profession.

THE DEVELOPMENT OF QUOTAS

The justification for affirmative action is that abandoning discriminatory practices is not enough to achieve justice for groups that have faced discrimination, for the effect of past discrimination will continue. This idea of affirmative action as necessary to correct past discrimination can be traced to labor relations law. When the National Labor Relations Board finds that an employer has been discriminating against union members or those trying to organize a union, he may be required not only to stop discriminating but to restore the persons discriminated against to the situation they would have held in the absence of that discrimination.[2]

This idea was incorporated into the great Civil Rights Act of 1964. This act banned discrimination in voting, places of public accommodation, public facilities, federal programs, federally supported public education, and employment; and it created the Equal Employment Opportunity Commission to enforce the ban on discrimination in employment "because of such individual's race, color, religion, sex or national origin." The words "affirmative action" occur in one place in the act, section 706 (g): "If the court finds that the respondent has intentionally engaged in or is intentionally engaging in an unlawful practice charged in the complaint, the court may enjoin the respondent from engaging in such unlawful employment practice, and order such *affirmative action* [my italics] as may be appropriate, which may include, but is not limited to, reinstatement or hiring of employees, with or without back pay, or any other equitable relief as the court deems appropriate." That is a modest kernel from which a general requirement of quota hiring by race or color may sprout, but it has. When courts find discrimination, they may, and do, order quotas; one black must be hired for each white until a certain ratio is reached, or whatever. After the Civil Rights Act was amended in 1972 to expand the powers of the EEOC to include public employers, many police and fire departments were placed under the requirement to hire by racial and ethnic category.

Was this what Congress intended when it wrote into the Civil Rights Act the provision for "affirmative action"? Certainly it intended that blacks or others who had suffered discrimination and as a result had not been given jobs or not been promoted should be given the jobs and promotions of which they had been unjustly and illegally deprived. It intended that members of minority groups should no longer face discrimination. Similarly, courts may require that a union activist be rehired or promoted; but they do not require that henceforth one union member be hired for every person not in the union until members reach such and such a proportion of the work force. But this is what judges who institute quotas under the authority of the affirmative action provision of the Civil Rights Act do, and this is one basis of statistical goals.

As yet only a small fraction of hiring in the United States takes place under a quota, under the authority given by the Civil Rights Act. And, it will be argued, this quota hiring is imposed only because of a finding of discrimination. However, it has to be pointed out that under the regulations of the Equal Employment Opportunity Commission a good deal in ordinary employment practices that ordinary people – and the Congress of the United States – might not consider discriminatory will be found to be discriminatory by the EEOC and the courts, and thus will trigger employment by racial and ethnic quota. There are two chief routes to finding discrimination that seem questionable (we would all accept another route, not in question here – that is, direct evidence of discrimination).

First, it may be found that an employer has not hired members of certain groups in proportion to their presence in the population or labor force or specific categories of certain occupations. This alone is often used as a demonstration of discrimination. But it may also have to be combined with other acts of discrimination that are charged, for recent Supreme Court decisions suggest statistical disparities alone may not be acceptable as evidence of discrimination.[3]

Second, it may be shown that the tests for employment used by employers are discriminatory. The guidelines that the EEOC issued to determine when a test is discriminatory have been upheld by the Supreme Court in the important *Griggs v. Duke Power* case of 1971 (401 U.S. 424). These guidelines tell employers that any test "which adversely affects hiring, promotion, transfer or any other employment or membership opportunity of classes protected by Title VII constitutes discrimination unless: (a) the test has been validated and evidences a high degree of utility as hereinafter described; and (b) the person giving or acting upon the results of the particular test can demonstrate alternative suitable hiring, transfer or promotion procedures are unavailable for his use." Or, as the Supreme Court said in *Griggs*: "The Act proscribes not only overt discrimination but also practices that are fair in form, but discriminatory in practice. The touchstone is business necessity. If an employment practice which operates to exclude Negroes cannot be shown to be related to job performance, the practice is prohibited."

The EEOC, supported by the courts, had established very stringent requirements for the use of employment or promotion tests that could pass muster as nondiscriminatory in order to pressure employers into abandoning tests and using racial and ethnic quotas in their employment practices. There is considerable evidence that this is just what the effect of the EEOC guidelines on testing has been. For example, one personnel expert is quoted as saying:

I had first assumed that the validation studies talked about in the EEOC Guidelines on Employee Selection Procedures would be required for all our employee selection standards and practices. Suddenly I noticed this was not the case. It was only those tests and procedures that had an *adverse impact* on the employment opportunities of protected groups that need to be validated.

If we dropped all discriminatory standards and changed all our procedures so that approximately the same proportion of all groups were proceeding through each step of our staffing procedures, there would be no adverse impact on any protected group, and we would not be required to conduct any validation studies at all. We would not be discriminating against any protected group, so the Guidelines would never be triggered.

Another is quoted as follows:

You can avoid violating Title VII and also avoid rocking the boat until you have enough hard data at hand to prove or disprove the actual relevance of various selection factors to the prediction of job performance for all groups. You do it by *temporarily equalizing* the impact of each factor being considered on each group in the applicant population while you study it.

For example, our company had been using a particular test to select employees for one job. Approximately 25 percent of the white males in the applicant population had been passing the text by scoring above a certain score. Now we just make sure that the top 25 percent of the applicants from each of the groups protected by Title VII also pass that test. We don't worry about what score becomes the cutoff for the various groups; we stick with the percentage passing from each group.[4]

Both these mechanisms for demonstrating discrimination and thus, on the basis of this demonstration, requiring quota employment are specifically forbidden by the Civil Rights Act under which the EEOC operates. Section 703 (j) asserts, "Nothing contained in this title shall be interpreted to require any employer . . . to grant preferential treatment to any individual or to any group because of the race, color, religion, sex, or national origin of such individual or group on account of an imbalance which may exist with respect to the total number or percentage of persons of any race, color, religion, sex, or national origin employed by any employer . . . " And Section 703 (h) asserts "nor shall it be unlawful employment practice for an employer to give and to act upon the results of any professionally developed ability test provided that such test, its administration or action upon the results is not designed, intended or used to discriminate because of race, color, religion, sex or national origin."

A second source of the new requirement to hire and promote on the basis of race and ethnic group is in practice the more important. It is the "affirmative action" requirements imposed on goverment contractors by an executive order issued by the President. The executive — the President — has the authority to determine the conditions under which the federal government will do business. When the federal government decides with whom it will or will not do business it exercises an awesome power: every big company, just about every university and college and hospital, and many nonprofit organizations are government contractors. And the federal government requires that the contractor not only refrain from discrimination by race, creed, color, or national origin, but, further, "take affirmative action to ensure that applicants are employed, and that employees are treated during employment, without regard to their race, creed, color, or national origin. Such action shall include, but not be limited to the following: employment, upgrading, demotion, or transfer; recruitment or recruitment advertising; layoff or termination; rates of pay or other forms of compensation; and selection for training, including apprenticeship." This is the language of Executive Order 11246, issued in 1965 by Lyndon B. Johnson. This order, the fount for affirmative action, did not give rise to any argument for affirmative discrimination: it used the language and the proposals of what was generally understood as equal opportunity. The passage I have quoted from the executive order may be obscure, but it is clear that it did not suggest that specific numbers of given groups would have to be hired or promoted.

It was under this order that the "Philadelphia plan" requiring building contractors to hire certain numbers of minorities was instituted. The building trades had long been considered most impervious to programs to overcome discrimination. This plan was upheld by the courts in *Contractors Association of Eastern Pa. v. Secretary of Labor*, 442 F. 2nd 159 (3rd Cir. 1971). But the extension of affirmative action into the controversial area of "goals and timetables," specific numbers that employers must try to hire or promote, derives from guidelines issued by the Department of Labor in 1971 to implement the executive order, though the approach was prefigured in guidelines of 1970.

EFFECTS OF THE QUOTA SYSTEM

The overall program of affirmative action operates under the Office of Federal Contract Compliance Programs in the Department of Labor, but the specific authority to review the employment and promotion practices of contractors and to negotiate and approve affirmative action plans is delegated to sixteen federal departments and agencies each of which supervises the affirmative action efforts of contractors in its area. Thus, the Department of Defense has a Director of Contractor Employment Compliance with an authorized staff of 565, the largest of the sixteen compliance staffs.[5] Thousands upon thousands of people are engaged, in the federal bureaucracy and by the thousands of contractors they supervise, in the work of affirmative action.

To what effect? Critics of affirmative action are to be found on two wings. On the one side are the watchdogs of affirmative action, civil rights agencies, civil rights advocates, minority and women's groups, committees of Congress. These groups are convinced that affirmative action is a great thrashing about and accumulation of paper signifying nothing. Thus, according to the criticism of the Subcommittee on Equal Opportunities of the House Committee on Education and Labor, since 1965 only eleven companies have been debarred from federal contracts, only one of which was large—Blue Bell, Inc., with 19,000 employees.[6] In an article arguing for preferences for minorities in employment, two law school professors assert that affirmative action plans "have been largely ineffective."[7] Marilyn Gittell argues that affirmative action has had no effect in higher education.[8] These critics of affirmative action defend its *objectives*, usually deny that programs call for *quotas* (since the programs themselves only demand *goals*, and government agencies make a great deal of the distinction), but nevertheless insist that desirable as these programs are, consistent as they are with the Constitution and the Civil Rights Acts of 1964, they are not effective because they are not forcefully carried out.

The other group of critics of affirmative action charge that it is imposing on government contractors the obligation to discriminate on grounds of race, color, and national origin; that it is all too effective in leading employers to consider in their hiring and promotion and firing the race, color, and national origin of employees, actual or potential; that it offends the Constitution's demand for the "equal protection of the laws" and the Civil Right Act's ban on discrimination in employment. And more than that, they say, by directly contradicting the hope of a society that operates without discrimination, it opens up other great social dangers. The chief critic of affirmative action in academic employment has been Sidney Hook.[9] I have criticized strong affirmative action in employment generally. There has been considerable though surprisingly muted criticism from business.[10]

At least as I see it, those who argue that affirmative action has achieved nothing for minorities, that it has been effectively countered by the actions of employers and universities, are in error. One reason they can advance these arguments is that so much of their experience and concrete evidence are drawn from higher education, a world with a number of distinctive features:

First, the criteria for academic appointments, vague as they may appear to academics, are specific and remarkably widely accepted. Thus, it is generally accepted that the Ph.D. degree and evidence of research are needed for initial appointments, and that further research resulting in books or articles is required for permanent appointments. If there are few people with such qualifications among some minority, a good deal of affirmative action may produce little in the way of appointments.

Second, appointments in universities, as compared to business and governmental institutions, are largely initiated by collegial peer groups, whatever the formal processes after their recommendations to higher authority. As a result, any appointment involves a wide participation. Departments are aware they must operate under some kind of affirmative action constraints. But since the process of appointment is not in fact under the full authority of administrators (as in business and government employment), the affirmative action plan that administrators agree to can be resisted by the departments that appoint on the basis of other criteria — academic, the supporters of this independence assert; old cronyism, its attackers insist.

Thus, the academic environment maximizes the opportunity for polarized views on the effectiveness of affirmative action. Because everyone is involved in the appointment process, everyone knows of the pressure from central administrators to give preference to minority candidates; but since everyone is involved, the qualifications are relatively firm, and the number of qualified persons from some minority groups is few, the administrative pressure may not lead to a rapid increase in minority faculty members. So one side can claim that affirmative action is a fraud; the other, that great pressure is being exerted by government officials and administrators to subvert academic standards.

The general result of affirmative action, however, is quite a different matter. It is not true that there have been no or minimal effects of affirmative action programs. Admittedly, any fact has multiple causes, and to demonstrate the effects of programs is not easy or unambiguous. Ideally, we would want to compare the employment and earnings at various occupational levels of minority and nonminority. We would want to compare those employers with government contracts and requiring affirmative action plans with those who had no contracts and did not have such plans (though even employers without government contracts might be subject to affirmative action plans because of state and local government contracts). In order to test the significance of statistical goals and timetables, we would want to compare the period between 1964 and 1970 or 1971, when employers were subject to Title VII of the Civil Rights Act and to the "soft" requirements — advertising, recruiting, and the like — with the subsequent period, when employers with government contracts were subject to the "hard" affirmative action emphasizing statistical goals, and when, in the wake of the *Griggs* decision, the pressure became stronger to hire by quota in order to avoid charges of and findings of discrimination. No analysis of employment and earnings data fully meets these tests, but various studies throw light on the matter.

One of the best to my mind is that of Richard Freeman,[11] who analyzes black progress in earnings and occupational position overall in the economy. While his data do not distinguish between employers subject and not subject to affirmative action, they do permit a comparison before and after 1969. Was black progress in earnings relative to white during the 1960s maintained during the weakened labor market in the early 1970s? He concludes that it was: "the gains in relative income of the late 1960s did not erode in the early 1970s, despite the weakened labor market . . . More important, perhaps, the figures show only slight, if any, lessening in the income increase. Of particular interest is the large increase in the ratio of black to white median usual weekly earnings from 1969 to 1974, which suggests that black wage rates went up substantially through 1974." If economic progress in a period of tightened labor markets and antidiscrimination legislation without statistical goals was sustained during a period of weakened labor markets and enforcement of statistical goals, these statistical goals presumably had some effect.

Another analysis, by Andrew Brimmer, does compare firms that report to EEOC (more than 100 employees, and one can assume that many are government contractors) with those that do not. Comparing employment in 1966 and 1974, he finds:

Black employment in EEOC-reporting firms rose much faster than employment in the economy as a whole. For instance, blacks accounted for 23 percent of the growth in jobs in EEOC-reporting firms, as compared with 15 percent in the total. Within the white-collar category, however, only clerical workers and sales workers recorded relatively larger gains on EEOC-reported payrolls (43 percent as compared with 21 percent and 12 percent as compared with 9 percent, repectively). In the case of professional and technical workers, EEOC figures shows blacks getting 11 percent of the increase in jobs, as compared with 14 percent for black professionals and technicians in the economy at large. The lag was especially noticeable among managers and officials. In the country as a whole, blacks accounted for 11 percent of the expansion; their share in EEOC reports was only 7 percent. In contrast, blacks got a much larger share of the new craft and service jobs in EEOC-reporting firms — for example, 27 percent of craft jobs, as compared with 15 percent for all firms; and 26 percent of service jobs, as compared with 11 percent for all employers combined . . .

On the basis of these figures, I conclude that the companies reporting under the EEOC requirements are opening jobs to blacks at a rate much faster than is true for all employers in the country as a whole. At the same time, however, it appears that the expansion is much slower in the upper reaches of the occupational scale than it is among job categories at the lower end. Thus, the task of occupational upgrading for blacks remains considerable.[12]

From this comparison of firms reporting to the EEOC with the economy as a whole, it would be a mistake to conclude that blacks are not making substantial progress in professional and managerial employment. This progress, however, has been largely in government employment. According to a study of college graduates by Richard Freeman, half of black males and 72 percent of black females work for government at all levels, compared with 27 percent and 56 percent of white males and females. The demand for black college graduates has been so great that black males may expect to earn 9 percent more than white males with a degree. These general findings of black progress continuing through the first half of the 1970s are also supported by the analysis of Reynolds Farley.[13]

Other studies report on different parts of the problem, but seemingly none contradicts the general conclusion that substantial progress took place in the relative earnings and employment and occupational position of the largest minority, blacks, that this progress has continued in the 1970s, and this progress has apparently been greater among firms reporting to the EEOC than others.[14] Stronger evidence is the experience of employers themselves. As against universities, where one may argue whether the statistical goals of affirmative action plans are "goals" or "quotas," large employers make no bones about the matter (though for legal reasons some may gag at the word): large hierarchical organizations have quotas imposed either by consent decrees or by affirmative action plans.

The largest private corporate employer in the United States (A.T.&T.), the steel industry, and many other employers, public and private, operate under court orders setting quotas for the employment of minorities. These are not set on the basis of formal findings of discrimination as such. Rather, charges of discrimination by the EEOC or Department of Justice have convinced the employers they would very likely be found guilty of discrimination if they were to contest them, and their liabilities for back pay would then be severe; undoubtedly, one reason they accept consent decrees is because the costs would be greater if they contested the charge in court. In consent decrees the corporation is assigned what are formally "goals" rather than "quotas", but with a judge reviewing progress reports it is a distinction without a difference.

But consent decrees cover only a small part of employment in the United States, with a much larger part covered by the affirmative action programs, which in theory also set goals rather than quotas. If we look closely at how these goals are actually met in industry, it is again very hard to see any significant difference. One well-known affirmative action program is Sears' "Mandatory Achievement of Goals" (MAG). As the country's largest retail employer, Sears has 376,000 employees. "The basic policy," the program asserts, "will be at the minimum to fill one out of every two openings with a minority man or woman of whatever races are present in your trading/hiring area."[15] An account in the newsletter *World of Work Report* describes how MAG works:

Unit managers must maintain the *existing* representation of minorities and women in filling job replacements. More important to bring about change, 50 percent of *all job openings* are to be filled by members of underrepresented groups. The manager has a *choice* from which underrepresented groups he can select. In categories of *nontraditional* jobs, where qualified or qualifiable candidates from underrepresented groups are in short supply, ratios of 20 percent are applied.

A local manager can exercise a *bypass*, or deviation from these ratios, only by demonstrating a good-faith effort first to hire from any of the underused groups, or where a clearly more qualified candidate is found. In MAG's three years of operation, hundreds of bypasses have been permitted, but the total is still tiny in comparison with the 150,000 or more people Sears hires for full-time or permanent part-time work in a single year under MAG requirements.

The importance of the flexibility allowed by the bypass and by the manager's choice among underrepresented groups is, according to Ray J. Graham, MAG's creator and Sears' director of Equal Opportunity, that "MAG avoids the charge of being an illegal quota by its flexibility and by the inclusion of a 'safety valve' if qualifiable candidates can't be found. Sears feels that generally they can be found.[16]

Under a charge of discrimination by the EEOC since August 1973, Sears is still trying to avoid litigation by continuing to negotiate with the EEOC. This may explain why Sears is a leader in affirmative action. But General Motors, Ford, and General Electric are laboring under the same charge; and other big corporations follow their cases closely and adapt their practices to avoid what can be expensive and damaging findings of discrimination. The practices of large companies that have in effect turned goals into quotas are not unique to Sears and other major companies facing EEOC charges. From discussions with personnel officers I get the impression that these practices are general.

ARGUMENTS FOR AFFIRMATIVE DISCRIMINATION

Unfortunately much of the discussion of these issues is clouded by evasion and lies (understandably: the government agencies are arguably engaged in breaking the law, as are the employers that adopt group-preference hiring), so that one must engage in a kind of detective work to establish that these practices are indeed widespread. But if one has established that government agencies have increasingly imposed on employers practices that in effect require them to take account of the color and national origin of prospective and present employees in hiring and promotion, the question arises: Is this a good or a bad policy? The claim that it is a good policy rests on a number of arguments, all of which can be effectively countered.

1. *Certain groups fall below the average in income and occupation, and they will not reach the average positions unless employers are forced to give them preference.*

It is common sociological knowledge that some minority groups, even in the face of discrimination, have improved their circumstances and indeed achieved more than the average income and occupational status. The groups—now called "the affected classes"—that government agencies have stipulated as particularly protected by antidiscrimination law have also, if variably, made progress. Thus, blacks were making considerable progress in the 1960s, before the introduction of statistical requirements. Indeed, good research shows that discrimination against young blacks of equivalent education and family background was a thing of the past by the end of the 1960s.[17] The two chief groups of Asian Americans—Chinese and Japanese—were not behind other Americans in income and occupational status, having made great progress. Hispanic Americans were a diverse group: Spanish Americans had never considered themselves a disadvantaged minority; Cubans had made substantial progress and had no need of affirmative action; Mexican Americans had also been making substantial progress; and while Puerto Ricans were the worst off of groups of Hispanic heritage, it was not at all clear that discrimination was the root of the matter. American Indians were indeed poorly off.

The response to this argument, then, is that some groups were no longer disadvantaged and others were making progress, so that the argument that statistical goals were required is grossly overextended in relation to all the affected classes.

2. *Equity demands that each group show the same average performance as any other group or the average of all groups.*

The objective of average income and occupation for each group is not dictated by equity. Income and occupation are based largely on education. Length of education and achievement in education vary greatly among groups, and for different reasons. Income and occupational prestige also depend in large measure on unknown factors; Christopher Jencks has suggested luck, Daniel P. Moynihan proposed pluck, and there are other candidates. While one might want to eliminate the effect of luck on income and occupation (though lottery ticket buyers would probably object), it is hardly likely it would be to the good of society to eliminate pluck. Groups vary by amount of education, quality of education, geographical distribution, occupational experience, distribution by age, and many other factors that properly affect income. To eliminate all these as elements from the overall score of a group would result in an even more peculiar and inefficient economy than we have. Further, some groups — even those bearing the badge of discrimination — have achieved more than equality. Does equity require that their income and occupations be cut down?

3. *The avoidance of resentment, rebellion, and perhaps revolution by deprived groups also requires that government ensure average income and occupational distribution for each group.*

Undoubtedly a permanently depressed group might become resentful, rebellious, riotous, criminal. Any multiethnic democracy demands equal treatment among groups. But the alternative to statistical goals, as I have argued in the answer to Point 1 above, was not stagnation; no one could say that blacks, the largest minority group, were stagnating in 1970. They were making rapid progress. There were two serious problems: the large proportion of female-headed families, whose members could not be effective in the labor force, and a very high unemployment rate among youth. Inevitably, affirmative action aided most those with education and qualifications. Just what assistance it has been to the two great depressed classes among blacks is questionable. Perhaps it has been of some help, but programs separate from and in addition to simple statistical requirements for employment are needed to deal with the economic and social problems of female-headed families and unemployed black youth.

4. *Discrimination is the cause of this failure to achieve an average position in income and occupation, and discrimination is illegal.*

Discrimination is an abomination. To label it *the* cause of the economic differences between groups, even when it is extensive and pervasive, is a gross oversimplification. See the comments in answer to point 2 above.

5. *The practices that require preferential employment and promotion are in any case temporary and will come to an end when the disadvantaged have achieved equality.*

It is very hard to see how these programs will be temporary. Groups do not give up advantages they have once gained. Nor do government agencies give up the power of oversight once seized. When all affirmative action goals are fulfilled, it will still be necessary to maintain the pattern of hiring and promotion by ethnic group, because only so can one ensure that the delicate statistical balance achieved will be maintained.

ARGUMENTS AGAINST QUOTAS

The opponents of statistical goals make their own arguments against them. First, they argue that this approach must arouse resentment among those not included among the "affected classes." What is gained in calming intergroup relations by increasing the economic welfare of one group is lost by the increased tensions created, in the workplace and society generally, by this very preference. Second, it encourages other groups to demand the same protection of statistical goals. Many ethnic and racial groups not included in the initial list of "affected classes" can point to discrimination in their background. "White" is an amalgam that covers Protestant, Catholic, Jew, English, Scottish, Irish, German, Italian, Polish, Lebanese, and a hundred other stocks, most of which have had some experience of discrimination. Immigrants from India have recently been demanding inclusion among "Asian Americans" (they had been considered "majority white," and not an "affected class" under affirmative action), and there have also been scattered protests from those of Italian and Polish origin. Third, it puts the government in the business of determining who belongs to which racial and ethnic group, in order to decide who should get affirmative and who reverse discrimination. This is a position that government had abandoned by 1964, because the Constitution does not permit discrimination on grounds of race and ethnic origin. And, finally, it offends against what many have believed to be the main thrust of liberalism in America, the primacy of individual rights. The outrage an American feels when he (or she) is deprived of a job or a promotion because of his race or ethnic background is no less when that person is white than when he (or she) is black, or yellow, or brown.

A full consideration of the past and the present has been necessary to assess any future development. Let us outline the forces on both sides of the issue. If one begins with popular opinion, one will discover uniformly enormous opposition to affirmative or reverse discrimination. A 1977 Gallup poll reported that 83 percent of a national sample opposed these policies, only 10 percent favored them. The question set was: "Some people say that to make up for past discrimination women and members of minority groups should be given preferential treatment in getting jobs and places in college. Other say that ability, as determined by test scores, should be the main consideration. Which point of view comes closest to how you feel on this matter?" The major significant differences were by race — 64 percent of nonwhites opposed such policies, only 27 percent favored them.[18]

Interesting as these findings are, they are of hardly any weight in the actual development of policies. At the governmental level, the judiciary, the Congress, and the executive departments play the key roles, in roughly that order. The judiciary has shaped the present policies; it is also capable of reversing them.

Action by Congress is much less likely, for it would depend on the kinds of influences that are brought to bear on its members. Any new bill to clarify the meaning of the act of 1964 as amended in 1972, more specifically to rule out preference in employment, would be fiercely challenged by the civil rights organizations, a powerful lobby in Washington. Whether or not they (or any other lobby) really represent their supposed constituency hardly matters; as we have seen, on this issue they may not. But they do not depend on their constituents for votes or money. These organizations, supported by foundations and in some cases government grants, find it unnecessary to consult the views of those whose interests they assert they are defending. The great majority of the people who oppose such policies, on the other hand, are not organized to make their opposition effective. Business groups are critical but their position is likely to be dismissed as mere self-interest. Unions have opposed statistical goals, but those which might speak up before Congress would either be dismissed as themselves having practiced discrimination or be inhibited by their long-time alliances with civil rights groups.

Thus, as is so often the case with legislation, those who influence Congress are those who are most concerned regardless of popular opinion, which is unorganized. The principal strength of the civil rights groups consists not of money to support campaigns, not even so much of threats to organize voters against uncooperative congressmen. It consists of two chief elements. The first is access to the national media: if civil rights groups send out releases to the *Washington Post*, the *New York Times*, major TV networks, *Time* and *Newsweek*, AP and UP, denouncing new legislation as a weakening of laws against discrimination, this is the way the story will be reported; and most congressmen would not like to see themselves allegedly supporting discrimination. Second, the civil rights groups claim to hold the higher moral ground. An opponent must have a very clear sense of his case before he is willing to argue against such a claim. Who is willing to be for discrimination, against progress for blacks and Puerto Ricans? The fact that the policies of those who claim to be more decent are discriminatory and only doubtfully assist the deprived is not clearly known to the congressmen, and they hesitate to take on organized forces which can smear them in the mass media.

The weakest element in the entire political picture is the executive department. The EEOC is of course an independent agency, not subject to presidential control except through the appointment power; but the civil rights lobby can ensure that no President, whatever his views on reverse discrimination, would appoint to the EEOC someone who opposed strong affirmative action. The Office of Contract Compliance Programs, with its various affiliated offices in the other executive departments, directly administers policies of affirmative discrimination on the basis of implementing guidelines written under the pressure of civil rights groups, guidelines that the courts have upheld. They cannot be influenced easily in the way they implement these policies by higher executive authority — that is, the president and the cabinet officers — as was demonstrated during the presidencies of Nixon and Ford. Particularly in the latter administration, when the Secretary of Labor, the Attorney General, and the Secretary of HEW were all considered to be sympathetic to the position that reverse discrimination should be limited, it became manifest that the President and the executive departments, whatever their views, were powerless before the civil rights lobby and its two chief sources of power. And the effective control of how the mass media handle stories dealing with discrimination and the lobby's moral advantage have as yet barely been challenged.*

I have given great weight in the development and maintenance of reverse discrimination policies to the civil rights bodies. These are now much more numerous than the NAACP and the NAACP Legal Defense and Educational Fund, though these play a leading role. For example, one can consider as part of the civil rights lobby — and a very important part, because it is remarkably well funded — the U.S. Commission for Civil Rights, an independent government agency. That the civil rights lobby now favors discrimination is a difficult point to put across; few will attack it on this ground, and of those who do, few will be given wide publicity. The civil rights lobby monitors legislation and federal regulations more effectively than any

---

*The Carter administration and its officials had no desire to change these policies, which indeed they strengthened. The Reagan administration by contrast was critical of quotas during the campaign. Nevertheless, twenty-four months after Reagan took office, the structure of federal regulations and court decisions enforcing statistical goals and quotas stood intact, though the Justice Department had begun to intervene against quotas in selected cases. — N.G., 1983.

group opposing affirmative discrimination. Most significantly, it uses class action suits both to establish as law the principles of reverse discrimination and, by legal intervention, to require government agencies to carry out the law as it interprets it.

This analysis of forces suggests that it is unlikely that policies of affirmative discrimination will be abandoned. One could not count on Congress or the executive department. But the courts, to repeat, are erratic. They are controlled by the Supreme Court, where a 5-to-4 decision may reverse a complex set of policies being implemented by many thousands spending many hundreds of millions. No one can be sure this will not happen. The Supreme Court is a mysterious body, and many kinds of influences play on it. The kinds and quality of briefs it receives may affect it. Under the Ford administration, for a moment, it seemed possible that the Justice Department might support modification of the rulings that support reverse discrimination.*

But there are two other sources of briefs opposing reverse discrimination which may influence the Court. One — we should not put too much weight on this, perhaps — is business groups, who are caught between minorities claiming back pay and preferential treatment and individuals from the majority who can also effectively sue for back pay and jobs. It is hardly possible for business to be happy about a situation, such as the one A.T.&T faced, in which it had to give both back pay to the minorities and women it promotes and damages for discrimination to majority males with greater seniority and better qualifications. And yet a court case required it to do just that. In *McAleer v. A.T.&T.*, 416 F. Supp. 435 (1976), a District of Columbia court required the company to pay damages to McAleer, but said the consent decree was also valid and therefore he should not get his promotion.

More significant, to my mind, is the break in the civil rights

---

*Under the Reagan administration, we can expect some briefs critical of statistics as tests of discrimination and of statistical goals as remedies for purported discrimination. But these would undoubtedly be more convincing to the Court if the administration first changed the regulations that in effect impose statistical requirements. — N.G., 1983.

coalition. The Jewish groups, in particular — the Anti-Defamation League of B'nai B'rith, the American Jewish Committee, the American Jewish Congress — are not happy with reverse discrimination. When it is applied in a situation to which Jews are particularly sensitive (admission to medical school, say), they take a strong and uniform position. All supported Allan Bakke in his suit alleging that he was not admitted to the medical school of the University of California at Davis because a number of places were held specifically for minority groups. How far they would go to intervene in employment cases is another matter. But legal commentators seem to agree that decisions in an educational case, such as *Bakke*, may have influence on what is legal and constitutional also in employment. If there is any halt or reversal in the development of practices of affirmative discrimination, then it will have to be because of court decisions; and if these decisions begin to change, it will be in large measure because dominant opinion on civil rights is no longer uniform, and is split on whether preferential employment on the basis of race and ethnic group is a proper response to discrimination and disadvantage.

[1979]

10

Who's Available?

ONE OF THE KEYSTONES of affirmative discrimination is the analysis that employers are required to carry out of "availability": They must determine how many people, from each protected group, are "available" for the jobs they have, and determine if their work forces reflect this availability. It is the disparity between numbers from each target group actually employed and their presumed availability that drives the machinery of statistically oriented affirmative action.

The fundamental assumption behind the required analyses of availability is that work forces at all levels should replicate the proportions in the labor force of certain specified minority groups and women, and that a failure to reach these levels in any work force, while not necessarily making a prima facie case for discrimination against minorities and women, is cause for suspicion and in any case requires correction. Affirmative action plans often go beyond the requirement for replication to call for the kinds of actions by employers that would force or speed up changes in the composition of the work force. For example, they may require that 20 percent of the places in occupational categories in which there have previously been no or few women be filled with women. The assumption behind this kind of demand is that previous discriminatory practices have discouraged women from entering these occupations, so one must do more than proportionally represent women already in them. One must encourage women who would not have considered the occupation in question to enter it by creating a special demand, and perhaps (as in consent decrees, awarding back pay to members of a category) a special reward.

The fundamental challenge to the requirement that work forces should reflect availability is that the differences among ethnic and minority groups, and men and women, are real differences, deeply based, and that requiring any fixed proportions of one group or another to be hired or promoted inevitably means that employers must act as if these differences do not exist. In trying to reach certain goals based on availability analyses that ignore these differences, employers will inevitably incur unexpected costs. When employers base their hiring and promotion decisions not solely on the judgment of whether an individual is the best one for a certain job, but on other considerations, such as representation by race and sex, there will be an increase in the cost of recruiting, hiring, and in general, the cost of doing business. This is justified on the grounds that a fair treatment of individuals in this country under the Constitution, antidiscrimination laws, and government agency regulations requires such a replication of the labor force among the employees of each employer, and that these costs are well worth bearing.

If differences among ethnic groups and between men and women are deeply based, however, and if there are reasons aside from discrimination why minority groups and women show distinctive patterns of distribution in jobs, then the effort to change the distribution may be futile as well as costly. It may engender side effects in the form of resentment among both "protected groups" and the "majority" that no one engaged in the fight against discrimination and for greater equity for minority groups and women would want to see.

One may argue that the right kind of availability analysis would obviate any of these negative results. If one could encompass in one's availability analysis every factor that in the mind of a presumed supreme and omnicompetent labor force analyst explains why individuals of one group or another look for or take one job or another, then the problem in theory disappears. The all-knowing labor force analyst would take into account, in setting his affirmative action target figures, the effect of all those factors, such as age, education, experience, residence, and more subtle factors of the type I discuss later in this chapter. Thus, the target figures would simply describe what would happen in the absence of discrimination to the distribution of groups in the labor force.

Yet it is utopian to believe that we can know so much, and even more utopian to believe that the government's affirmative action officer and the private company's personnel department would agree on the analysis. It is in the interest of government agencies trying to increase the number of minorities and women employed or promoted to take the most expansive view of availability: to select those availability figures which argue that a large pool of available employees exists that is not being tapped. It is in the interest of the employer seeking to reduce the costs of recruitment, training, firing, and the carrying of less efficient employees to select those figures which show the pool is small, for the smaller the pool, the smaller his target and the greater his degree of freedom in hiring and promoting. But I would argue that no matter how refined the availability analysis, in the present state of knowledge the realities of group difference will finally make the achievement of the task difficult, expensive, and in a variety of ways counterproductive.

One example of a fairly successful effort to reduce the required goals by refined availability analysis is that of the University of California at Berkeley, which, by analyzing the number of women and minorities available for different academic fields, was able to show that availability in most fields for most groups was so tiny that relatively few hirings in the affected classes would enable its faculty to match the availability pool. The University of California was able to do this because in the case of academic disciplines there have been developed fairly specific criteria that define whether one is eligible for employment or not (the Ph.D. degree), and there are statistics for each field, which tell us how many in each protected group are to be found. Having found that the burden was not onerous, the University of California at Berkeley was ready to stand content with the figures that emerged.[1] In the second part of this chapter, where I review the range of problems that afflict any availability analysis, it will be seen that even the University of

California's elaborate and expensive undertaking does not really provide good grounds for setting, for example, a female target for civil engineering or a black goal for teaching a Middle East language.

This pattern describes much of the struggle between government compliance officers and company personnel officers. The compliance officers will choose that definition of the availability pool which shows "underutilization." Thus, there will be disputes as to the geographical range of the availability pool. If going to a larger pool will show underutilization, compliance officers will try to choose that; if going to a smaller area demonstrates the pool is large, they will choose that. And similarly, as to the kind of specifications for the jobs involved, they will choose that specification which shows greater availability rather than lesser. Where availability on any ground is minuscule, as in the case of women for many occupations, they will point to the large proportion of women generally in the labor force to argue for special efforts that will induce women to enter certain occupations in which they have been all but absent.

There are three possible approaches to this issue, inevitably intertwined, but also distinguishable. The first is constitutional and legal: What is evidence of discrimination or insufficient affirmative action in the absence of clear discrimination? The second is economic: What are the costs or benefits of any effort? The third type of approach may be broadly considered sociological: What generally *explains* the distribution of ethnic and minority groups in occupations? How potent are these explanations? To what degree is it reasonable to try to overcome the given distribution of any group at any time? This last question also brings us back to the constitutional and legal issues — what *part* of the distribution is attributable to discrimination? — and brings us back also to the economic question — what is it worth spending to overcome the given distribution? The constitutional-legal and economic considerations are also interconnected. While government regulatory agencies and courts generally refuse to take into account economic considerations when a basic constitutional right, in this case the right to be free of racial and ethnic-group discrimination, is at issue, (for example, the refusal of the courts to be bound by economic considerations in school desegregation orders, where the plea of inability to provide buses, transportation, new schools, police protection, and the like is not allowed), at some margin a cost might limit a presumed right. Ten thousand dollars to get one new minority employee might not stop a court, but $100,000 might.

In this chapter I will focus on the broad category of sociological considerations, and within this I will concentrate mostly on the issue of racial and ethnic-group variation in jobs. I will have something to say about the differences between male and female occupational distribution, but this raises different kinds of issues. The largest minority group, blacks, makes up only 11 percent of the population and labor force. Women make up half the population and two-fifths of the labor force, so that potentially very high goals may be set for increasing employment of women. Further, the distribution of women in specific occupations is more divergent from that of men than the distribution of protected minority groups is from that of "whites." Women are undergoing a revolution of self-image and expectation which has, for example, sharply increased applications and admissions to law and medical schools. There is great uncertainty about what women want, or will want (or more exactly, what proportion of women will want what kind of relationship to labor force and specific occupations). Thus, while some of my specific comments may apply to male-female differences, I consider this a rather different kind of issue, and will devote most of my attention to the minority-group issues.

The remainder of the chapter is divided into two parts. In the first I discuss generally what we know about the varying occupational distributions of ethnic and racial groups. (I use the terms "ethnic" and "minority group" to refer to groups that are defined by a presumed commonality of descent and a degree of common culture — these groups are also variously called races, nationality groups, national origin groups, and so on.) In the second, I make some specific criticisms of the presently accepted techniques for determining availability, and argue that such techniques are grossly flawed, possibly improvable but not enough to make them worthwhile, and that they should be abandoned as a requirement of affirmative action.

The most crucial point about the occupational distribution of ethnic groups in the United States is that this distribution is only in part — and probably for most of the protected groups in small part — owing to discrimination. It is, of course, to the interest of the regulating agencies to insist that any deviation from some norm must be explained by discrimination, as this is the basic legitimation of government requirements for goals and quotas, whether set under affirmative action or Title VII of the Civil Rights Act of 1964. The norm that these agencies would like to set is the one that shows the greatest possible amount of discrimination under their reasoning. For example, the Equal Employment Opportunity Commission asserted, in the landmark case it brought against A.T.&T., selected as the largest private employer in the country, "One can assume that, absent employer discrimination, the percentage of minority employees in a company's work force should roughly approximate the percentage of that minority in the relevant population, especially if the jobs the employer has to offer require no particular skills."[2]

The actual role of discrimination in explaining variations in any group of employees in any company both from the population percentage (as in the above quotation), or from the labor force can be extremely variable and is very difficult to determine. The first crude efforts to explain "what else" besides discrimination might explain a difference would include length of education (a very important component in determining what kind of job a worker gets), quality of education, family background (which may be measured by parental education or occupation or income, or may be significant in ways independent of all these but inaccessible to most quantitative research), previous experience, and elements of work attitude and work orientation that may be related to or independent of any of the preceding.

Some part of a variation in occupation and income from

some norm is due to discrimination, but it is difficult to quantify that part, and scholars have come up with rather different answers. Depending on the group involved (and the part of the country it lives in), the element may be very large (blacks in the South), or very small or nonexistent (Spanish-surnamed groups of Cuban or other Latin-American middle-class background in most of the country).

We are only at the beginning of an understanding of the role of discrimination. There are numerous studies of blacks, fewer of Mexican Americans and Puerto Ricans, still fewer of other Spanish-surnamed groups, few that are useful for American Indians — census statistics on Indians are particularly poor — some for Chinese and Japanese, far fewer or none for groups that are presently included among Asian Americans and are significant for some occupations in some parts of the country and will become more significant with time (Filipinos, Koreans, and Indians and Pakistanis and Bangladeshis). There are different dependent variables that may be used to test for discrimination, and the results may be different depending on the dependent variable chosen. A group may score high on occupation (that is, concentration in occupations of high status and high earnings), but lower than expected on earnings. This was one of the findings of studies based on the 1960 census for Japanese and Chinese. Contrarily, undoubtedly one could find groups — particularly if one disaggregated the "other" majority — who showed the reverse pattern: higher income than expected on the basis of occupation (perhaps, for example, Eastern European groups with strong positions in the unionized sectors of various occupations).

Nevertheless, a few findings are interesting on this question of the role of discrimination in the overall measure of occupations and earnings. Orley Ashenfelter observed as long ago as 1966 that one-third of observed occupational differences between minorities and whites were attributable to years of formal schooling.[3] By the early 1970s Richard Freeman could no longer observe much influence of discrimination on the earnings and occupational position of young blacks; using other data, Robert E. Hall and Richard A. Kasten agreed.[4] More recent work by Freeman shows that by 1969 young black college graduates did better economically than whites.[5]

This work on the effects of discrimination on income and earnings for blacks does not account for the substantial effect *past discrimination* has had on the position of *older blacks*. But overcoming this raises, first, complex constitutional-legal questions (as indicated in recent Supreme Court decisions on seniority), and second, economic and social questions related to the issue of how one can really make up for the effects of past discrimination, if one considers that some part of income and occupation is properly explained by work experience, which those discriminated against in the past have been prevented from getting. In other words, we may break up a minority group into two parts: one part consisting of persons whose education and work experience and other occupational background features suggest that they should have higher occupations than they do, and another part consisting of persons in occupations of low income and status, but whose education and work experience do not present any argument that they should hold higher positions. Affirmative action goals may be the right policy response to the problems of the first group; they may be futile for the second, and perhaps monetary compensation for past discrimination is the proper response for them.

When we come to other groups, the question of the effect of discrimination on economic position is much more mixed. Spanish-surnamed Americans, to take the second-largest minority group, must be disaggregated to make any sense of their economic position. The largest among these (Mexican Americans) are characterized by substantial class and cultural (for example, language) differences that must play a significant role, aside from any discrimination, in their economic position. Many are in an illegal position as immigrants, and many are of poor educational background. Those raised in the United States show low educational achievement and high dropout rates. (One can argue that this is the result of discrimination in schooling, but to what extent is it an employer's responsibility to disregard the effects on capacity for work in different occupations of educational inadequacy, regardless of its cause?) As their educational achievements increase and they overcome the impact — significant for all groups — of poor English-language skills, it is questionable whether any discriminatory effect on earnings and income could be demonstrated. Puerto Ricans show a somewhat different pattern, with higher educational achievement in Puerto Rico, but the general picture is similar. Geographical concentration in the New York metropolitan area, which has been losing jobs at a substantial rate, as well as in other Northeast metropolitan areas where economic growth has lagged, has undoubtedly contributed to the poor economic achievement of Puerto Ricans.

As for other Spanish-surnamed groups, the fact that they are included in this "protected group" simply compounds confusion. There is no evidence that Cubans, immigrants from Spain and their children, Nicaraguans, Colombians, and others have suffered from discrimination on account of national origin. Their pattern is very much an immigrant pattern in which their progress is related to how long they have been here and to original class background and occupation. Cuban experience is similar to that of other immigrant groups — except for a somewhat more rapid rise, perhaps owing to greater governmental assistance and in part to the unintended impact of affirmative action.[6]

American Indians raise a more complex issue. They are not immigrants who came to this country seeking work in a modern economy. They have remained outside this economy in very large numbers, largely it would appear by choice. When they have attempted to enter the modern job economy, they have often met discrimination. But it is no easy matter to determine the degree to which their high unemployment and low earnings are to be ascribed to discrimination, or to poor education (and discrimination is only one factor explaining why this education has been poor) and specific cultural orientations.

Chinese and Japanese were the two dominant elements in the affected class of "Orientals" when this class was first set up for reporting purposes — later to be used for affirmative action purposes — after the passage of the Civil Rights Act of 1964, but since then three other categories of Asian immigrants have grown rapidly because of the new provisions of the Immigration Act of 1965 — Filipinos, Koreans, and persons from the Indian subcontinent (Indians, Pakistanis, and Bangladeshis). A fourth

Asian group has sprung up full blown as a result of the disastrous close of the Vietnam war. All these groups will grow rapidly, because the immigrants are young and of an age to have children, and because the flow of immigrants will continue to be substantial.

For these groups, a rather special issue is raised in considering the impact of discrimination on occupational and income status. The average occupational status of the Chinese and Japanese, and the immigrants from the subcontinent of India among the newer groups, is *higher* than that for Americans in general. There is no question there *has* been discrimination against Chinese and Japanese, including substantial and severe state discrimination. Nevertheless, they show "over-" rather than "under-" representation. Thus, of 181,000 employed Chinese-Americans in 1970, 5,060 were college teachers, 4,000 were physicians or dentists, 8,900 were engineers — all proportions considerably higher than are found in the population generally.[7] The Japanese occupational level was higher than that of whites as early as 1960.[8] An index of representation in the general schedule grades of the federal civil service shows Orientals overrepresented by 80 percent. Interestingly enough, American Indians are overrepresented by 175 percent, and even blacks are overrepresented by 14 percent. But while blacks are concentrated in the lower grades, Orientals are found fairly evenly throughout the system, except for the very top grades, G.S. 16–18, where they only reflect their proportions in the population generally.[9]

When a history of discrimination is associated with "more than equal" representation, one questions the usefulness of a requirement that in any occupation where a given group shows less than equal representation, an effort be made to achieve equal representation. This would be difficult for employers. Presumably one would have to ask Chinese and Japanese to leave more lucrative and higher-status careers as professors, doctors, engineers, and civil servants, to staff occupations as skilled or unskilled workers, or whatever other category they were found to be "underrepresented" in. Here we find one of the anomalies in affirmative action, one of particular significance when men, who generally hold better-paying positions and positions with higher status, are required to be recruited into job categories held predominantly by women (for example, the requirement on A.T.&T. to achieve certain percentages of men in telephone operator jobs).

Other groups aside from those protected under affirmative action also show a pattern in which, despite discrimination, we find "overrepresentation" in preferred occupational categories. It is well known that Jews have faced substantial discrimination in this country, discrimination well documented in the past by Jewish defense groups. Nevertheless, they are highly concentrated in the fields of business (as independent entrepreneurs) and the professions. While the census does not give figures on Jews, as it does on Chinese and Japanese (because they are considered "races," while Jews are not), other data are evidence of this "overrepresentation." Thus, the largest study of college and university faculty shows that Jews, who make up less than 3 percent of the population, make up 8.7 percent of college faculties, 19 percent of faculties in elite colleges and universities, and in certain fields—medicine and law—reach truly astonishing proportions of faculty—22.4 and 24.9 percent, respectively.[10]

Does one limit affirmative action only to those groups discriminated against as a group that have *not* overcome underutilization? An interesting question of equity is raised here, for by taking this position one seems to argue that discrimination is all right, as long as individuals of the group discriminated against overcome the handicap of discrimination. But would they have not been even further ahead had they not faced discrimination?

But aside from this rather abstract issue of justice, the fact is that in the sphere of real interests and political action it will probably be difficult to confine affirmative action to those groups who have been discriminated against but have not overcome discrimination. First of all, the protected groups, we have pointed out, already include groups who have probably not suffered discrimination at all (such as Cubans). Second, if a group gets the protection of affirmative action because it is "related" to a group that has been discriminated against (as Cubans are "related" to Mexican Americans), other groups with the same claim to "relationship" will also demand protection. Thus, immigrants from the Indian subcontinent were formerly considered by the Office of Management and Budget, for purposes of minority reporting, "white" or "Caucasian" or "other." This agitated some Indian groups who demanded they be included in the "Asian" affected class. Other Indians objected that they did not want "minority status," because their economic status was already high. Indians have recently been reclassified by OMB, as a result of this pressure, as "Asians and Pacific Islanders." Is this a marginal problem? It is not when we consider how many groups may demand inclusion in affected classes on the basis of past discrimination, despite present circumstances, or on the basis of a relationship to groups that already are an affected class.

Unless we understand the factors that lead to "over-" as well as "under-" utilization, it will be difficult to find effective policies to change occupational distribution. There is no easy answer to this question. Discrimination can only explain the underutilization of those discriminated against, and the overutilization of those favored—it cannot explain the reverse facts. In addition to the examples of the overutilization of those discriminated against, there is equally significant evidence of the underutilization of those who have not faced racial or national-origin discrimination. Farmers in this country—one of the poorest of occupational categories—have generally been disproportionately of old native stock. The poorest farmers, indeed, have particularly been those of old native stock (Southern, Appalachian, backwoods New England), while the more prosperous have generally been those of immigrant stock (German, Scandinavian).

Discrimination is a factor in occupational distribution. In some cases, it is almost the total explanation, as when by law and custom groups are forbidden education for certain occupations, entrance or licensing in them. For some of the groups benefiting at present from statistical goal requirements, this was the case in the past in the United States. The occupational consequences of legal and customary limitation of opportunity can be long and severe. On the other hand, they can also change rapidly when the laws and practices that limit a group change, and even in the absence of strong governmental remedial measures. Thus, in the decade of the 1960s, before statistical goals or quotas for employment had become widespread, there was substantial change in black occupational distribution. Between 1960 and 1970, for example, black male professionals as a percentage of all black workers almost doubled, for 3.1 to 5.9, while white professionals as a percentage of all white male workers increased from 10.3 to 14.3. Black craftsmen increased from 9.8 percent to 15.3 of black male workers, whites from 19.6 to 21.2 percent of white male workers. Black female private household workers dropped from 35.7 to 17.9 percent of black female workers, and black female clerical workers increased from 7.6 to 20.7 percent of all black female workers.[11] Such rapid changes in occupational structure can also be documented for other minority groups, in the period before goals and timetables were widespread as means of implementing affirmative action.

Consider the Chinese occupational distribution, depicted in table 1. Clearly many things have affected this development: not only the decline in discrimination against Chinese during and after World War II, but also the immigration of more educationally qualified Chinese with the lessening of immigration restrictions after World War II, the increase in proportion of native-born Chinese, changes in the American occupational structure, and so on. What did not have any effect on the changing occupational structure for this group clearly was the emphasis on goals and timetables based on availability, an approach that was scarcely in place in 1970.

Because, then, of the many influences bearing on occupational distribution, one may expect to see substantial differences between the occupational structure of any two groups, even if discrimination is not involved. In this country, such matters as period of arrival in this country and the occupational structure and opportunities of that period, places of concentration, educational and occupational background in home countries, attitudes toward education, attitudes on suitable kinds of work

Table 1. Occupational distribution of Chinese Americans, 1940–1970.

	1940	1950	1960	1970
Professional and technical	3%	7%	18%	26.5%
Managers	21	20	13	9
Sales	11	16	7	4
Clerical	11	16	14	17
Craftsmen	1	3	5	5
Operatives	23	17	15	15
Service	30	29	19	19
Private household workers	6	3	1	1

Source: Betty Lee Sung, Chinese American Manpower and Employment (New York: Praeger, 1976), p. 75.

for men and women, and many other factors will shape an occupational distribution. Differences will often lessen as the first generation gives place to the second and the second to the third. In some cases they may actually increase, but in no case will they disappear.

It is scarcely necessary to document the obvious, but since the presumption of randomness in occupational distribution as "normal" is so widespread among the enforcers of nondiscrimination and affirmative action, a few examples of the obvious will be given. E. P. Hutchinson analyzes census figures on the occupational distribution of groups of immigrants and their children in the United States.[12] He establishes an index number, which shows the difference between the *actual* distribution and what the distribution would be if it paralleled the national occupational distribution. In the latter case, the index number would be 100. An index number above 100 shows "overrepresentation;" an index number below 100 shows "underrepresentation." Consider the occupational distributions of the children of Finnish and Greek immigrants in 1950 as indicated in table 2.

Thus, 36 percent more children of Greek immigrants were in professional and technical occupations than one would expect on the basis of random distribution, while there were only 11 percent more children of Finnish immigrants in these categories.

Table 2. Occupational distribution of the male children of Finnish and Greek immigrants to the United States (1950).

	Children of Finnish immigrants	Children of Greek immigrants
Professional and technical	111[a]	136
Farmers and farm managers	81	9
Managers, officials	63	147
Clerical and kindred	93	112
Sales workers	40	143
Craftsmen, foremen and kindred	114	66
Operatives and kindred	125	101
Private household workers	98	—
Service workers, excluding private household	60	265
Farm laborers and foremen	90	22
Laborers and foremen	159	75

Source: E. P. Hutchinson, *Immigrants and Their Children, 1850–1950* (New York: Wiley, 1956), pp. 220–221.

a. Entries are Hutchinson's index numbers: the index is 100 for a group whose occupational distribution matches the national distribution; an index above 100 indicates "overrepresentation"; an index below 100, "underrepresentation."

Forty-seven percent more of the children of Greek immigrants were managers and officials than one would expect on the basis of random distribution, but the children of Finnish immigrants were severely underrepresented in this important category, having only 63 percent of their expected number.

Similarly, if we go to a single metropolitan area and compare groups that arrived at roughly the same time and met probably similar degrees of discrimination, we also find great differences in occupational distribution. For example, Jewish and Italian immigrants immigrated to New York City during the same period and probably met roughly similar degrees of prejudice and discrimination. If we look at their occupational distribution, however, we find substantial differences between them.[13] Thus, in the New York–Northeastern New Jersey metropolitan area in 1950, 3 percent of Italian immigrant males and 6 percent of their children were in "professional, technical and kindred" occupations, but the figures for U.S.S.R. immigrant (mostly Jews) and their children were 9 and 19 percent. And at the other end of the scale, while 14 percent of the Italian immigrants and 9 percent of their children were laborers, for U.S.S.R. immigrants and their children the figures were 2 and 1 percent.

Conceivably this is something that, as a matter of public policy, we would want to correct, to make the distribution of groups in occupations more equal. Undoubtedly where very large groups are disproportionately concentrated in poorly paying occupations, this creates discontent, resentment, and social conflict. Insofar as any part of this distribution is owing to discriminatory acts, it is also illegal. But one may question whether major restructuring of the occupational distribution in the name of overcoming discrimination, when discrimination has had only a minor effect in creating that distribution, is a reasonable public policy.

But we can also raise a narrower question: What are the technical difficulties in the way of actually establishing a suitable "availability" figure to serve as a target for occupational redistribution, and can they be overcome? I discuss here seven problems in setting a goal based on availability that seem evident to the sociologist of ethnic groups and ethnic-group difference.

1. *Unreliability of census and other sources on availability owing to ambiguity of ethnic-group membership.* There is considerable ambiguity for many individuals as to the group to which they belong. In particular, there is considerable overlap between black and some Spanish-surnamed or Hispanic groups, and the latter and American Indians. Since this ambiguity affects three of the four ethnic categories that are the object of affirmative action, this is not an unimportant problem. A Bureau of the Census technical paper shows substantial inconsistency in how the same individuals report their ethnic origin

between two reporting periods. The percentages of persons reporting the same origin in March 1971 and March 1972, among the categories relevant for affirmative action, were: Puerto Rican, 96.5; Negro, 94.2; Mexican, 88.3; Cuban, 83.3; Spanish (total), 78.9; Central or South American, 47.3; other Spanish, 32.0.[14] Professor Martin Trow of the Graduate School of Public Policy, University of California, Berkeley, director of the largest study every undertaken of American faculty, which surveyed 60,000 faculty members in 1968-69, reports that when it comes to small numbers (and for protected groups in specialized categories the numbers are always small), the error rates in reporting are large. As is well known, there are other problems of reliability, in that substantial numbers of blacks, particularly young males, are missed. Substantial numbers of members of Hispanic groups are also missed. The errors increase as one proceeds to smaller geographic areas, or goes to more detailed information on education, labor force status, occupation.

Undoubtedly one important source of error, owing to the varied ethnic statuses people may properly claim because of mixed or uncertain origins, is the creation of government incentives — as inclusion in affected classes for affirmative action might be interpreted — to classify oneself in one category as against another. Another source of error or at least variation and unreliability, is the change in attitudes of persons in certain groups to the desirability of presenting oneself as a member of that group, with negative attitudes leading people to classify themselves out, and positive attitudes leading to classify themselves in. These sources of error based on self-classification can be enormous. Between 1960 and 1970, for example, American Indians increased more than 50 percent, undoubtedly because many people who had not previously identified themselves as such decided to do so.

2. *Aggregating subgroups into protected groups.* Each category for affirmative action is itself a congeries of distinguishable ethnic group or subgroups. Some of the difficulties of categorization and grouping are illustrated by government agencies' efforts to deal with this problem. Thus a memorandum from Phil J. Davis (4224–4), Director of the

Office for Federal Contract Compliance, dated February 18, 1975, tries to deal with the problem, but bears the interesting note " . . . the attachment should not be distributed in response to inquiries. Rather, specific responses should be formulated consistent with the attachment." When one reads the attachment, one understands the embarrassment in making it public: (This memorandum has now been superseded; the problem it illustrates has not.)

Blacks should include persons of African descent as well as those identified as Jamaican, Trinidadian, and West Indian.

Spanish surnamed should include all persons of Mexican, Puerto Rican, Cuban, Latin American or Spanish descent, including all persons whose native language, cultural heritage, and/or ancestry are rooted in Spain or Latin America.

American Indians should include persons who identify themselves or are known as such . . .

Asian Americans should include persons of Japanese, Chinese, Korean, or Filipino descent, or whose appearance reveals oriental, Polynesian origin.

Persons of Indo-European descent, e.g., Pakistan and East Indian as well as Malayans, Thais, and others not falling within the above are regarded as white.

One reads such a document with astonishment. Note, for example, the confusion between race (appearance) and language. In what sense are "East Indians," presumably persons from the subcontinent as well as Indonesians, of Indo-European descent? Indians include speakers of Indo-European languages (as well as others who are not); Indonesians have no connection at all with "Indo-Europeans," linguistically or otherwise. The document unfortunately leaves out Vietnamese, of whom 150,000 were shortly to descend on these shores.

The main problem with the categorization is that each group contains ethnic groups with diverse patterns of occupational distribution and income, that is, less and more successful groups. Some of the groups (Spanish-surnamed and Asian) also mix subgroups that have suffered discrimination and subgroups that have suffered less or perhaps no discrimination. One can thus envisage, in the most extreme case, employers selecting employees from each category who are already part of a group with substantial occupational and economic success, and who have not suffered from discrimination. Thus, an employer could in theory fulfill a goal for blacks with immigrant West Indians of good education and strong work orientations, for Hispanics with middle-class Cubans and Colombians, for Asian Americans with Chinese and Japanese. What happens then to native American blacks, Mexicans and Puerto Ricans, Filipinos and Koreans? The latter may well be worse off because the former have been given a "premium" that is not warranted.

These confusions are compounded if, as seems to be happening with immigrants from the subcontinent of India, groups that can claim some relationship of geography or language to a group already included in the affected classes (the Indians are certainly "Asian") raise successful claims to be brought in. There is no reason to think this process will have any natural end if statistical goals for affected classes are continued. One can envisage Portuguese Americans demanding as much as Americans stemming from Spain have; after all, they already include Cape Verdians, mixed with Africans, and there is, in any case, a substantial Moorish (African) admixture among Portuguese. French Canadians and Cajuns could also make claims. Spokesmen for Italians and Poles have raised questions. Since the present classes already include the more and less prosperous, and the more and less discriminated against, why not?

While some groups will demand inclusion in the protected classes to get the benefit (or avoid the costs) of not being listed in the majority, other groups, seeing themselves lumped with a more successful and achieving group, will try to become a "protected group" on their own to maximize the benefit of a goal specifically for them. This is no idle possibility: Filipinos, the third most numerous Asian group, and rapidly growing through immigration and natural increase, have already tried. "Filipino-Americans sue U.S. Job Panel," read a headline in the *Wall Street Journal* of June 12, 1974:

The Equal Employment Opportunity Commission was charged in a class action civil rights complaint with discriminating against some

600,000 Filipino-Americans on the basis of non-identification of Filipino-Americans in various EEOC forms.

Public Advocates Inc., a nonprofit public-interest law firm, filed the complaint on behalf of 40 Filipino-American organizations and 100 individual complainants. The complaint asks the EEOC to separately identify Filipino-Americans in its employer reports in states with either 10% or 100,000 Filipino-Americans. Currently, Filipino-Americans are usually lumped in the "Oriental-American" or "Spanish-surnamed" categories.

Non-identification of Filipino-Americans deprives them of equal protection under various civil rights laws, according to Robert Gnaizda, attorney for the complainants . . .

The complaint said that Filipino-Americans are the fastest-growing major minority group in the U.S. As a direct or indirect result of the "exclusionary practice" of the EEOC, the complaint continued, Filipino-Americans lose an estimated $820 million a year in salaries.

3. *Compatibility of available statistics, census or otherwise, with categories established for affirmative action; differences between different government agencies' classification of protected groups.* Different government agencies may accept the same definitions of protected groups for purposes of goals or quotas, but it is likely that some differences exist among them. In any case, it is certainly the case that employers trying to establish the appropriate categories for job applicants, test takers, hirings, promotions, firings, follow different procedures in classifying foreign-born Africans, various types of Spanish-origin groups, various types of Asian and Pacific groups, people of one group carrying names because of marriage that suggest another group, and so on. Nor is there any reason to believe that the categorization procedures of regulating agencies, which may vary among themselves, and the procedures of employers, which certainly vary among themselves, are compatible with the categorization procedures of the census, the major source of statistics on minority groups, or the procedures of the host of private and semipublic agencies that keep records on different professions, occupations, numbers of individuals preparing for given occupations and degrees, and numbers receiving diplomas and other credentials.

Yet employers must set goals for protected classes based on some available statistic; in the best of circumstances, it is from the census, but it may have to be derived from many other sources — private surveys, professional association lists, health and welfare survey studies, and so on. All of these are likely to handle the problems of ethnic categorization in different ways. Undoubtedly the employer will try to show the maximum number of hirings and promotions from the protected groups, and if a person falls in two or more, will place him or her in that category which best improves his showing. But even the most objective effort to determine "availability" will be flawed if the census categories are not compatible with those which regulatory agencies set up as protected groups. And since we as yet refuse in this country to hand out identity cards in which the race and ethnic group of individuals are officially and unambiguously determined by appropriate government agencies, it is not easy to overcome this problem.

4. *"Creaming," and its effect on availability analysis.* The employer is not prohibited from getting the best employees he can, even while operating under goals or quotas. The effects of this are various and complicated. One effect is that those employers who first enter the market to seek out minority employees may be rewarded with the best; if they have begun vigorous recruiting campaigns under court order or under affirmative action pressure, those originally most guilty of neglect in affirmative action or of discrimination may be those who get the best employees. Another may be that those companies found most culpable and under greatest pressure may draw off the better employees through premiums and other actions, leaving the most innocent with the worst. As the search goes on, and on the assumption that the market works this way, subsequent employers are left with substantial numbers apparently available, but these may include less and less adequate employees. Consider one example of the operation of this kind of effect from a different but related field: As major law schools and medical schools have vigorously entered the market for black students, the quality of those available to Howard University Law School, which has never discriminated, and has always been available to black law school

students, has declined. In the 1960s, Howard Law graduates passed the bar at rates of 80 to 90 percent. By 1970 the success rate had dropped to 60 percent; by 1971 to 47 percent, by 1972 to 35 percent. There has probably been the same effect on the traditional black medical schools.[15]

5. *Two distinctive patterns of minority employment — self-employment and government service — and their effect on availability.* It is quite characteristic for some minorities of limited education and poor language facility who have been affected by discrimination to be highly concentrated in occupations that permit self-employment, for example as proprietors of small enterprises — retail stores of all types, service establishments such as laundries, junk and scrap metal collection, and the like. Ivan Light, who studied this pattern of entrepreneurial concentration (as has Mabel Newcomer), wrote:

As Mabel Newcomer has observed, the persistent overrepresentation of the foreign born in business is not a testimonial to the entrepreneurial drive of the foreign born, nor an invidious commentary on the lethargy of native-born Americans. Compared to the native born, the foreign born have received less schooling and hold less impressive educational credentials. They possess fewer higher-priced salable skills. They experience discrimination because of their accents or ethnicity. Hence, the foreign born find in self-employment relatively better income and status rewards than do the native-born persons who have advantages in the labor market.[16]

This pattern continues today. The *New York Times* has noted, in a story titled "Vegetable Stores Provide a New Start for Korean Immigrants," "If Il Y. Chung were Chinese and he had immigrated here, he might well have gone into a coffee shop or delicatessen. But he is Korean and so he has entered the newly popular Korean-American enterprise: he has opened a fruit and vegetable store."[17] This pattern will, of course, increase the proportion of managers among the foreign born, and if the pattern continues into the second generation, as it often does, among their children as well.

It may also create a bias toward self-employment as they or their children enter professional and other occupations, as will, for some groups, the continued reality or fear of discrimination. Strong family connections for some groups will also encourage self-employment when these businessmen or their children become professionals. (The *New York Times* story continues: ". . . Mrs. Chung is going to night school this summer and hopes to become a certified public accountant. Then, she hopes to work while her husband goes back for a doctorate in political science.") Thus, the minority-member professional will be more typically in practice for himself or with a partner rather than a member of a large firm. This pattern has been typical for Jews, Chinese, Japanese, Armenians, Lebanese, and some other groups, some of which are in protected groups.

An alternative path to employment for minorities has been government service, where discrimination has been less evident in the past than in private employment. Thus, during the Depression, Jews in large numbers entered government service. Forty-eight percent of black male professional, technical, and kindred workers, and 24 percent of black male managers, work for government, while the comparable figures for all males are 30 and 12.5 percent respectively. Government employs 67 percent of black female professionals, compared to 31 percent of all female professionals, and 35 percent of black female managers, compared to 17 percent of all female managers.[18] Orientals are to be found in government service at a rate 80 percent higher than their percentage in the population.[19]

These two kinds of concentrations will affect the willingness of minority members in certain occupations to enter private employment with large companies; they may find the rewards and security of government service, or the freedom (and conceivably the opportunity for higher rewards) of self-employment more attractive, and this undoubtedly acts as an upward bias on the apparent "availability" of managers, professionals, and possibly other categories of employees as given by census labor force statistics.

6. *Relationship between larger occupational categories and detailed occupation in census statistics, and in protected groups.* Any census or other listing of occupations must place together related occupations. At the same time, any ethnic group will

show a distinctive distribution among occupations and detailed occupations. Availability of any group on the basis of statistics of an occupational category may be grossly distorted if the employer in question looks for occupational specialities within that group to carry on his work. While, of course, skills are transferable, there are undoubtedly limits to transferability and costs to employees and employers in transferring from one specialty to another. Presumably if one makes the occupational classification more and more refined, one will reduce the chances of error in determining availability. But then, as one makes the occupational classification more and more refined, the chances of finding availability statistics decline, as does their reliability.

To take one example from a closely related field, statistics showed that fewer female applicants than male applicants for graduate work were accepted at the University of California, Berkeley. This seemed strong evidence of discrimination by sex until it was pointed out by researchers that in each department to which females applied for graduate work, equal or higher proportions of females were accepted. The problem is solved when one notes that female applicants preferred graduate school specialities (such as English) which accepted smaller proportions of all applicants for study.[20] One could undoubtedly find similar cases in industry that could be explained by the actual numbers of persons with specific occupational specialities.

7. *Age in labor force statistics; space in labor force statistics.* The distribution of any group in occupational categories by age is likely to be distinctive: for one group, managers will be old (the immigrant proprietor), for another young (new college graduates). The pattern of age distribution is a factor that would have to be considered in availability: it is on the whole young workers, entering the labor force or changing jobs more rapidly, who are available. This factor would inflate availability for some categories, deflate it for others. Once again, reliability of figures on age would decline as the number in the group surveyed diminished.

Ethnic groups differ, too, in their spatial distribution, within the country, within regions, within metropolitan areas. Undoubtedly they also differ in their attitudes toward the appropriate distance one will travel when seeking a job, accepting a job, or commuting to a job. This is a well-worn area in the arguments over availability statistics between compliance officers and company personnel officers. But the issue of differing orientations or tastes, distinguishing between groups, is also important. Ethnic groups vary in the degree to which they are willing to move away from family and relatives when seeking work and housing.[21] This is also a feature that distinguishes men and women, insofar as higher proportions of women seek part-time jobs, show more movement into and out of the labor force, and have greater family responsibilities. Availability of different protected classes may vary considerably if one takes this factor into account.

These seven problems are in no sense exhaustive. Nevertheless, they are enough to suggest that there are severe difficulties in establishing a figure of "availability" for ethnic and racial categories that one can have confidence in, and that there is legitimate room for substantial disagreement over what the "true" availability figure is, if one could determine it. What does this tell us about the present requirement that, nevertheless, employers establish, to the satisfaction of government affirmative action officers, availability figures for the many protected race, ethnic, and sex categories, for each occupational category, for each labor market? Undoubtedly one response — the present response dictated by federal policy, since goals set on the basis of availability are a requirement for an affirmative action program — is nevertheless to go doggedly about the task of setting a number for each job title, for each protected group, to do the best job possible, and to keep on improving our capacities. The issues I have raised in this chapter suggest many lines of productive research to improve availability figures; whether government, industry, or any other source is willing to foot the bill for the extensive research necessary to improve availability figures is another question.

But another approach would be to accept the fact that human capacities and human understanding are limited, and that availability is a subject for research by skilled economists and sociologists, not something to be fixed by government officials — or business personnel officers. But if we abandon hard figures, what happens to affirmative action?

Unfortunately, affirmative action — which means a wide range of actions on the part of employers to increase the number of minority employees — has become fixated on the hard number, the goal, as its true test. There can be another, and better test, for affirmative action. That is, what processes and procedures does an employer use in searching for, selecting, hiring, training, promoting, firing employees? We know a great deal about the effect of these procedures on minority employment. It is now common knowledge that employers should seek minority employees where they are to be found. Their advertising and recruiting should show that they welcome minority employees, they must review their testing and selection procedures for unconscious bias (let alone conscious bias), and the like.

Affirmative action might then eschew the will-o-the-wisp objective of the "true" availability figures, and accept the position that the true test of availability is what happens when employers make serious, earnest, and unbiased efforts to overcome all discrimination, conscious and unconscious, to cast the nets of publicity and recruiting as widely as possible, neglecting no area or source where employees may be found. "Result-oriented" sounds good, but if it means that we are capable of establishing a hard and fast figure of availability, it merely fosters illusion. Under process-oriented rather than result-oriented affirmative action procedures, we may well find that some employers in some job titles have fewer minority employees than a crude availability figure suggests, and others have more. But why should that surprise or offend us? If groups are real, then we must accept differences among them. It should not be the task of government to eradicate these; its task, and its mandate, is to eradicate discrimination.

Clearly the chances of the latter approach becoming reality, that is, of affirmative action becoming limited to advertising, recruiting, seeking, training, with a line drawn against its using statistical goals and quotas, is politically unlikely, and will not depend on a demonstration of technical difficulties, as they appear to a sociologist of ethnic groups, such as I have developed here. However, when one considers the other two perspectives that are relevant in judging the desirability of goals and timetables, the Constitutional and the economic, one may discern possibilities of limiting what is, to my mind, an enterprise that refuses to take into account the facts of ethnic group difference.

[1977]

11

Liberty, Equality, Fraternity

— and Ethnicity

IT HAS ALWAYS been difficult for Americans to understand the revolutionary slogan of France, "liberty, equality, fraternity." The first two terms are clear enough: they frame the central issues faced by society and polity in the modern age, neatly juxtaposed and in some sort of inevitable conflict. We all understand that the desire for liberty — for freedom of action — regularly comes into conflict with equality, the overwhelming tendency in modern society to ensure that each man (and woman, and perhaps child) count for one, and no more than one. The conflict can be more or less sharp, but it is impossible except through sophistry to eliminate it. During the days when the New Deal was for the first time trying modestly to redistribute income in the United States — through such programs as the WPA, aid to poor farmers, social security, aid to dependent children, unemployment insurance, public housing — the notion that the freedom of individuals was in some substantial measure reduced by the modest taxes that were then required for these jointly determined national efforts to introduce a minimal level of decent living seemed extreme, ideological, and outlandish. The inexorable growth of such programs and the inevitable addition to them of new programs (in health care, food distribution, work training) have substantially increased the burden of taxation, and they make less outlandish the notion that when the government deprives one of income in favor of some publicly accepted program of redistribution of goods, services, or income, it is taking away from "liberty" in order to increase "equality." But it takes a Milton Friedman or a Friedrich Hayek to get angry about this kind of restriction of liberty in favor of equality. Taking away some of one's income and property is still — *pace* John Locke — the most modest and acceptable form of reducing liberty in favor of equality.

It is other kinds of deprivation of liberty that more properly arouse concern and anger. The restriction of liberty of religious and political discourse, publication, and participation is what first and principally aroused the defenders of liberty and the philosophic formulators of a defense of liberty. But between the restriction of income in order to assist in achieving a greater equality and the deprivation of the freedoms of speech, and movement, and of religious and political activity, there remains a huge range of governmental action to promote what would appear to many to be legitimate equality. It is in this middle range that new issues have quite suddenly emerged in the United States in the past ten years. Here, perhaps, that obscure third term, "fraternity" — which the French felt they needed, and we felt we didn't — now becomes important.

Undoubtedly the revolutionary French felt a term like "fraternity" was necessary to express their objectives for a good society because there were such radical social divisions among the French, divisions going back deep into their history, expressed in law, dividing them into estates with different rights, privileges, ways of life, and expectations. These would be swept away. In the United States, in contrast to eighteenth-century Europe, a remarkable social uniformity prevailed. There were no titles — except those brought over from Europe; law did not govern and regulate social status. There was only one great division in society — that between the slave and the free. But among the free, according to most observers — it would, of course, hardly seem so to us after two hundred years of further progress in our expectations of, and the reality of, equality — a remarkable equality and uniformity prevailed. Even those few legal distinctions that still existed among the free (on the basis of religious affiliation or wealth) did not long survive the Revolution.

In the eyes of foreign visitors, "fraternity," in the form of the democratic intercourse among white and free Americans, was already so far advanced as hardly to need assertion as a distinctive goal. The chasm between black and white, slave and free, seemed too great for any ideal of fraternity to bridge. "Liberty" and "equality" alone seemed sufficient for the new nation. It was within these two terms and with these two terms that the United States tried to deal with the greater diversity that arose among the white and free population with the rise of immigration and the creation of a great nation drawn from more varied ethnic sources than any other in the world.

Until, perhaps, the mid 1960s; then the effort to deal with the varied facts of ethnicity and race within the framework of liberty and equality alone broke down. I do not believe we have yet reached any consensus as to how to overcome the breakdown, but the third term, "fraternity," while it does not give us a solution to the problems that have arisen, suggests something about their nature. In a word, "fraternity" in the United States — as against an ethnically homogeneous nation such as France — faces two ways. On the one hand, it suggests a united nation; but, on the other, it reminds us that the basis of fraternity in the United States is narrower than the whole nation. I will explore this two-faced nature of fraternity later in this chapter. The task now is to describe why "liberty" and "equality" became insufficient to encompass the racial and ethnic crisis of the later 1960s.[1]

It had been expected that they would be: that the freedom to vote, to enter public places without stigma or limitation, to enter schools of one's choice, to organize politically without fear of economic and physical reprisal, that is, a full equality of blacks and other groups in every realm of public activity, would solve the crisis. To ensure this liberty and equality, some of the most radical legislation in American history rapidly moved through Congress: in 1964, a civil rights act banned discrimination on account of race, color, religion, and national origin in places of public accommodation, in public education, in federal programs and federally assisted programs, and in most areas of private employment; in 1968, discrimination in the sale or rental of most housing was added; in 1965, a striking measure swept aside state or local action to limit the right to vote — all state or local powers to regulate the franchise were automatically suspended if the proportion of people voting fell below 50 percent of those eligible on the basis of age and citizenship alone.

All these sweeping actions were upheld by the courts as constitutional. They seemed to most people to raise no problem of conflict between "equality" and "liberty," though undoubtedly the legislation — and its subsequent interpretations — infringed strongly on the liberty of employers, renters and sellers of housing, and proprietors of places of public accommodation to exercise discriminatory tastes. This seemed an infringement modest enough to bear in view of the great public good expected from this legislation.

But the achievement of equality in a multiethnic society turned out to be a rather more complicated matter than the public opinion that supported the civil rights legislation of the 1960s had expected. In its simplest form, the unexpected issue was as follows. Equality had regularly expanded its meaning. Among large groups of the population, it no longer meant a formal public equality but a *concrete* and *actual* equality. However, as was soon clear, the right to entry (as well as actual entry) into schools without discrimination was in fact quite different from the right to equal test scores and equal achievement; the right to employment without discrimination did not mean that the average income of each group or its distribution within occupations would match that of every other group; the right to rent and purchase apartments and houses did not bring with it the income to afford the apartment desired; the right to register and vote did not necessarily mean that equal proportions of each group actually did register and vote and exercise "equal" political power.

The reason that "equality of opportunity" did not automatically bring "equality of results" lay in the concrete differences that had developed in, and characterized, different racial and ethnic groups. And thus the two faces of fraternity came into conflict: the national fraternity which meant that all would be equal and alike was inhibited by smaller circles of fraternity, built around race and ethnicity, which created their own cultures, values, aspirations, and behaviors, and which, whatever their superficial similarities (didn't everybody watch the same television shows?), ensured an actual difference.

This conclusion as to why the new liberty and the new equality of opportunity did not result rapidly in an actual measured equality in such key social indicators as education, wealth, occupation, residence, and voting was not uniformly accepted as the correct one. The public authorities were in any case expected to be formally blind to group differences — neither religious, ethnic, nor racial differences were to play any role in public law after the middle 1960s, except to facilitate the elimination of differences in achievement among groups (and except for the idiosyncratic and special position of American Indians). Since public law banned discrimination, the government decided to take *all* evidence of difference as a signal of *possible* discrimination. If there were more blacks in a public school or college than their proportion in the school population, if the number of eligible voters who actually voted in Brooklyn fell below the suspect 50 percent mark, if there were fewer blacks (or some other group that was the special object of government concern) employed in some occupation than their numbers in the population made plausible, if blacks (or some other groups) were not evenly distributed throughout a metropolitan area, this could, in the light of American historical practices, mean actual and current discrimination or, failing that, the heritage of past discrimination. That it could result from any other cause than intended discrimination was difficult for public officials and courts to recognize.

The law developed at different rates in different realms. Since the law required it, government needed to make no complicated argument to intervene in setting local voting requirements if the proportion of voters fell below 50 percent of those eligible. In the case of schools, the law as interpreted by the courts put on the school boards the burden of proof in explaining departures from an even racial distribution; they would then have to show that the deviations had not occurred as a result of any discriminatory public action. In the case of employment, employers were narrowly ringed with guidelines set by government departments, administrative agency decisions, and court judgments: in effect the burden of proof was on them, too, to demonstrate that deviation from some statistical norm was not the result of discrimination.

A broad general principle began to emerge, underlying all these areas of policy: any deviation from statistical parity could, and should, be interpreted as owing to unconstitutional discrimination. If it was not the discrimination of the current school board, or employer, or housing manager, or local jurisdiction that was responsible, then it was the discrimination of their predecessors, for whom redress must be made; if it was not the discrimination of school boards or employers or housing managers at all that was responsible, then some other branch of government must have created the illegal discrimination. Thus it was perhaps the discriminatory behavior of realtors (governmentally licensed — and therefore acting in some respect as public agents) excluding blacks from good residential neighborhoods with good schools that was responsible for poor school performance by black students; or perhaps it was the schools, improperly segregating black children, that were responsible for their poor performance on tests for employment; or perhaps it was employers, improperly discriminating against blacks, who prevented them from acquiring the income that would permit them to move into better neighborhoods and get better schooling; and so on and so on.

In each case in which numbers showed that a group had not achieved parity by some measure, some showing of governmental dereliction could be made. Perhaps it could not be shown that the specific responsible agency of government had directly discriminated (Discrimination I), but some other agency might have contributed to, or led to, improper representation in the first area (Discrimination II), and, even if no governmental agency at all had contributed to the result, some occupation or profession that was either governmentally licensed or governmentally affected (almost everyone, it turned out, might be discovered to be the beneficiary of, or a contractor for, government services and thus in some sense a government agent) might have contributed (Discrimination III), and so on and so on.

The secondary boycott is considered an unfair labor practice: one cannot picket the employer who simply does business with the employer against whom one has a grievance. But this principle plays no role in discrimination law as elaborated by government agencies and the courts: if there is inequality, someone is responsible and someone must be found to provide redress. But at the bottom of such an approach is one unexamined assumption: that all groups would, in the absence of discrimination, be distributed equally in all realms of society. To what extent this is the assumption of the "common man," I do not know; but it is certainly the assumption of government administrators and judges, and even, surprisingly enough, of many social scientists studying group differences, who might be expected to take the reality of group differences more seriously.

Thus, consider one scholarly definition of "racism": "Whatever acts or institutional procedures help create or perpetuate sets of advantages or privileges for whites and exclusions and deprivations for blacks." The sociologist Robin Williams comments that, by this definition, "racism is being practiced whenever white parents aid their children to get a good education, assist them in locating jobs, or allow them to inherit property. No doubt unequal advantages are involved in these practices, but how is clarity served by lumping them together with gross and explicit racial exclusion and denials of opportunity?" [2]

In other words, the basic assumption of antidiscrimination law, as it has evolved in the hands of government agencies, has been upheld in the courts, and has been argued for by legal and social science advocates, is that whatever differences among groups are found in the key areas of modern life, they are in the first instance — and unless proved otherwise — to be attributed to unconstitutional discrimination by government or by private parties that could be and should be restrained by government. Alternative interpretations are barely considered. Indeed, any discussion of them is likely to create such a storm of protest and charges of racism that in effect the field is held secure for this one central interpretation — one that contradicts everything we know about human diversity — that all differences are created by the intentional design of governmental authorities.

The reality that many people try to resist is that equality of opportunity and of treatment, insofar as we can measure it, will not automatically lead to an equal outcome for all groups — at least not rapidly. It appears that the simple liberty to compete, regardless of our effort to equalize the starting points, will lead some students to move far ahead and will prevent an equal outcome. We will find the same patterns in economic life: a measured equality of starting point seems to have only a modest influence on eventual outcome, as measured by income and occupation.[3]

The liberty to compete educationally and economically will lead to inequality, even starting from an equal position, and even, indeed, taking into account the fact that some groups start with initial handicaps of private and public discrimination. It is well known that minorities in many countries are disproportionately successful educationally or economically even though such minorities face discrimination. These minorities include Jews, Lebanese, Chinese, Indians, Armenians, Ibos, and many other groups, though no one makes the claim that persons from these groups are uniformly successful in all circumstances. This is not to say that the discrimination such groups have faced, and do face, is irrelevant to success educationally and economically: even the groups that are disproportionately successful, one assumes, would have achieved more in the absence of discrimination.[4]

If, then, liberty leads to inequality, even when an initial equality exists, even indeed when certain achieving groups are handicapped severely (of course it is more common for handicapped groups to fall behind, but as we have seen this is by no means always the case, nor are the exceptions inconsequential), a dilemma is created for a democracy that judges its success by the degree to which each group approximates the average in key indicators of success and well-being. If, further, lawyers insist that any difference that exists is attributable to an unfair and now illegal discrimination by public authorities and private individuals and institutions, and no cause of group difference other than discrimination, past or present, is admitted, legal reasoning will simply lose touch with reality.[5] For one overwhelming fact undermines interpretations of difference as owing to discrimination: Some minorities that have met discrimination have not only achieved equality but more than equality in many significant measured areas.

When reality is ignored or suppressed, and illusion prevails, there are good reasons for it. There is one basic fear that motivates this denial of reality: if one admits that differences between groups are real, and admits they may be based on something other than discrimination, one opens the way to the possibility of attributing these differences to genetic inheritance that cannot change except over many generations. This would mean giving up the hope that over time a rough equality in group distributions would emerge through competition among individuals, and it would mean, perhaps, accepting the justice of differences that do exist because they are based on inborn competence. (Even if this were the cause of differences, the justice of such an arrangement could of course be denied, as it is by John Rawls and others.) In nonessential areas of achievement, ethnic differences may be admitted and accepted — the achievement of blacks in basketball and baseball, of Jews in chess and classical string playing in the past, of Koreans and Japanese in classical string playing today, and the like. No one seems much concerned that admitting the existence of such differences may open the way to genetic explanations. But in the major areas that give power and prestige — education, income, occupation — we find a denial that inborn differences can be large or important.

Unfortunately one cannot reassure those who are frightened of the possibility that significant differences of achievement in education, the professions, and income may have a genetic basis. This is not absolutely impossible. But at least the matter is sufficiently complicated to require a very long time indeed before we can move from what we know about human heredity and its complex interaction with environment today to a conclusion as to what, if any, part of human differences in living societies can be attributed to heredity. We have gone only a few steps on that road—steps dogged by the insistence of many, scientists and nonscientists, that we must not proceed further for fear genetic grounds of difference may be more sharply revealed. One can reassure those with such a concern that we seem far from any such resolution today.[6]

The fear that some biological and hereditary component to human group differences may be found is not only based on concern for the achievement of a wider and more stable equality: a pseudoscientific theory of fixed biological characteristics in races was the starting point for Hitler's monstrous doctrines and the ensuing horrible massacres. And yet it may be argued that no biological theories were needed for the other massacres of peoples that have taken place in the past—differences of religion, language, wealth, caste, or what you will have been sufficient to mark off one group as different from another and to lead to cruel treatment rivaling Hitler's intention, even if no one has yet rivaled him in the technical means for the carrying out of hate.

Among those seeking greater equality the fear of group differences now spreads to *any* effort to explain difference, even if it has nothing to do with biology. During the years when social scientists tried to combat the racist theories of Nazism, they emphasized other, more plastic sources of human difference, which could be summed up in the term "culture." Franz Boas, Ruth Benedict, and other distinguished anthropologists felt that if they could persuade people that differences among groups were not genetic but cultural—based on the transmission of custom, practice, values, ideals, rather than genes—that people would be more tolerant of difference, would understand that individuals are not fated biologically to be what they are, that group characteristics can change rapidly as environment, incentives, and policy change. In the days of Hitler, to speak of race was retrograde, to speak of culture was progressive.

Today, it is considered almost equally retrograde to speak of culture: Culture is also not accepted by much educated opinion as a legitimate explanation of difference in place of an explanation based on public or private discrimination. That groups may differ in tastes, values, practices, stemming from history and custom is considered almost as dangerous a suggestion as that groups may differ because of genetic selection. There was, after all, no hint in Daniel P. Moynihan's famous report on the Negro family that anything aside from slavery and discrimination had shaped it, but he was nonetheless attacked as a racist. The hope of Boas and Benedict that an emphasis on environment, nurture, and culture in explaining differences would be compatible with a liberal and progressive outlook has foundered since about the middle 1960s, for such a doctrine appeared, by explaining, to justify differences: only if differences were owing to discrimination was the dangerous possibility eliminated that they could be justified by being shown to have some rational and functional explanation.

We may see coming up on the horizon new scientific explanations for difference, and one wonders what *their* fate will be. Thus, as against either hereditary or cultural or general environmental explanations of differences in intelligence, we now have the beginnings of a ver specific kind of explanation based on family size. This is also environmental, but in a rather narrow sense. There is some evidence that intelligence declines regularly with size of family or origin. One theory that seems to have considerable merit explains this decline by family configuration: the larger the family, the less the influence of adults and older children in raising the intellectual level of the immediate environment of each subsequent child. This family-size factor seems to be at work even after one takes account — as one must — of the well-known large socioeconomic influence in measured intelligence. If one takes into account that size of family varies greatly across ethnic and racial groups, one has a totally nongenetic explanation of differences in intelligence among groups, and if one takes the position that education is relevant to some tasks in some degree, one can explain some part of occupational difference.[7]

This explanation of differences in intelligence is too recent and too little known — compared with genetic and looser cultural and environmental explanations — to have aroused much response, but one can hazard the prediction that it will have no happier a fate than genetic or cultural explanations. The family-size theorists may also discover to their astonishment that they are "racists," illogical as the label may be, merely because they give *some* explanation for human difference that is not simply discrimination.

The fear of the recrudescence of racist theories is the first reason for the denial of difference; this becomes expanded into a fear of cultural explanations which seem to justify differences; and finally a fear of any kind of rational, systematic, and functional explanation of difference, whatever it is. Difference itself is the enemy.

A second current approach to explaining the differences generated by liberty is to argue that, whatever they may be, they are too insubstantial to account for, or justify, differences in education, occupation, and income. Thus Samuel Bowles and Herbert Gintis argue that differences in educational achievement play no role, functionally, in making one person more effective economically than another. Rather, differences in socioeconomic background generate unimportant differences in educational achievement, which are then used as an excuse to maintain privilege in a meritocratic society which could not take social origins directly as a legitimate source of difference of reward. Or the tasks of modern complex societies, it is argued, are not as solidly based on training and capacity as we have been led to believe—many people can perform them, and educational differences are simply used as an excuse to select those who have already been assigned a privileged place by birth. These arguments are ultimately based on empirical findings regarding the real differences in achieved position attributable to educational achievement independently of socioeconomic background, and—a more difficult task—the real contribution of merit—whether developed by education or only recognized by it—to productive tasks. They may be weakened by further research.[8]

There is a third contemporary approach to rejecting the significance of group differences: this neither denies them nor depreciates them, as do the first two approaches. It simply asserts that whatever the differences among individuals (and presumably among ethnic and racial groups) may be, there is no legitimate theory of justice by which these differences — whether biological, or cultural, or based on effort, or on luck — can be used to reward individuals differentially. Our passion for egalitarianism is such that the theory that best expounds this point of view has been seized upon with enthusiasm,[9] even though it has not been without critics arguing against it on various grounds. What is most striking about the theory for our discussion is its denial of any ground for differential reward, unless it benefits the least advantaged. Whole bodies of morality are thus swept aside. Inherited beauty and physical capacity, developed charm or wit should be no basis for differential reward (even though it is not this kind of difference that agitates people — people in general seem least resentful about the differential rewards of entertainers and athletes).[10] What is startling is the broad acceptance this notion of the separation of merit from return has achieved, despite the fact that the notion that merit should be rewarded plays a substantial role in every traditional system of morality, and even in the system of morality that can be drawn from Marx. P. T. Bauer writes, arguing against Gunnar Myrdal:

Why should everybody be entitled to substantially the same income, simply by virtue of being born, and regardless of conduct, motivations, faculties and contributions to the economy? Why should it be inequitable that people who revere animal life, or who do not let women work outside the home, or who do not exert themselves greatly, should have lower incomes than do others who do not impose such restraints on themselves? Or why should it be inequitable that the Chinese in Malaysia and Indonesia, or the Indians in Burma, or the Europeans in South Asia should earn higher incomes than do the indigenous populations, when they work harder, often face great hardships, and incur risks far from their countries of origin?[11]

Presumably when these questions were asked P. T. Bauer thought they were, at least in part, rhetorical. It has now been explained — and broadly accepted — why reward should be separated from effort.

The question raised by this excursion into recent intellectual history is what kinds of differences among people a contemporary society, and the modern mind, will be able to tolerate. Undoubtedly our level of tolerance for difference (or inequality) has been greatly reduced when considered in the broad reach of history. All societies, except perhaps some of the most primitive, have shown substantial differences in the enjoyment of basic goods—food, clothing, shelter, sex, knowledge, prestige, and the like. These differences have generally been justified by tradition, and in more complex societies they have been further justified by resort to religion—inequality was the will of God or the gods, who in their wisdom had determined this state of affairs. With the secularization of the world this would no longer do, and rational and functional explanations of differences were consequently developed. They have received surprisingly wide acceptance among the common folk, who believe that success is the result of merit and hard work, along with a good deal of luck, and are not inclined to argue about it. But these explanations have less power among the better educated, who find rational and functional explanations inadequate.

When these inequalities coincide with ethnic-group lines, tolerance of difference declines still further. Then even the common folk, in groups that on the average have less, will be unwilling to accept the legitimacy of the prevailing distribution. Or, perhaps, at one level, they accept its legitimacy; people in groups with less are remarkably candid in attributing the circumstances of their group to its characteristics. "We don't work hard enough," "we just like to sit around in the sun and sing and dance," "we spend all our money on cars and women," "our kids don't buckle down in school," "we don't stick together and help each other," "we distrust each other"—one will run into such statements among the less successful groups in many societies. But, at another level, people in such groups also recognize the benefits they may get from their political power—if they are in a majority or in sufficient numbers to cause trouble—or the power of the prevailing ideologies generated among the more highly educated, which tells them they are unjustly deprived and have a right to as large a share of the good things as anyone else. It would take an act of heroism for the first kind of explanation of ill fortune, based on observation (as well, of course, as on stereotype), to stand up against the second—and it does not.

And here we return to that ambiguous and obscure term, "fraternity." It appears that, so long as a group is bound by some sense of fraternity, it will tolerate substantial differences *within* the group. In contradiction to what the Marxists expected, class feelings, which divide ethnically homogeneous peoples on the basis of income, education, and life style, have not developed the strength and passion of ethnic feelings, which group people on the basis of presumed origin. When ethnicity coincides even to some extent with class feeling, however, dangerous conflicts erupt. Most developed societies have about the same amount of inequality, as measured by the distribution of income, and about the same amount of social mobility, as measured by the opportunity of persons of lower income and occupation to rise to, or see their children rise to, higher positions. But it is in those societies which are sharply divided ethnically that a politically powerful demand for a full, measured equality among groups has become potent. One can present as examples Canada and Belgium, prosperous nations that do not suffer from any more marked a degree of inequality than, let us say, Australia or Holland. Yet, because of the lines that divide Canada and Belgium into two language communities, we have had the rise of movements insisting that any inequality between the two language communities in any key area is not to be tolerated and must be overcome, whatever the cost to efficiency. And so we have the division of the library of the University of Louvain. Interestingly enough, if Canada and Belgium *were* to be divided into two countries, if "fraternity" could be reestablished by creating successor states to the present bilingual states, the demands for equality within the successor states would be reduced. Inequalities that differentiated people within the newly ethnically homogeneous states would be considered more acceptable than the inequalities that separated one ethnic community from another in a single state.

The point is that fraternity reduces the intensity of feelings against inequalities. The examples are numerous: One is angry at the foreign colonial administrator who enjoys a high standard of living; one is not angry at people of one's own group if they take over these positions, maintaining — or even expanding — inequalities. One is angry at the foreign Indian or Chinese merchant, even if his standard of living is only minimally above that of the indigenous majority and even if it is based on an observably longer and harder work day. But one is not angry when the new national monopoly over trade distributes rewarding positions to members of the majority group, conceivably increasing inequality when measured as a return for a unit of work — for it is now an inequality whose sharp edge is reduced by the feelings of "fraternity."

Ethnic conflicts over issues of inequality are given a peculiar complexity in the United States because we have never been sure whether we ought to add to "liberty" and "equality" a "fraternity" that encompasses all the people. Great numbers of American have always been excluded from participation in the fraternity, some completely (American Indians, blacks, Mexican Americans, Orientals) and some only partially (Catholics, Jews, and immigrants from almost any country outside Northwestern Europe). The thrust of American society was steadily to expand the definition of groups eligible to become full Americans and fully to participate in a common society. In the civil rights acts of 1964, 1965, and 1968, and in the immigration act of 1965, division on the ground of race or ethnicity in any public sphere and many private spheres was no longer to be recognized. All were to be equal — the first step toward fraternity. If indeed a stronger national fraternity had come into being, our attention would now be focused less than it is on the relative standing economically and educationally of blacks, Mexican Americans, Puerto Ricans, and other groups, and more on divisions of class. But it is clear that only a partial, even if a real, fraternity exists among Americans of diverse race and ethnic background. It is a real fraternity — we have never come close to the dangers of political division that have threatened, and still threaten, Canada, Belgium, the Soviet Union, Nigeria, and other ethnically divided societies in which the sense of fraternity is more sharply limited by ethnic boundaries than it is in the United States. We have created an American people, and Americans of any ethnic group become aware of it when they are in contact with foreigners. One of the interesting discoveries of black writers of the 1960s traveling in newly independent African states was how much they had become "Americans" and were no longer in any social or cultural sense "Africans." Probably Irish Americans visiting Ireland, Polish Americans visiting Poland, and Jewish Americans visiting Israel discover the same thing.

But it is also a partial fraternity. Very often the more significant fraternity is the ethnic and racial group, not the whole society: the ethnic neighborhood, the church, the self-consciously ethnic organization. So we are suspended, it appears, between the clearly ethnically divided societies — which must, if these societies are to remain together, overcome inequalities between the self-conscious groups — and a homogeneous society, in which concern for inequality is less intense and is focused in any case on the class divisions rather than the ethnic divisions of the society.

In a society of the first type, the achievement of equality among different groups is such an urgent task, if political resentment is not to lead to unmanageable conflict, that one resorts to public action determined directly by this objective: quotas in higher education, quotas in government employment and programs, and funds specifically earmarked for one group or another. But we in the United States shrink from fully embracing such measures, for we are not sure we are that kind of society — or want to be — as against the more homogeneous, fraternal one we have tried to become, in which the individual is treated simply as an individual, without regard for ethnic characteristics.

The significance of the recent developments in law that have succeeded the antidiscriminatory legislation of the 1960s is that they have raised sharply the question of which way the United States is to go: toward an ever increasing attention to the inequalities among ethnic groups, leading to requirements for government and private institutions to overcome such inequalities and, in doing so, to treat persons on the ground of their race, color, and national origin. Or toward a society in which we take for granted an increasing "fraternity," a more homogeneous society, in which each individual is already presumed to be part of the overall fraternity and is thus to be treated — as the mid-1960s legislation ringingly insisted — "without distinction of race, color, national origin, or religion."

To many — and, indeed, to the official branches of government, the executive and the judicial in particular — this dilemma is no dilemma. Of course, they say, our objective is "the equal treatment of the laws," a society and a polity which act "without distinction of race, color, national origin, or religion," but in order to achieve such a society we must steadily test, through statistical analysis, whether such equal treatment exists, and if it does not, we must ensure that agencies operate on the basis of ethnic distinction until equality is reached and there is no longer reason to operate on the basis of ethnic distinction. In other words, we are told, we record the race and ethnicity of school children and college students and employees only to ensure there has been no discrimination, and we require school assignment and college and professional-school admission by race and employment by race only until such discrimination has ceased. Thus we do not move toward an ethnically divided society by making ethnic distinctions for education and employment and various other realms, we are merely engaged in a temporary process to eliminate the effects of discrimination. This is the reasoning, and it is broadly accepted: the leaders of the less successful ethnic groups themselves insist that their objective is not quotas but equal opportunity, that the setting of racial quotas for school assignment and racial goals for employment is meant only to achieve the situation in which the strict bans on public action on grounds of race and ethnicity that Congress inserts regularly into its legislation can come into effect.

I believe the argument is wrong, for two reasons. The first is that we cannot easily draw a line separating those groups that are to be favored by having their progress monitored, and by tailoring official action to speed it up, from those that should not be so favored. Our recent history suggests how hard it is to draw such a line. Originally school desegregation was meant to apply only to blacks. School-desegregation law has now spread to include Mexican Americans, Puerto Ricans, any group of Spanish surname, Chinese, and Japanese — and the last few groups, at least, have often resisted the imposition of school-desegregation quotas that required them to attend schools outside their neighborhoods. There is no reason why the spreading judicial requirement of dispersion should not be applied to French Canadian students, Portuguese students, and other definable groups.

Originally the Voting Rights Act of 1965 was meant to apply to blacks. In its extension in 1975, American Indians, Spanish-surnamed groups, and Orientals were all brought within its purview. On the basis of a statistical test for their presence, election materials must now be translated into various languages for the benefit of groups that have not been shown to vote less than others, or to have any restrictions, official or unofficial, placed upon their voting.

Originally affirmative action was meant to apply to blacks, American Indians, Spanish-surnamed, and Asian Americans. But the last two include groups that do not seem to suffer from any distinctive employment problems based on their ethnic background. Polish Americans, Indians (from India), and other groups either are on the way to being included in some affirmative action plans, or are arguing they should be.[12] Our problem is that we are not a federation of peoples (like Canada or the Soviet Union) but of states, and our ethnic groups are already too dispersed, mixed, assimilated, integrated to permit without confusion a policy that separates out some for special treatment. But if we try, then many other groups will join the queue, or try to, and the hope of a larger fraternity of all Americans will have to be abandoned.

The second reason the argument is wrong is that the means by which these policies attempt to promote the end of nondiscrimination will themselves become ends, for it is hardly likely that a benefit once attained — the benefit of special treatment — will easily be given up.

The misfortune we risk in the new policies is worse than that of being divided into two, or three, or some other relatively small number of ethnic categories for different treatment; we are already too mixed and too diverse for that. What we risk is a real Balkanization, in which group after group struggles for the benefits of special treatment on the basis of some claim — which too many can make — to discriminatory treatment to some degree, if not now then at some time in the past.

"Fraternity" has two faces: There is the small fraternity of the group, the manufactory of distinctive customs, attitudes, and values which, when exercised in the larger society, makes it the most unlikely thing in the world that each group will show the same profile of education, employment, wealth, and political influence. Many such groups exist in the United States, though inevitably over time and through the influence of the larger society their distinctiveness is reduced. We have always considered this to be a positive part of the experience of American life. On the whole, American opinion has favored this development: without demanding the utter reduction of ethnic distinctiveness, we looked with favor upon the rise of a single American people. But now the differences created by this small-scale "fraternity" have led to demands and policies that increasingly weaken the possibility of the rise of a larger fraternity. We have faltered — and now are not so sure we were right in creating institutions such as the English-language common school to Americanize, often in a rather roughshod fashion, the immigrants and the separate racial and ethnic groups.

To live with the two fraternities — the fraternity of the racial and ethnic groups and the fraternity of the larger American society — means to acknowledge, and to accept, differences that are not the result of unfair discrimination but are themselves the result of a concrete group life. Every contemporary society tries to reduce differences and inequalities, and ours should too. But what is problematic is the attempt to treat every difference as the result of discrimination and as a candidate for governmental action to reduce it. In a multiethnic society, such a policy can only encourage one group after another to raise claims to special treatment for its protection.

And that, one fears, would only be the beginning. The demand for special treatment will lead to animus against other groups that already have it, by those who think they should have it and don't. One sees the opportunity for the growth of antagonisms with a potentiality for evil that all such ethnic and group antagonisms possess. And the fact that among the victims might be that old elite that practiced discrimination in the past and that might therefore in some sense "deserve" its fate would scarcely reassure us: as in Lebanon today, the former discriminators and the discriminated against would go down together.

Thus the rising emphasis on group differences which government is called upon to correct might mean the destruction of any hope for the larger fraternity of all Americans, in which people are tied to one another in what they feel to be a common good society, and in which the tie is close enough to allow tolerance for their range of differences.

[1976]

IV

THE INTERNATIONAL

PERSPECTIVE

12

The Universalization of Ethnicity

ARE THERE some large discernible trends in the world — political, social, economic — that are leading in general to an accentuation of ethnic conflicts?

Admittedly, there are problems involved even in the exact determination of whether there is or is not an increase in "ethnic conflicts." Thus, we have the persisting conflict between French- and English-speaking groups in Canada. Is that an "ethnic" conflict, or a "language" conflict, or the struggle of a "suppressed nation" for independence? We have the division between "Indian" and "Spanish" elements in a number of Latin American countries. Are those "ethnic conflicts"? We have the tragic conflict between Protestants and Catholics in Northern Ireland. But isn't that an essentially "religious" conflict? We have the movements for Scottish and Welsh autonomy in Great Britain; Breton and "South French" movements in France; the strain between Northern and Southern Italy. Some observers would define these as "regional" rather than "ethnic" movements. In each case an outlying section of the country has not shared in the prosperity of the center, and this seems to have awakened some long dormant ethnic consciousness. One doesn't know whether the group pressing for autonomy or more central government funds feels deprived because of an ethnic difference, or because of regional discrimination. The group has a choice as to which basis of deprivation it will emphasize.

I will not continue this tour around the world, but if I did we would find a host of conflicts in which race, religion, region, and nationality are involved. Consider the continually recurring conflict between the Kurds of Iraq and the Iraqis (they share the same religion), and between the Muslims and Christians of the Philippines. In both cases an international element enters into the conflict — because there are also Kurds in Iran and Turkey, while the Muslims of the Philippines are linked (by religion as well as by former political connection and culture) with North Borneo which is now part of Malaysia. Indonesia is also involved, at least distantly — because under its previous ruler Indonesia dreamed of a "greater Malay empire" which included Malaysia and the Philippines.

Let me try to clarify these varying bases of group division which seem so diverse and to justify a usage, which may seem to some to be too imperialistic, in which I label them all "ethnic." The term "ethnic" refers — and this usage by now is quite common among sociologists and other social scientists — to a social group that consciously shares some aspects of a common culture and is defined primarily by descent. It is part of a family of terms of similar or related meaning, such as "minority group," "race," and "nation"; and it is not often easy to make sharp distinctions between these terms.

"Race" of course refers to a group that is defined by common descent and has some typical physical characteristics. Where one decides that a "race" ends and an "ethnic group" begins is not easy. Clearly, Swedes are (on the average) physically somewhat different from Frenchmen or Italians; but we normally don't use the word "race" to describe these differences. In European usage, on the other hand, at least until the time of Hitler, "race" was rather unselfconsciously used to describe what we would call "nations" — such as in the phrase "the genius of the French race." *Race* tends to refer to the biological aspect of group difference, *ethnic* to a combination of the cultural aspect plus a putative biological element because of the assumption of common descent. It is possible for a race not to be an ethnic group. In some descriptions, Brazilians of the predominantly Negro race do not appear as an ethnic group because they are not aware particularly of a common culture different from that of other Brazilians. This is also because they do not have a corporate self-identity as a distinct group, even though *individuals* are aware of their physical characteristics and are aware that these physical differences tend to be associated with some common group characteristics (such as poverty). Recent accounts from Brazil seem to suggest that blacks in Brazil may be becoming an ethnic group. This would fit in with one major theme of this chapter: that is, that the ethnic group is tending to become, in many countries, a more significant basis for social organization and for individual identification.

"Race," then, refers to something more grossly physical than ethnic group. "Religion," another significant basis of human organization, seems on the face of it a very different matter from ethnic group. Religions, in common understanding, are based on conversion and individual allegiance. The great trans-national religions — Christianity, Islam, Buddhism — include individuals and groups of every race and ethnic group. In the specific realities of social intercourse, however, religious groups very often act as, and are felt as, ethnic groups. The over-whelming majority of people, after all, are born into a religion, rather than adopt it, just as they are born into an ethnic group. In this respect both are similar. They are both groups by "ascription" rather than "achievement." They are groups in which one's status is immediately given by birth rather than gained by some activities in one's life.

Religions are generally in any given setting specifically associated with a defined ethnic group. Thus, in the Sudan and in Chad, Arabic-speaking groups in the North (which are Muslim) contrast with Negro groups in the South (which are pagan or Christian). In Nigeria, the Northern language group (or tribal, or ethnic, group) of Hausa is Muslim, while the Ibo and Yoruba are Christian. Thus, when a Hausa meets an Ibo, they assume the other's religion is Muslim and Christian, respectively. In the United States, Poles are almost all Catholic, and Swedes are almost all Lutheran — if, that is, they have any religious connection. Aside from the normal close connection between religion and ethnic group, religion in itself is culture-forming, and thus makes ethnic groups.

Thus "religion," except for periods of conversion and expansion, when members of many ethnic groups may be swept up in a religion, is in social context a category that acts very much like what I have called "ethnic group."

Perhaps the most difficult question in setting a boundary to the term ethnic group is that of its relationship to *caste*: groups defined by birth and by origin from some distant ancestors, intermarrying, traditionally fixed in a hierarchy from upper to lower, and limited to specific occupations. "Caste" is identified primarily with India, but there are other examples, such as the Eta or Burakumin of Japan.[1] The Jews in medieval and in early modern Europe were treated as a caste—they had a fixed low hierarchical position, intermarried, were limited to certain occupations, and had about them (to Christians) an air of ritual impurity.

Castes (theoretically) are permanent. One cannot "convert" to another caste, as presumably Jews could convert to Christianity, and thus lose the disadvantages of being Jewish. But it should be recalled that even converted Jews were viewed with suspicion in Spain, and they were never considered really as good Christians as the others.

This fairly lengthy introduction is, I feel, necessary in view of widespread confusions, and in view of the fact that I will be referring on occasion to religious groups, racial groups, tribal groups, language groups, and be calling them all ethnic groups. Let me try to justify this very inclusive term by answering the obvious question: What is *not* an ethnic group? Do I set any boundaries to the term? Yes, I do. After all, distant as our studies as sociologists are from the most respectable sciences, our terms must have some clear definition, and one means of making a clear definition is to set a boundary.

There are two important social forms that are *not* ethnic groups. One of them is the political community; the state and its members.

Americans very often call a state a "nation," but in most European languages the nation refers very specifically to the ethnic group, the state to the formal political organization that grants citizenship. The close link between nation and state arose because in the course of European history, and in particular in the nineteenth century, with the rise of nationalism, every nation demanded its own state. This led to the creation of modern Germany and Italy, the formation of ethnic European states out of the Ottoman Empire, the breakup of the Austro-Hungarian Empire into its ethnic components, each organized as a state, and the creation of ethnic nation-states out of the western borders of the old Czarist empire. The United States is perhaps unique among the states of the world in using the term "nation" to refer not to an ethnic group but to all who choose to become Americans. "The American nation," a perfectly legitimate term, is not limited in its usage to those of a given heritage. Despite this, Woodrow Wilson (with his emphasis on national self-determination) insisted that every *other* ethnic group, under no matter what political organization, should have its own state. The vital contrast between nation and state was obscured in large measure between the two world wars when so many of the independent states of the world were organized on the basis of a single dominant ethnic group. Those who remained as ethnic minorities within such states hoped for eventual reunion with the nation-state that represented their own ethnic group.

In the post-1945 world, the close link between state and nation, which had dominated the state-making efforts of the post-1918 peacemaking (and of the politics of Europe between the two world wars) was again broken. For most of the new states that were formed out of the colonial empires were *not* "nation states," that is, states representing a single ethnicity. And yet the world, in revulsion to war and conquest, had become strangely enough strongly attached to "old boundaries"—any boundaries, set any way. The scores of new states formed out of the colonial empires simply accepted the old accidental colonial boundaries. These new states then were faced with the problem of—as they and others saw it—becoming "nations," molding people of different ethnic groups into "Nigerians," or "Kenyans," or some other people.

The problems of the newly independent states of Asia were somewhat different. There were ancient cultural traditions or imperial state boundaries which did not make frontiers quite as arbitrary as they were in Africa. But even there — in Pakistan, India, Burma, Indonesia, Malaysia — the problem of creating a single nation became a severe one, varying in intensity from country to country. The problem in each case was: Would older identities — religious, linguistic, racial, and caste — submerge themselves in a new national identity? Or would they become (to use our problematic term again) *ethnic* identities, with some possible claim to their own kind of state existence? Would they soon be demanding political recognition of their separateness, with perhaps an ultimate claim to the right of secession?

One social form, then, that is not an ethnic group is the state. This is so despite the fact that in European thinking (and, to some extent, in Asian) it is generally taken for granted that the ideal form of the state is one in which there is a state for each ethnic group, and one ethnic group for each state. In the circumstances of Africa, this is almost impossible — the conflict in creating any such format would be unbearable, and it has accordingly rarely been attempted.

There is certainly a tension between ethnic groups and states. As each state tries to become a nation, it attempts to reduce the intensity of subordinate ethnic claims. The problem is that both ethnic groups and states make claims to *ultimate loyalty*. And the state inevitably comes into conflict with any social form that has a competing claim to ultimate loyalty. At one time this competing claim was most strongly put forward by religion. With the decline of religion this competing claim is most strongly put forward by *ethnicity*.

Rupert Emerson has defined the Nation as a "terminal community — the largest community that, when the chips are down, effectively commands men's loyalty, overriding the claims of both the lesser communities within it and those that cut across it within a still greater society."[2]

A sound definition, from a European perspective, neatly separating French loyalty from the lesser loyalty of being Gascon or Burgundian, or the larger loyalty of being European or Christian. But when applied to Nigeria or to Malaysia it simply leaves us uncertain as to what the nation is. As Clifford

Geertz writes: "[It seems] to leave such questions as whether India, Indonesia, or Nigeria are nations to the determination of some future, unspecified historical crisis."[3]

States, then, are not ethnic groups, though the linking term "nation" can be taken as one or the other. Nations are not necessarily ethnic groups, though those that are not coterminous with an ethnic group try to create a new national identity, which (if they succeed) becomes a new ethnicity.

There is one other crucial boundary limiting ethnic groups. Social classes are not ethnic groups. One is not born an unskilled worker, a clerk, a professional. One is born into a family whose head may hold such an occupation. Some social theories insist that this means, in effect, that one's future occupation and income are fixed by birth. But if this were really so, we would not be so interested in "social mobility." Social mobility refers specifically to movements between the strata of society, from one occupation, income level, education standard, to another. Social mobility is one term that cannot be used to refer to the change of one ethnic group into another. Other terms are necessary. Just as "social mobility" applies specifically to the *class* phenomena of society, so do "assimilation," "acculturation," "conversion" apply to the *ethnic* phenomena. These are rather more exceptional processes than those of social mobility. They are not accepted—or expected—processes. It is true that peoples assimilate to other peoples, and do change their ethnic identity over time. But it is more or less expected that the ethnic stock remains immutable.

Thus "ethnic group," in my usage, refers basically to the vertical divisions of a society in contrast to the horizontal divisions. The horizontal divisions refer to *class*; the vertical divisions to *ethnicity*. Sometimes they coincide, as in the case of the Negroes in the American South, all of whom were by definition for a long time in the lowest class (or, in view of their inability to rise, caste). And yet the distinction was plain. As the blacks rose, socially, to become doctors, professional persons, and white-collar workers, their *class* changed. But their *ethnic group* remained the same. Even in India, the classic land of caste, one observes a similar phenomenon. The correlation between caste and class becomes somewhat weaker over time. The caste groups do become, in my definition, "ethnic groups." Perhaps the best indication of this is that they are increasingly called "communities" as the social position of their members becomes more diverse.

It is along the boundaries between ethnic group and state (on the one hand) and between ethnic group and social class (on the other hand) that we have witnessed in the past two decades· some striking new developments. These developments have made *ethnicity* a new and problematic force in internal and international relations. Let me state a proposition in connection with each boundary.

The first proposition is on the relations between states and ethnic groups. The old hope of nationalism, accepted in the peacemaking after World War I (and to some extent after World War II) — for each nation a state, for each state a nation — has receded into the distance. It becomes more and more difficult to grasp it effectively as a basis for international organization. A number of developments have led to the recession of this model.

1. Too many new states have been created that are not, and cannot in the foreseeable future become, states of a given ethnic group. I refer primarily to the new states of Africa, and to some extent to those of Asia. In these cases, we have seen the rise of a new concern with "nation-building." We have also seen the hopes for nation-building complicated or foundering on the basis of old lines of division — racial, religious, linguistic, tribal. Each division has taken the common form of ethnic group.

2. We have been surprised by the rise of new ethnic or quasi-ethnic identities and the sharpening of old ethnic identities in those states which were considered either models of contemporary modern nation states, or successes in having subordinated their ethnic divisions to the "terminal loyalty" of the nation. Consider for example that model of patriotic commitment in World War I — Belgium. Look at it today: increasingly divided between groups that place their terminal loyalty more and more in the ethnic group of Fleming or Walloon. Consider Canada in World Wars I and II, with its apparently total com-

mitment to war for the sake of the ethnic Motherland. See how delicately it now tries to reconcile the claims of its French-speaking and English-speaking citizens. Consider the remarkable, if still far from signal, success of Scottish nationalism on the island of Great Britain, whose ethnic divisions seemed a few decades ago fully reconciled in the new identity of being "British." The United States was never a nation state, but certainly we have not seen as sharp a challenge since the Civil War to the "terminal loyalty" of Americans as we saw in the rise of the militant black power movement (with its search for an alternative loyalty, marked even by such national symbols as a separate flag) or in the rise of new Mexican American and American Indian militant movements. Those states which are effectively single ethnic groups avoid such divisions. But few are so fortunate as, say, Sweden, or postwar Poland, made "pure" by massive population transfers. As old divisions in some states sharpen, other states worry whether their old seams will rip open.

3. Many even of those older states that were ethnically homogeneous have become ethnically more heterogeneous as the economic developments of the postwar world have led to enormous migrations of labor. In West Germany, by the mid-1970s there were 2.4 million "guest workers," principally from Turkey, Yugoslavia, Italy, and Greece, forming 12 percent of the labor force, and in some areas considerably more. Germany cannot do without them; and more and more the guest workers settle down with their wives and children. Switzerland has, proportionately, even more. France has taken its foreign workers in large measure from Algeria, Spain, and Portugal. England has seen a substantial migration from the West Indies, Pakistan, and India, creating a permanent "coloured" population. In each of these countries the specific numbers and legal statuses vary; but in each of them a once remarkably high degree of ethnic homogeneity has been reduced by the introduction of new ethnic elements. The United States, from being an exception in the world because of its formation as a state out of many different elements, becomes more and more typical — as England struggles with its own color problem, France wonders

about the "integration" of the Algerians, and Germany considers how to educate the children of Turks and Yugoslavs.

4. The efforts of states, new or old, to achieve "ethnic purity" are *not* leading to ethnically homogeneous states. Burma expels its Indians; Uganda evicts its Asian community, and other African states may do the same to theirs; Poland ejects even the pitiful remnants of its once large Jewish community; and the Jews of other Eastern European states have migrated in large numbers to Israel. But ironically, the attempts of some nations to become "ethnically pure" only complicate the problems of others. Britain's Asian community grows; and new Asian communities are established in other European nations, as a result of the expulsion of Asians from Africa. The Jews leaving Eastern Europe enter an ethnically mixed Israel, which is not — and never will be — without a large Arab population. There is still much debate over the origins of the Palestinian refugee problem and the causes that led Arabs to flee the emerging Jewish state. Whatever the reasons, undoubtedly many Jews believed that their problems in creating a new state would be simpler if they did *not* have a large Arab minority. But the creation of Israel as a 90 percent Jewish state also created a Palestinian diaspora. The Jews are now matched in their dispersion by resident Palestinian groups in many countries, one of the developments that makes the struggle between two peoples in the Middle East a world-wide one.

Aside from the fact that each nation's ethnic purification leads to another's greater diversity, one senses that the effort at purity, for most states, is a lost cause. The divisions in Uganda between blacks of different tribes are potentially far more severe for that state than the division between all blacks and Asians. Few black African nations are ethnically homogeneous. The attempt to create some degree of homogeneity by the expulsion of Asians seems as futile as an effort to empty the sea.

Resident aliens have been expelled from a number of African states. In November 1969, the Ghanaian government gave all resident aliens, African and non-African, two weeks to obtain residence and work permits or leave the country. The police were given broad powers to search out and arrest aliens lacking the required papers, and bands of citizens attacked alien traders in public markets. Although a few aliens died in the Ghanaian expulsion, conditions for Nigerian traders expelled from Congo-Zaire were even worse. Those who were released after a year in detention reported numerous incidents of torture and death plus confiscation of all assets. Public pressure in the Ivory Coast led to expulsion of Togolese and Dahomeyans employed in the Ivory Coast civil service since colonial days.[4]

I have said enough, I hope, to give some plausibility to my first proposition. In the world as it is developing, despite tendencies to make some states "ethnically pure" (particularly in the newer states of Africa and Asia), more and more states become *multiethnic*. This is, in part, because of the universal commitment against boundary changes to make ethnic group coincide with state. (How many interstate boundaries have, after all, been changed since the end of World War II? Fewer I would guess than in any period in history.) It is also because of the extensive international migration of labor (a migration that is almost the equal in scale to that which transformed the United States), and because old ethnic divisions emerge in old states and new ones are created in new and old states.

And now to my second proposition on the relations between ethnicity and social class. This, too, has developed in unexpected ways. My proposition here is that the socialist hope for a transnational class struggle, based on class identification, never came to pass. Instead, it has been replaced by national and ethnic conflicts to which combatants have often tried to give a class character. The first great defeat of the socialist hope was in World War I, when the large Socialist parties of Germany and France became patriotic, and fought on the side of their respective bourgeois governments against their national enemies (instead of, as Socialists hoped, together with their "class comrades" of other nations against their respective bourgeoisies). The second great defeat came with the rise of the Third International under Soviet Russian domination. Despite the heightened rhetoric of class warfare that characterized the Third International's Communist parties, it became increasingly evident that they were serving the national interests of Russia. After World War II, Communism was more and more closely integrated into a number of national movements. Chinese, Yugoslav, and Cuban Communism were clearly as Chinese and Yugoslav and Cuban as they were Communist. The language of international class warfare still persists. The reality however is quite different, for it masks the state interests of Russia, China, and the minor Communist powers. The antagonism of the classes and the opposition of their interests are severe in many countries (particularly the non-Communist countries of the developing world), but in most countries national interests and ethnic interests seem to dominate over class interests. India, despite its severe internal class conflicts of interest, is never so united as when it is fighting China — or Pakistan. We have witnessed some classic class warfare in recent decades, in particular in China and Cuba and in some other developing-world countries. But we have rather more frequently seen severe ethnic conflict and even bloody ethnic warfare.

Marxists try to interpret all conflict as class conflict. Indeed in the ethnic conflicts of the postwar world there is always a class component. One group is more prosperous, owns more of the means of production, or is a more effective competitor in economic activities, than another. Economic interest undoubtedly plays a role in ethnic conflict. But this is far from saying ethnic conflict is simply masked class conflict. What, in the conflicts of Catholic and Protestant in Northern Ireland, of Hausa and Yoruba versus Ibo in Nigeria, Hutu versus Tutsi in Rwanda, Chinese versus Malay in Malaysia, Anglophone versus Francophone in Canada, and so on, is the "terminal community . . . that . . . effectively commands men's loyalty"? I would say it is increasingly the *ethnically* defined community rather than any exclusively *interest*-defined group. The evidence for this is too strong to be dismissed.

In the light of these two propositions — that ethnicity becomes less and less coincident with state boundaries, and that ethnicity becomes a stronger basis for "terminal loyalty" than class — we can proceed to draw some consequences of importance for international relations.

Let me first recall—and put to one side—the more traditional and better-known relations between ethnicity and international relations. These relations can be described as the effort to make ethnicity coincide with state borders. It has taken the form of *irredentism*—where one group, subjects of a state dominated by a different group, tries to rejoin the major part of the ethnic group in another state. Its other form is national independence movements, where an entire group is subject to a state dominated by another.

Obviously such situations are real problems and still occur. But they, I would suggest, are perhaps steadily less important in the relations between ethnicity and international conflict—because of the previously mentioned fact that state borders have become oddly immutable. After World War II, many states became independent; some states had revolutions; some partition lines between states established after the war became international boundaries; and some states were partitioned. But even the newly partitioned states (Viet Nam, Korea, Israel), in which new boundaries had to be established, have found it difficult to get those boundaries to take on the same immutability as the boundaries created by post-1918 and post-1945 settlements. Multiethnicity used to appear as irredentism. We can still find some classic irredentism—for example, the case of the Somalis in Ethiopia. But, increasingly, what we would once have called irredentism must be called simply multiethnicity. There is no easy way to make ethnic boundaries and state boundaries coincide. Ethnic groups, owing to migrations and economic interrelationships, are less and less definable by physical boundaries.

It is these new tendencies toward *multiethnicity* (combined with other social developments) that, in my view, create new problematical relations between ethnicity and the interstate system.

One of the most important of these developments is the creation of an international system of communications. It makes the spread of ideas and ideologies from one state to another, from one troubled situation to another, ever more rapid and effective. Ethnicity, as a part of culture, always had to be taught. But it used to be taught by parents to children, by teachers to students, by leaders to followers — in other words, in traditional settings. More and more, ethnicity and its possible implications are taught by the mass media. One group learns from another, and picks up its language, its demands, its resentments, its forms of organization. It has become commonplace to say that the blacks have taught through their example other ethnic groups in the United States to raise certain demands, to use a certain language, to feel resentment at exploitation and subordination in contexts they had previously accepted. This is obviously true. What is striking to me is how much the movement of black militancy in the United States has affected other groups in *other* countries.

In the West Indies, we have seen the emergence of "black power" movements — a rather unlikely term, since these movements are directed against black ruling classes as well as white economic interests in largely black societies (but the power of the American term, spread by the mass media, was evidently irresistable). In Canada, the French Canadians had their own reasons for resentment at the dominant position of the English-speaking Canadians; but one of the best-known books about their situation called them "white niggers." Similarly, Northern Ireland has its own deep conflict, and it has an even longer history than that of blacks and whites in America. But the Catholic movement was first called the "civil rights" movement, in clear imitation of the black "civil rights" struggle in the United States, even if it is arguable how much it owed to the inspiration of this struggle. The "Oriental" Jews in Israel (of lesser education, income, and power than the "Western" Jews) had their own grievances. But actions that led to world-wide attention were initiated by "Black Panthers," again the borrowing of a term from the American struggle. And, similarly, the developing color conflict in England has been influenced, on the part of the colored groups, by developments in the United States, and on the part of government, by the actions taken in the United States.[5]

These examples of the international communication of ideas, slogans, demands, with one ethnic group and one ethnic struggle influencing another, also reflect of course the dominant position of the United States in the international configuration of communications. But the communication is not, I believe, all one way. One example of an ethnic struggle that has had some effect on other intergroup relations is the Israeli-Arab struggle. As I have pointed out, both groups have international diasporas. The image of the Palestinian Freedom Fighter became for a while almost as heavily imprinted on world public opinion as the images of a Martin Luther King or an Angela Davis. The two diasporas internationalize the struggle. The Palestinians find their targets in many countries.

But the internationalization also means that it is copied, and that it influences other ethnic conflicts. The black militants in the United States and the Croatian nationalists in Sweden both borrowed the technique of "skyjacking" from the Palestinians. The Israeli-Arab struggle leads to a tension between radical groups and Jews in the United States, in France, in Germany, because the Far Left identifies with the Palestinians. The Jews of Poland, completely assimilated, are accused of Zionism in the wake of the 1967 war (and in their emigration add to the small Jewish community of Denmark). In Africa, black states were once divided between support of Israel and of the Arabs. They were variously affected by the historical memories left by Arab conquerors, missionaries, and slave traders; by white European colonialists; by their current ideologies; and by the cash or credits one or the other party could give them. There were reverberations of the faraway struggle in the local internal politics of African countries. President Amin of Uganda accused the Israelis of trying to overthrow him, while Uganda's former president, Milton Obote, accused Amin of using Palestinian liberation forces in carrying out genocide against his opponents.[6]

The new patterns of communication are, I believe, one of the most potent forces in insuring that ethnic concerns and ethnic issues will remain serious forces and will indeed grow in seriousness. The increasing ease of air travel — combined with the existence of wide economic disparities between nations and the comparatively liberal attitude toward immigration of European states and other states with populations of European origin

—guarantees that every ethnic group can develop a diaspora. It thus makes the problems of each ethnic group a matter of significance to more than one state and its neighbors. The ease of air travel also means that ethnic struggles can be fought out on a world-wide stage, involving nations that are on the surface completely removed from the struggle. The Israeli-Arab struggle has, perhaps, had the widest geographical scope. Letter-bombs explode in England, India, and Malaysia; Cypriots, Greeks, Turks, Israeli diplomats are seized in Thailand; Israeli athletes are killed in Munich; Arabs are shot in the streets of Paris and Rome. The Indian-Pakistani struggle also has its international scope, as young Pakistanis are killed in the attempted seizure of Indian offices in London. Croatians, now settled in Sweden and Australia, carry on their warfare against Yugoslavia. This led to a protest from the Australian Prime Minister to Yugoslavia because "Croatians of Australian· citizenship" were executed in Yugoslavia. And within Australia, the conservative opposition protested against government investigations of the Croatian nationalists.[7]

Thus a number of factors, it seems to me, are leading to the internationalization of ethnic conflicts, to a "universalization of ethnicity."

1. There is, first, the increasing difficulty, if not impossibility, of making ethnicity and state coincide. The United States, as a nation formed of many peoples without territorial concentration in any part of the country, first demonstrated this impossibility. It had to become a multiethnic society. Now England, France, Germany, the nations of old Europe, the developing nations of new Africa, the ancient nations of Asia are all forced more and more to come to terms with ethnically mixed populations, whose mixture (as long as the world remains open or free to travel and settlement) must grow.

2. A second element in the growing internationalization of ethnicity is the rapid growth of international communications. This has made the creation of ethnic diasporas easier. It has created multiethnic societies in homogeneous ones. It has also meant that the images of identity and struggle are now spread

everywhere, with significant effects in heightening ethnic consciousness and strengthening it in its conflict with other claims on terminal loyalty.

3. About a third factor leading to the internationalization of ethnic conflict I am less certain. But I think I can at least propose as a hypothesis that we are, increasingly, refusing to accept as moral — and by "we" I mean what may be vaguely called an international community of public opinion — the exploitation or persecution of an ethnic minority by a state. We increasingly refuse to accept this as an "internal" matter. The international relations of South Africa, Rhodesia, and Portugal were decisively affected by their racial policies. Soviet Russia has been insistent that all conflicts affecting its ethnic groups are purely internal matters — but the Russian Jews have successfully challenged this position by making their demands for emigration a matter between states (in this case, the United States and Russia). The treatment of American Negroes certainly affects America's international image — the cases of Angela Davis and other black militants received (if possible) more attention in Western Europe than in the United States. The developing world has tried to argue that its ethnic conflicts should be left to themselves, and that the outside world should not intervene. But it was impossible to keep the situation of Bengalis in Pakistan an "internal" matter (even though many people argued that for the "peace of the world" it should be so considered). No ethnic issue can remain simply an intrastate issue, in part because of the growing number of diasporas, but also perhaps because of the developing world conscience which tries to reconcile state claims with ethnic claims that are felt to be legitimate. Nigeria was, perhaps, most successful in "internalizing" the civil war against the Ibos; and the outside world stood aside, too, from the sanguinary conflict between Hutu and Tutsi in Rwanda. But even in that distant and obscure struggle we have seen the United States criticized (*New York Times*, June 11, 1973, "U.S. Held Remiss in Burundi crisis") for not playing a larger role. Thus it is not only international diasporas but also a globalized conscience which serve to universalize ethnic conflict.

What I have discussed up to now — migrations, international communications, world conscience — all leave aside the initial question: Why have ethnic identities and demands become so significant in the first place in so many different countries, with such varied historical backgrounds and economic and political institutions? Can we find any *general* developments that have accentuated the role of the ethnic, and in general made it more salient?

This is an enormously difficult problem, and various theories or fragments of theories have been propounded. Perhaps the most ambitious general theory argues as follows. In the modern world there is a loss of traditional and primordial identities because of the trends of modernization. This means: urbanization, new occupations, mass education transmitting general and abstract information, mass media presenting a general and universal culture. Now all this *should* make original ethnic identities — tribal, linguistic, regional, and the like, all the "primordial" identities — weaker. However (as this argument runs) in mass society there is the need in the individual for some kind of identity — smaller than the state, larger than the family, something akin to a "familistic allegiance." Accordingly, on the basis of the remaining fragments of the primordial identities, new ethnic identities are constructed. Thus, the varied tribal groups in the cities of Africa form ethnic associations and merge into larger groups — which seems to be the origin of the large tribes (for example, Hausa, Ibo, Yoruba). The process is similar to that which affected the transatlantic European migrants from East European and Southern European villages — in the United States they developed a special Polish, Italian, Slovak identity. The trends of modernization, even while they do destroy some bases of distinctive culture and distinctive identity, create a need for a *new kind of identity* related to the old, intimate type of village or tribal association. Thus does the new ethnic group, as a political and social possibility, come to life.

This is one of those large social theories which seem impossible to test, to validate, or to refute. It makes sense. The worldwide scope of "ethnicization" is matched by developments that are considered causative and are themselves of a world-wide scope.

One other general theory might be mentioned. Egalitarianism is the dominant social philosophy in the world, and it comes in all forms. Egalitarianism legitimates a group's demands that its deficiencies (in income, occupation, political power) be made good, and *now*. It justifies the expulsion and liquidation of trading and merchant peoples (such as Asians in Uganda). Why, however, does not the egalitarian thrust emphasize *occupational* and *class* identities more? Why does it not lead to more class conflict, and less ethnic conflict?

This is the heart of the darkness. Why *didn't* the major lines of conflict within societies become class conflicts rather than ethnic conflicts? It is of paradoxical interest to note that in the developing world the dominant ideology among students is Marxism. Yet the dominant political forces have been, first the drive for independence, then the defense against and attack on neocolonialism, then conflicts with neighbors, along with efforts to create a "national identity" at home. In most developing countries Marxism remains the ideology of the students and often of the ruling group—but ethnicity is the focus around which identity and loyalty have been shaped. Sometimes the two themes of class conflict and ethnic conflict are merged (as in the Chinese theory of the Third World as a rural world exploited by the urban developed world). It would seem that if class conflict is to be made at all effective it must now be joined to ethnic conflict—as in the case of the revolutionary Cubans who, in liquidating their own middle class, insisted they were also fighting the North Americans (imperialistic, racist, and arrogant).

Admittedly the powerful thrust to egalitarianism *can* be attached to class conflict as well as ethnic conflict. Ethnic conflict, however, seems to have become more effective than class conflict in reaching and drawing upon the more emotional layers of the human and social personality. Class conflict is rational—it is based on the defense and expansion of interest. Ethnic conflict is rational in this sense, too—but it fuses with the rationality of class conflict a less rational, an irrational appeal, that seems to connect better with powerful emotions.

Is this because it brings to mind such primal things as the shape of one's body, one's image and color, one's language and religion, the earliest experiences in the home and in the family?

It would seem that the rallying cries that mobilize the classes have, in recent decades, had less power than the rallying cries that mobilize the races, tribes, religions, language-users — in short, the ethnic groups. Perhaps the epidemic of ethnic conflicts reflects the fact that leaders and organizers believe they can get a more potent response by appealing to ethnicity than they can by appealing to class interest. In the best of cases, the appeal is a double one, since almost every ethnic group is disadvantaged in relationship to some other; and so, if class interest and ethnic interest are appealed to together, the white European (and his descendants wherever they may be) can everywhere be marked as the enemy.

If ethnicity is a permanent part of the modern world, and if the multiethnic form is increasingly common within each nation (owing to the factors I have been describing), then each country needs new approaches to the handling of multiethnic conflict. In the historic past, powerful and forceful assimilation was a dominant approach, combined with permanent subordination of certain groups considered inferior. Neither approach will survive long in the contemporary world. The spirit of egalitarianism assures us that each individual and each group will make its claims to just and equal treatment and will find strong support for its claims. Perhaps the answer to multiethnicity in each country will be a situation in which each group has guaranteed rights and guaranteed shares in the economy, the polity, in social life. It is possible to emphasize different parts of this solution: either guaranteed shares for each group, or guaranteed rights for each individual and each group. The United States in the past seemed to find the approach in terms of guaranteed rights more congenial than the approach in terms of guaranteed shares; but recently Americans have begun to take individual rights less seriously, and to take group shares more seriously. I think the American experience will prove to be only one of the possible ways in which a modern state deals with the problems of multiethnicity. Our experience — since we are the most diverse and complex of multiethnic societies — may serve as a model for some, may at least serve as a storehouse of trial-and-error experience for others who come to view what we have done and consider whether they should go and do likewise.

Yet aside from conflicts *within* nations, the world-wide spread of ethnicity as a significant basis for political action raises serious questions about the relations *among* nations. In a world in which Marxism competed with liberalism, the problems of ethnicity, as a source of conflict within nations and among nations, have generally appeared as simply a leftover, an embarrassment from the past. It is my conviction that they must now be placed at the very center of our concern for the human condition.

[1975]

13

Individual Rights against

Group Rights

The United States today is in the midst of a great national debate which must have bearing, in time, for any nation that is composed of many ethnic and racial strands — and that means the great majority of the nations of the world. The debate, which takes place in the executive, legislative, and judicial branches of government, in the scholarly periodicals and the mass media, among unions and employers, in schools and universities, centers on the meaning of justice for minorities that have previously been treated unjustly. What it has done for us is to underline how simple were our understandings of the problems of racial and group discrimination in 1964, when one of the major pieces of legislation in American history, the Civil Rights Act of 1964, was passed.

In 1964, in the United States, ending discrimination seemed a simple matter. Presumably one could recognize a discriminatory act — not hiring blacks, or not promoting them, not paying them more than X dollars, or not allowing them into this college or hospital. And one could devise penalties to punish such acts. Many cases are brought every day under the Civil Rights Act of 1964 and other pieces of legislation, federal and state, that ban discrimination, and many people who have been discriminated against find relief under these acts. The penalties are sufficiently severe — in particular, the granting of back pay for a period of years to individuals who have been discriminated against in employment — to make employers careful to avoid discrimination. The effects of the act, it has been argued, were evident in a marked improvement in the numbers of blacks employed in better jobs after 1964.

Individuals take these actions to complain against discrimination, in order to vindicate rights that have been denied because of a group characteristic. Can we, however, solve the problems of group discrimination by using the language, and the law, of individual rights?

In that question is encapsulated the dilemma of justice for discriminated-against minorities. The individual has received discriminatory treatment because of a group characteristic. The law is written so as to vindicate the rights of individuals. But can the rights of individuals be vindicated, can the effects of past discrimination on the groups be overcome, if only that individual who takes action on the basis of discrimination receives satisfaction and compensation as the result of his individual charge of discrimination? Does not every other individual who is a member of the group also require satisfaction and compensation? But if the whole concept of legal rights has been developed in individual terms, how do we provide justice for the group? And if we provide justice for the group — let us say, a quota which determines that so many jobs must go to members of the group — then do we not, by that token, deprive individuals of other groups, not included among the discriminated-against groups, of the right to be treated and considered as individuals, independently of any group characteristic?

These are the issues that have arisen in the United States. I would like to break them down into a number of questions:

1. Why are our laws written as if the problem of discrimination is one affecting individuals; why do we in effect assert that justice in the face of discrimination is justice for the individual, rather than a new and equal status for the group?

2. Can laws and practices written as if the grievance is borne by individuals overcome the effects of group discrimination and provide satisfaction to groups?

3. If, alternatively, we provide compensation to individuals

on the basis of minority-group membership, have we deprived individuals of majority groups of rights?

4. Is there any general principle that can guide us as to when we should try to overcome discrimination by concentrating on the rights of individuals, and when we should try to overcome it by concentrating on the rights of groups?

Let me explain the perspective from which I will approach these questions. I am a sociologist, not a political philosopher or a lawyer. As a political philosopher or a lawyer, I would try to find basic principles of justice that can be defended and argued against all other principles. As a sociologist, I look àt the concrete consequences, for concrete societies, of different policies. And here one major principle guides me. It is whether those practices lead to a general acceptance of the policies meant to overcome discrimination as good and decent policies, and lead to the widest measure of acceptance, among minorities as well as majorities. That may be denounced as a purely pragmatic or "functionalist" principle, which leaves aside the great objectives of equality and justice. But these objectives are incorporated in that principle, too, because people today will not accept arrangements that maintain great inequalities and that offend strongly their sense of justice. These are key realities to be taken into account in using the pragmatic principle I have proposed: what policies to overcome discrimination give us the opportunity to best satisfy all the groups of a multiethnic society so they can live in some reasonable degree of harmony?

It is an interesting problem to ponder why it is that the deprivation of individual rights on the basis of some group characteristic — race, religion, national origin — is nevertheless treated in law, at least in American law, as a problem of protecting the rights of an individual. The Fifth Amendment to the constitution, which limits the federal government and provides the language used in the Fourteenth Amendment, the foundation of constitutional protection for blacks and other minorities, reads: "No *person* shall . . . be deprived of life, liberty, or property, without due process of law" (my italics). And the Fourteenth Amendment, adopted to protect the rights of the newly freed slaves, reads:

No State shall make or enforce any law which shall abridge the privileges or immunities of *citizens* of the United States; nor shall any State deprive any *person* of life, liberty, or property, without due process of law; nor deny to any person within its jurisdiction the equal protection of the laws" (my italics). Citizens, persons—this is the language designed to defend a group, blacks, and which by extension of activist Supreme Courts defends the rights of Chinese, Japanese, Indians, Mexican Americans, Puerto Ricans, aliens, women, and many other groups defined in various ways. The same kind of language is to be found in the Civil Rights Act of 1964 and the Voting Rights Act of 1965; they refer to no single group. The legislation, just like the constitution, attempts to be colorblind in a society where color and national origin are key realities determining in some measure the fate of the individuals of any group.

It is not only the constitutional and legal language that attempts to overcome the problems of group prejudice by guaranteeing the rights of individuals; the most important American philosophical contribution to the problem of justice in recent times, John Rawls's *A Theory of Justice*, also ignores the problem of justice for groups, as Vernon Van Dyke points out in perceptive essay:

[Rawls] stipulates that those in the original situation "should care about the well-being of some of those in the next generation" . . . but he does not make a comparable stipulation about racial, linguistic, religious or national groups that are weak or disadvantaged or that cherish or want to preserve their distinctive characteristics and identity . . . I do not see in the book a single reference to differences of language. Race is mentioned mainly to be ruled out as a ground of discrimination. Religion is mentioned at a number of points, but almost always with the individual believer in mind rather than the collective body of the faithful.[1]

It is an intriguing problem, and undoubtedly the answer is that the language and theory of the protection of human rights developed in a time and place (England in the seventeenth century) when the issue was seen as one of deprivation because of conscience, because of individual decision and action, rather than one of deprivation because of race, color, or national origin. England was relatively homogeneous, *except* for religion and political attitudes which largely flowed from religious conviction. These were seen as individual decisions, and protecting diversity was seen as an issue of protecting the diversity that flowed from individual decisions.

But what of that diversity that flows from the accidents of birth into a preexisting community — defined by race, national origin, or religion? As Van Dyke reminds us by pointing out that Rawls in speaking of religion has "the individual believer in mind, rather than the collective body of the faithful," religion involves not only individual choice, but in the great majority of cases faith determined by birth, just as much as color or mother tongue is determined by birth. This makes it very different from an act of individual conscience, as one can well see when one considers the meaning of Catholicism and Protestantism in Northern Ireland, of Islam and non-Islam in Malaysia. It would be play-acting in these countries to try to solve the serious problems of group conflict by legislating the freedom of the practice of religion, for that is not the issue. The issue in these countries, and in other countries where religious conflicts take on what I would call an ethnic character — that is, conflicts of groups of contrasting cultures defined by birth — is the relative economic and social positions of the two religious communities, not the free practice of religion.

Is there an alternative legal and constitutional language to protect individuals who are penalized because of a group affiliation? Of course there is. It is the language that specifically guarantees the rights of groups, by name, that specifically reserves for groups a certain proportion of posts in government, in the civil services, in the universities, in business. This kind of approach to group rights is clearly just as compatible with a regime committed to human rights as the approach that focuses only on the individual. In one measure or another, we see this kind of approach in Canada, Belgium, India, Malaysia. Yet in the United States the attempt to reserve places, by number, in key areas of political life and economy is strongly resisted as a subversion of individual rights. And indeed, the revolutionary effort in the middle 1960s to establish a firm legislative basis for overcoming discrimination against blacks and other minorities expressly used language that protected the individual, carefully avoided specifying in any legislation what groups were to be protected, and specifically banned any approach that emphasized reserving places for different groups. This was the clear intention of Congress, and the American people, majority and minority, when the Civil Rights Act of 1964 was passed. To protect against the possibility that the act might make possible a group remedy—let us say, quotas for employment for some groups that had been discriminated against—this was specifically forbidden in the act. Perhaps that demonstrated the general naiveté that prevailed as to what would be necessary to raise a whole group that had faced discrimination over a long period of time. I have already pointed out that in other nations a different approach has been taken to the problem of raising a group—an approach that has straightforwardly adopted numerical quotas to ensure that appropriate numbers of the group received the benefits of education or employment. And so we have "reservations" for scheduled castes and tribes in India, and special programs to increase the number of Malays in higher education and business employment in Malaysia.

As against this group-based approach, the American approach, both in legislation and in the important Supreme Court decisions that preceded and succeeded it, used the language of individual rights. It was in each case an individual that brought suit—*Brown* v. *The Board of Education*, *Griggs* v. *Duke Power*. One must neither overestimate nor underestimate the significance of the language and law that emphasize the vindication of an individual's rights. One must not overestimate it: it was organizations representing group interests that were sought out by individual plaintiffs, or that alternatively sought them out. It was the resources of groups that were required to argue cases up to the Supreme Court. It was the position of the entire group that one hoped to raise by individual test cases. If Brown could not be segregated on the basis of race, neither could White or Wilkins or any other black. If Griggs could not be denied a job because the test he took for employment did not properly test his aptitude or capacities for the job in question, neither could any other black be denied employment on that basis.

But we should not underestimate, either, the significance of the individual aspect of these rights. Each case goes into the individual's account of discrimination, the damage to the individual. And even if the justices know well that by acting against an individual complaint of discrimination they are raising the status and enhancing the rights of an entire group, it was expected — certainly in 1964 — that these rights would become effective because *individuals* would claim them, and because they would now be treated as individuals, without distinctions of color or national origin.

Could such an approach to overcoming group discrimination — the approach that assumed that individuals would act to vindicate their rights, and that actions of individuals would overcome the deprived status of groups — really be effective? One of the main charges against the enforcement provisions of the Civil Rights Act of 1964, as written and intended by Congress, is that it is unreasonable to expect that a group would overcome a heritage of generations of discrimination by the actions of *individuals* to acquire, on their own initiative, education, jobs, political representation. It was for this reason that the agencies involved began to take actions that aroused a good deal of dissent in Congress.

To begin with, they began to require that large employers take censuses of their employees on the basis of race and ethnic group, in order to make a preliminary assessment of whether certain groups were absent or underrepresented in certain levels of employment. Note that the first step in requiring these reports was to decide which groups an employer would have to report upon. The legislation was silent on which particular groups were protected from discrimination — all individuals were protected from discrimination on the basis of race, color, national origin, religion. But in order to set up a system for employer reporting, some groups had to be selected, by administrative regulations, as being the particular focus of Congressional attention. It was a rather strange categorization of groups that the enforcing agency adopted for reporting. There was no question that Negro Americans were the major concern of the Congress, as they were the major target of discrimination. Thus employers were required to report on the number of Negro employees. Mexican Americans and Puerto Ricans, two large groups of lower than average educational and occupational achievement, were incorporated into a new category of "Spanish Surnamed" or "Hispanics," which also included anyone with a Spanish name, whether his or her origin was Spain or Cuba or some other place. Finally, a fourth category was defined, "Oriental" or "Asian American," which consisted principally of Chinese and Japanese. All the rest were "others" or "white." Educational agencies required reporting on the same categories from colleges and universities and schools.

The problem of the reporting system was, first, that it created amalgams by including groups that had presumably faced discrimination and those that had not (for example Mexican Americans and Cubans); secondly, that it set up a category composed of groups (Chinese and Japanese) that had faced discrimination but had nevertheless already overcome the handicaps of discrimination to score higher in education and occupational achievement than the "others" who were to serve as a benchmark by which to determine statistically the elimination of discrimination; thirdly, that it excluded some groups that felt they too, whether in the past or the present, had faced discrimination. Thus Americans of Italian and Polish and other Slavic origin have often felt they have faced discrimination; but they were lumped with the "others." Jews have certainly faced discrimination but were also included among "others." In effect, the enforcing agencies had created two kinds of groups by this system of reporting — those which were its peculiar concern as objects of possible discrimination, and those which were of no concern at all and received no recognition as facing possible discrimination. A new form of the famous Orwellian principle was introduced: all groups were protected against discrimination according to the law, but some groups according to the enforcing agencies were more protected than others. Drawing a line between the first and the second was no easy matter in a complex multiethnic society where group prejudice has a long history and where it would be a foolhardy social analyst who would claim that only the four affected categories defined by the enforcing agencies were even today subject to discrimination.

A second problem arose with the reporting system: it was used to make presumptions of discrimination. While the law rejects the notion that statistical disparities alone are evidence of discrimination, this in effect is how the agencies enforcing civil rights laws acted. They took statistical disparities as evidence of discrimination, and tried to pressure employers, public and private, into overcoming them by hiring on the basis of race, color, and national origin — exactly what the original Civil Rights Act of 1964 had forbidden.

But was there any alternative to censuses of given groups and presumptions of discrimination on the basis of disparity? The defenders of this approach pointed out that to attack discrimination in any other way was costly to the individual who had faced discrimination and uncertain of satisfactory results. The individual would have to complain of discrimination to the enforcing agency, wait for investigation, conciliation, a final decision of whether his case was sound, possibly subsequent court proceedings. Or alternatively he would have to begin litigation on his own. And once having initiated a case, how was an enforcing agency or a court to settle the question of discrimination? Discriminatory acts could be rationalized away, concealed behind other ostensible bases of action, dissembled, would be difficult to determine precisely. It was easier to go to the numbers.

Was then the Congress simply naive in its assumption in 1964 that discrimination was not to be overcome by seeking disparities and imposing quotas? I think not. There were two important reasons why such an approach could be defended. The first was that in a democracy each group wields political power. That political power would in many cases prevent the bland hiding of discrimination behind rationalizations. With political power would come political representation and representation in the government service (where political considerations directly dictate appointments at the highest levels, and are influential at lower levels). Even without the warrant of specific law, political representation would lead to some rough justice in the distribution of government jobs, contracts and favors so that each group would get a share. Thus, in determining candidates for public office, parties often use as one principle the "balanced ticket" — each major group is represented on the party list of candidates — for in a two-party system each party must appeal to almost every group. Representation in elected office means influence in making political appointments to government service. Political appointees in government service hand out contracts, place government money in banks, provide benefits of various types to businesses, universities, schools. In effect, political representation is seen as a key to more general representation of all the major segments of a society. And the Civil Rights Act of 1964, supplemented by an extremely severe Voting Rights Act of 1965, ensured that all obstacles to the registration and voting of minority groups would be swept away, as indeed they have been.

The second reason why Congress might well have believed that a purely individual approach to overcoming discrimination was not utopian was that other groups that had faced discrimination in the past — Jews, Chinese, Japanese — had, even without the powerful assistance of federal civil rights legislation, risen on the basis of individual initiative. If discrimination was illegal, if penalties for discrimination were, even if at only the margin, severe, would one not expect that the initiative of blacks, Mexican Americans, and Puerto Ricans would also operate to raise them politically, educationally, and economically?

Was this faith justified? It would be possible to answer that by studying intensively progress made by minorities in the six years between 1964, when the Civil Rights Act was passed, and 1970 and 1971, when policies based on requiring employment to reach statistical goals or quotas became increasingly common in the United States owing to the regulations of executive agencies and the rulings of federal courts. This is not the place for such an examination. Nor do we have fully satisfactory techniques to separate out, in any social change, one cause from a variety of others that are operating. It was after all also during those years that black demands were most militant and the fear of urban riots and possible urban insurrections greatest. Nevertheless, it is my judgment that great progress was made in those years, and that the point of view of Congress on minority progress was vindicated by that progress: black political representation did rapidly increase (it has continued to increase), black movement into colleges and universities leapt upward, black progress in closing the gap in earnings between whites and blacks was substantial.[2]

Of course this judgment is disputed; there is a great battle of the statistics and their interpretation which I cannot go into here. But behind the battle of the statistics lie ideological orientations. Those who feel that American society is irredeemably racist, that the public opinion polls showing a decline in prejudice are simply deceptive, that progress for blacks and other minorities is impossible except through governmental intervention, try to find in the statistics the evidence that supports their judgment of no or little progress. Those who believe that prejudice and discrimination have declined in the United States, that the United States is still basically an open society in which deprived groups and immigrants can achieve equality with older settlers and groups, see in the statistics the evidence that vindicates their faith.

Aside from this basic orientation, there is another difference in view that separates pessimists and optimists. Those who believe that blacks have been severely damaged by centuries of slavery and discrimination and prejudice do not see how simply opening up nondiscriminatory opportunity can raise blacks (and one may, in lesser measure, make the same argument for other groups). Too many blacks are too crippled, the argument goes, to act individually to take advantage of new nondiscriminatory opportunity. And therefore one cannot count on individual initiative, one must assure by goal and quota that given numbers of blacks are employed, promoted, taken into colleges and professional schools.

This brings us to my third question. If we set a number, if we say one must employ one black teacher for one white teacher until the number of blacks reaches 20 percent of the teaching force—as a judge in Boston requires—or if we say that 16 percent of all places to a medical school must be reserved for certain specified minorities—as the Medical School of the University of California at Davis did—are we depriving the majority, the nonminority group, of any rights? The kind of action I have described is now widespread in the United States. Many police and fire departments must hire today on the basis of racial quotas, many teaching and supervisory appointments must be filled on this basis, many medical and other professional schools have goals for minority admissions. A major constitutional case, decided by the Supreme Court in 1978, dealt with this issue. This was the case of Allan Bakke, who applied for admission to the University of California Medical School, was denied admission twice, and claimed that his individual right to admission on a nondiscriminatory basis was denied because the school reserved 16 percent of its places for minorities.

Was it a fair claim he made? One could answer Bakke—and he was so answered, in many *amicus* briefs filed with the Supreme Court—that very few of the many applicants to medical schools are accepted in any case; that blacks, who form 11 percent of the population, have only 2 percent of the doctors; that these numbers will not increase unless a specific effort to reach a certain number of black admissions is made; that one cannot argue that there is a discrimination against the majority when they have 84 percent of the places.

But on the other hand, it can be argued that the black proportion in medical schools has increased greatly in recent years; that there are other ways of recruiting blacks to medical schools than by setting a fixed numerical quota; and that the constitution and the civil rights laws forbid discrimination against any *person* on account of race, color, or national origin, and this applies to whites, as well as blacks. Blacks were given the opportunity to enter the medical school both by means of the regular admission process, and by means of the special admission process for minorities, for which 16 percent of places were reserved. Whites were given the opportunity to enter the medical school only by means of the regular admission procedure. As a result, less-qualified minority applicants were accepted in place of majority applicants.

If one thinks of a rough justice proportioned according to the size of groups, then Bakke should have lost. There are very few black doctors; there should be more. But if one thinks of individual rights, the right to be considered in one's own person independently of race, color, or national origin, Bakke should have won — as, in a very narrow decision, he ultimately did.[3]

There are two notions of justice in conflict here, one which says justice is apportioning rewards to groups on the basis of proportionality, the other which says justice is to be color-blind, to consider only the individual. Bakke can say, "I don't care how many black and white doctors there are, I want to be considered for admission on my individual merits, independently of race. *I* want to be a doctor; it is not the white race that wants to be a doctor."

While it was an issue of admission to medical schools that has reached the Supreme Court, it is generally accepted that the principles governing employment and promotions are not very different. Here, too, one faces the same conflict: justice as proportionality by group or justice as the consideration of the isolated individual regardless of race, color, national origin, religion.

The American people, raised on the language of individual rights, are remarkably uniform in their views. The Gallup poll has shown that huge majorities of whites and substantial majorities of blacks are against preferential treatment on the basis of race (see Chapter 9). Individualism, one may say, is still strong in America.

It would be nice if we could avoid the dilemma, if individual choice in a multiethnic society, in the absence of discrimination, aggregated into a rough proportionality that meant justice satisfying both the individual and the group standard. But it doesn't — or it hasn't yet. That is the problem. Can we rest on principle when there are these substantial differences of representation between racial and ethnic groups? Or is it the task of a just society to make representation equal, even if this means the individual is not treated as an individual, but must be considered as a member of a group?

Is there a principle that suggests which course a multiethnic society will or should follow: whether to deal with discrimination and group difference by establishing defined places in government and economy for each group, or whether, alternatively, to emphasize the right of the individual to be considered without regard to group characteristics for election to office, for appointment to government posts, for employment, for admission to educational institutions? I have already placed in opposition to the dominant individual-rights approach that we see in the United States and, I believe, in the United Kingdom, in France, and in Australia, the approach in terms of rights for groups that we see, in different degrees, in Canada and Belgium, in Lebanon before its tragic civil war, in Malaysia and India. Undoubtedly if I knew more about other multiethnic states (for example Czechoslavakia and Yugoslavia) I could add more to the group approach. One may also add South Africa as a state committed to group rights — though the use of the term will certainly sound ironic here. The legitimation in South Africa for the removal from politics and the higher reaches of the economy of blacks, coloured, Indians, is that each group is distinct and to be kept separate. This rationalization can be seized on by the subordinate groups to demand group representation at the center.

Whether a nation elects to handle multiethnic diversity by formally ignoring it or by formally recognizing it has no bearing on whether it is a democracy or not: whether it be a democracy, a "people's democracy," a dictatorship, or an autocracy, either approach to multiethnic diversity is possible. What this suggests is that the *form* of a nation's response to diversity — individual rights or group rights — should have no bearing on whether we consider that nation responsive to human rights and to civil rights. Rather, we should realize, there are two quite distinct forms of response. In the United States, divided as we are by this issue, we seem to believe that one course upholds the

Constitution while the other betrays it, and thus that one course enhances democracy and equality in the United States but that the other course reduces it. I am a partisan of the individual-rights approach for the United States but given the diversity of handling these kinds of issues in other equally democratic countries of the world, I do not believe the issue can be decided in these terms.

I believe the key principle that does in fact and should determine for a multiethnic state — including the United States — whether it elects the path of group rights or individual rights, is whether it sees the different groups as remaining permanent and distinct constituents of a federated society or whether it sees these groups as ideally integrating into, eventually assimilating into, a common society. If the state sets before itself the model that group membership is purely private, a shifting matter of personal choice and degree, something that may be weakened and dissolved in time as other identities take over, then to place an emphasis on group rights is to hamper this development, to change the course of the society, to make a statement to all its individuals and groups that people derive rights not only from a general citizenship but from another kind of citizenship within a group. And just as laws and regulations are required to determine who is a citizen of the state and may exercise the rights of a citizen, so would laws and regulations be required to determine who is a citizen of a subsidiary group, and who may exercise the rights of such a citizenship.

If, on the other hand, the model a society has for itself, today and in the future, is that it is a confederation of groups, that group membership is central and permanent, and that the divisions among groups are such that it is unrealistic or unjust to envisage these group identities weakening in time to be replaced by a common citizenship, then it must take the path of determining what the rights of each group shall be. Thus, Canada sees itself a federation of two founding peoples, English and French; Malaysia cannot conceive of the dividing line between Malay and Chinese disappearing; Belgium tried to work as a unitary state, with the dominance of the French-speaking element, but once the Flemish-speaking element asserted its claim to equal rights, its constitution had to accept these two central elements in the state as permanent.

There are of course other important differences among multiethnic states: there are those in which one group was clearly subordinate, a minority facing discrimination; and there are those in which different groups did not see each other as arranged in a hierarchy of higher and lower. But in almost all multiethnic situations groups do rank each other. While the hierarchy may not be as absolute as it is in South Africa, or as it was in the southern United States, that is, a strict caste-like situation fixed in law, there is generally some sense of grievance by one group against another. But this issue does not affect the principle I have proposed. Groups that are roughly parallel in political and economic strength may nevertheless be so diverse, or consider themselves so different, that the idea of integration or assimilation to a common norm is inconceivable. This is certainly the case for Anglophones and Francophones in Canada, Flemish-speakers or French-speakers in Belgium. On the other hand, groups that are ordered in a hierarchy, that are considered "higher" or "lower," reflecting real and substantial economic and political inferiority, may nevertheless set as their ideal and ultimately expect integration into the common society. This was certainly the objective of the American Negro civil rights movements until the late 1960s — black leaders wanted nothing more than to be Americans, full Americans, with the rights of all other Americans. And this was also the objective of European immigrant groups to the United States, many of whom as immigrant and second-generation communities faced discrimination. Similarly, West Indian immigrants to Britain viewed themselves and, I believe, still view themselves as black Britons, wanting nothing more than full acceptance, the same rights in all spheres that all other citizens hold.

There is thus such a thing as a state ideology or a national consensus that shapes and determines what attitude immigrant and minority groups will take toward the alternative possibilities of group maintenance and group rights on the one hand, or individual integration and individual rights on the other. It is interesting to contrast immigrant groups, from the same background, in Canada and the United States. Canada, because it was already based on two founding, distinct national elements, gave more opportunity for incoming minority groups to select group maintenance as a possibility. Thus it appears there is somewhat less integration, somewhat greater commitment to group maintenance, among Slavic groups and Jews who went to Canada, compared with groups of the same origins that went to the United States. The United States, whatever the realities of discrimination and segregation, had as a national ideal a unitary and new ethnic identity, that of American. The United States was a federation of states which were defined politically, not ethnically; Canada was a federation of peoples, organized into different provinces. The impact of this originating frame for ethnic self-image can be seen on subsequent immigrants into the two countries. And, I would hazard, one can see the same difference in legal institutions, with a greater willingness in Canada formally and legally to accept the existence of ethnic groups, I would not exaggerate the difference, but it is there.

But what I would emphasize is that for some societies a choice is possible. There are facts and ideals that point both ways. And now I return to the United States. The society can go one way or the other, toward individual rights or group rights — which is why the division over the Bakke case was so intense, even among those elite, educated elements of the society that in the 1960s, during the civil rights struggle, formed a solid phalanx of one opinion in favor of individual rights. In the United States, coexisting with the facts of eager immigrant groups entering the country, becoming Americanized, rising economically, socially, politically, were the equally powerful facts that the status of blacks, of Chinese, of Japanese, of Indians was defined in law, in racial terms, for purposes of discrimination and segregation. And coexisting with the overarching national goal or image of one nation, of individuals endowed with equal rights, was a minority sentiment — encouraged undoubtedly in part by discrimination — in favor of cultural pluralism, the maintenance of group identity. A large body of opinion in the United States always fought discrimination and segregation as a betrayal of the American ideals of individual rights and equality. In the middle 1960s, with the passage of the Civil Rights Act of 1964 and the Immigration Act of 1965, which eliminated all references to race and all quotas on the basis of nationality, it seemed as if the individual-rights ideal had triumphed. But then, as we saw, the question came up of how to achieve practical equality, and we began to slide again toward group definition, this time for purposes of correction and benefit, rather than for purposes of discrimination and segregation.

Clearly one key issue is whether previously subordinated or separate groups can envisage progress under a course of individual rights. Gordon P. Means puts the issue well:

A good case can be made both for and against special privileges. Such a system can be an effective strategy for inducing rapid social change, in settings where cultural variables need to be taken into account. Without preferential privileges, there may be no inducement for improving the opportunity structures of deprived or encapsulated cultural and ethnic groups. Where group identity and communal and ethnic prejudices permeate a society, it is naive, if not hypocritical to talk about the equality of opportunity based upon individual achievement and universalistic norms.[4]

I would emphasize the words "where group identity and communal and ethnic prejudices permeate a society." If in a society the groups are sharply divided from one another, so that their boundaries are clear, are firmly set by law or custom, are not expected to become permeable; and if they live in a long historical tradition in which group identification has been used and is used for purposes of discrimination and separation, there may be no alternative: special preferences may be necessary to protect the inferior group and to foster intergroup harmony. Thus we must determine an issue of fact. But we must also determine an issue of direction. Because if inferiority and difference are being overcome, we must consider the negative consequences of selecting the path of group rights and preferences, and we would wish to avoid them if possible. As Means continues, "Yet, when all has been said, it must also be acknowledged that the system of group special rights does involve considerable social costs and is a rather crude strategy for inducing social tranformation."

An Indian Supreme Court justice has also suggested language helpful in confronting the dilemma. The case before him dealt with special preferences which were originally granted to the most backward castes, but which — a tendency one might expect in the case of special preferences — have become more expansive to include other less backward castes and classes. Justice Krishna Iyer wrote:

The social disparity must be so grim and substantial as to serve as a basis for benign discrimination. If we search for such a class, we cannot find any large segment other than the scheduled castes and scheduled tribes.[5]

This is a test we can apply. Is the social disparity so grim and substantial that there is no alternative to benign discrimination?

We now understand the basis, in facts and ideals, that will move a multiethnic society in one direction or another. But what are the implications of choosing one path or another? If we choose the group-rights approach we say that the differences between some groups are so great that they cannot achieve satisfaction on the basis of individual rights. We say, too, that — whether we want to or not — we will permanently section the society into ethnic groups by law. Even if advocates of group rights claim this is a temporary solution to problems of inequality, as they do in India and in the United States, it is inconceivable to me that benefits given in law on the basis of group membership will not strengthen groups, will not make necessary the policing of their boundaries, and will not become permanent in a democratic society, where benefits once given cannot be withdrawn. In effect, American society, which was moving toward an emphasis on individual rights in which group affiliation and difference were to become a matter of indifference to the state, in which the state was to be concerned only that such affiliation did not affect the fate of individuals, will become something very different if it continues to move along the path of group rights. More groups will join the four already selected as special beneficiaries. And with every movement in the direction of group rights, the individual's claim to be considered only as an individual, regardless of race, color or national origin, will be reduced, as more and more places are reserved to be filled on the basis of group affiliation.

When a society, such as American society, faces both ways, with one tradition insisting on a unitary identity, and another — a minority tradition — arguing for cultural pluralism, with many groups barely differentiated from each other in wealth and power, but others lagging much further behind, there is no escape from difficult choices. Are the differences among groups in American society "so grim and substantial" that there is no other course but special privilege? To me, and to other analysts of the American scene, the speed with which gaps between blacks and whites — and gaps between most minority groups and the rest of the society — are being closed in political representation, in income, in education, is rapid and satisfactory. To others, these changes are paltry and insignificant. To me, too, the overall direction of American society has been toward a society with a common identity, based on common ideals, one in which group identities are respected as private and individual choices but in which these identities are strictly excluded from a formal, legal, consitutional role in the polity. To others, the fact that groups were in the past legally defined for purposes of discrimination and segregation and exclusion is sufficient reason why we should resurrect legal group definitions for purposes of reparation and compensation.

The choices we are now making on the difficult issue of individual rights versus group rights will tell us which view of American society will prevail, and what, in consequence, the fate of individual rights in American society is to be.

[1978]

14

Federalism and Ethnicity:

The American Solution

To COUPLE federalism and ethnicity immediately suggests one familiar solution to the problem of a state containing a number of ethnic groups varying in language, culture, religion, average income, occupational structure, history, and self-image, or some of these, and attempting to retain the force of a single nation acting, in certain key spheres, as a unitary state. The solution is to make the boundaries of the constituent federal units coincide with the boundaries of each ethnic group. And so we have the familiar cases of Yugoslavia, Czechoslovakia, the Soviet Union, India, Canada, Belgium, Switzerland, in each of which the boundaries of some of the federal components making up the union are also boundaries of a cultural sphere that it is expected will be dominated by a single ethnic group. Such a solution tries to divide parochial matters, of interest to one of the ethnic groups that make up the state, from national matters. Thus the political unit of a given ethnic group can settle, without disturbing the rights of other ethnic groups, the question of what language will be used in the schools, courts, and legislation; the central federal authority can deal with monetary matters and finance, foreign affairs and defense. And it is hoped that tranquillity will result.

There would still be problems: even when ethnic groups occupy compact geographical areas, their boundaries are not so sharp and distinct that minorities of one group will not be left in a political unit designed for another group. Migration may be expected to increase the diversity of groups within any federal unit, and so to raise the difficult issue of "minority rights," the national rights of migrants of one ethnic group in a political unit that another ethnic group dominates. And finally, making ethnic boundaries coincide with political boundaries increases the fear of separatist and secessionist movements, for the ethnic group adds to its force as a social unit with the additional force of a political unit that it dominates.

So we have another familiar but opposite solution, particularly in states in which the antagonisms between ethnic groups established compactly on a territory seem dangerous: Political lines for constituent units of the federal state are drawn so as to break up single groups and combine different groups (as in Nigeria).[1]

These are two approaches to the problem of politically structuring a single state consisting of a number of ethnic groups. But these two rather straightforward alternatives are possible only because in these states ethnic groups *are* concentrated on their own territory. Great difficulties are created as migration and urbanization mix up the groups. What are the rights — linguistic, civil, national — of group A when its people have left its territory and migrated to that of group B? And thus we have the question of the rights of the French-speakers who have migrated over the border of Quebec into neighboring Ontario; of the Tamil-speakers of Maharashtrian Bombay; the problem of the Baltic states of Estonia, Latvia, and Lithuania and of Central Asian states in the Soviet Union in maintaining their national cultures as the numbers of Great Russians increase among them; of the rights of blacks, assigned to Bantustans in South Africa, when they live and work outside the borders of these ministates, and the like.

In the United States, the situation is quite different. Our federalism preceded the creation of much of our great ethnic diversity. It is true that at the time of the creation of the union in the late eighteenth century there was already a large slave population, a smaller American Indian population. There were also immigrants from a variety of places. The largest concentration was of Germans in Pennsylvania, but there were also Dutch in New York and small numbers of other groups. The white population was, however, overwhelmingly from the British Isles and of various Protestant faiths. (There were then marked divisions among the colonists from the British Isles — English, Welsh, Scots, Irish — and this contributed to ethnic diversity. But America became more diverse after mass immigration.) The boundaries of the colonies had not been shaped by ethnic conflict or ethnic concentrations. They were lines on a map drawn through territory inhabited by Indians. When Tocqueville toured the United States in 1831–1832 he was scarcely aware of any European ethnic diversity in the United States. Tocqueville and Beaumont were concerned with the fate of the blacks and Indians; no other issue of ethnic diversity came to their attention. The new states of the expanding union were established for the most part in territories inhabited only by Indians and occasional white hunters, trappers, and settlers, and the fixing of their boundaries was unaffected by ethnic considerations. In Louisiana the United States did annex a small French-speaking community. Only in the Southwest did the United States annex territory with a substantial foreign population, aside from American Indians. In the territory taken from Mexico there were established Spanish-speaking Mexican populations in California and New Mexico.

In general, however, there is little coincidence between ethnic groups and state boundaries. The typical picture of ethnicity in federal America is the wide distribution of many groups throughout the national territory, with concentrations it is true here and there, but concentrations generally not so large that a single group could expect to dominate a single state or group of states. The creation of American ethnic diversity came largely through immigration, and after the formation of the union and the creation of new states. In the absence of ethnic and racial concentrations dominating one or more states, and of ethnic concentrations that could claim national rights on the basis of settlement on American territories before they became part of the United States, it became difficult for most groups to envisage claims to national rights — for example, the right to use their language in a state's government, or to establish institutions reflecting their distinctive ethnic culture, or to secede.

There are three important exceptions to this general picture of the establishment of ethnic groups through immigration, broadly distributed throughout the United States, and without the opportunity to claim national rights on the ground of settlement before the establishment of the authority of the United States. First, as I have already pointed out, there was a Spanish-speaking population, with preexisting rights, settled in the Southwest. The story of these rights (the use of Spanish in state government, in public education, in courts) is a complicated one. As white Anglo populations grew, rapidly in California because of the discovery of gold, less rapidly in New Mexico, the Spanish-speaking were gradually deprived of these rights; today, a hundred years later, under quite different circumstances, these rights are being revived. Texas, already a free republic, had very few Spanish-speaking Mexicans when it was annexed by the United States; but a very large Mexican population grew up over the years through immigration, and here, too, the history has been one of early deprivation of rights, and recent creation of new rights.[2]

Second, there were the black slaves concentrated in the Southern states. The close identification of the problem of slavery and later the problem of civil rights and formal and practical equality for blacks with the Southern states continued for generations. It was only in the South that the possibility — or, if one wishes, the fantasy — of an independent nation or autonomous state drawn on ethnic and racial lines, separated from the United States, could arise. The Confederate States of America was created to protect slavery. But one can also see it as an effort to create a new political unit for a nascent ethnic group. The South was relatively unaffected by European immigration; it was somewhat distinctive in religion, dialect, and customs; and of course slavery made it different in politics and culture. Had it survived, we would have had a nation in which a huge black population, a majority in many areas if not in the nation as a whole, was dominated by a white population somewhat different in culture, language, religion, and ethnic background from the industrial, commercial, and family-farm North.

Closer to our own times was the idea of creating a black state in the South. I will not evaluate here how practical such a possibility ever was. It played an important role in the thinking of the American Communist Party about the black problem in the 1930s. It arose again as a possibility in the late 1960s, as a heightened black nationalism swept through large sections of the black population. But by then it was clearly too late; heavy emigration of blacks from the South had greatly reduced the black population as a proportion of the whole. While still more highly concentrated in the South than in any other section, blacks nowhere formed a majority of any state, though they formed majorities in many counties, often contiguous.[3]

In recent years a second possibility of black autonomy on the basis of black population concentration has developed, because of black concentration in central cities, in some of which they formed majorities by 1970 (Washington, Atlanta, Newark, to list the largest), in others of which they are expected to soon reach a majority. The possibility of some degree of separate political control arose. There was the wildfire spread of a movement for "community control," with variable results, and some fictional fantasies of a separate black state created in the ghettos of large cities.

But the issue in these cases does not reach fully to the question of federalism, for with black concentration in central cities there was no longer any possibility of dominating as a majority one of the constituent units of the United States, a state, with all the rights of such a unit as fixed permanently in the Constitution. Cities are after all creatures of states. In this new stage there was only a question of whether blacks would dominate some city governments, as Irish Americans, Italian Americans, and Polish Americans, where they were sufficiently numerous, dominated other city governments. In this case, the black situation becomes similar to that of other ethnic groups. We no longer have a group so concentrated in an extensive territory that it can conceive of a separate state. Rather, we have groups so broadly distributed throughout the United States and so intermingled with others that the questions of the relationship between federalism and ethnicity quite change their form.

I will come to these new and more distinctly American questions shortly. At this point, let me complete my catalogue of those groups which were so concentrated in given territories that the hope, possibility, or fantasy of a separate national state reflecting a single group and divorcing itself from the United States could be envisaged.

The third exception to the general rule of the broad distribution of ethnic groups, along with the Spanish-speaking of the Southwest and the blacks of the South, are the American Indians. Their political status has been a varying one, and in fact has never been settled. Indian treaties suggested they were separate nations or political entities. Whatever the legal weight of these treaties, Indians were treated as wards of the United States, and concentrated in reservations in which power was held by white American authority. In one state, Oklahoma, there was a sufficient concentration of Indians for a while to raise the possibility that this might become a state dominated by that group. But everywhere they were too few, too limited in resources of every type, to play a substantial political role. In the past fifteen years, however, as American consciences have awoken to the condition of minorities who have been stripped of rights and property, American law has been employed to return to American Indians as corporate groups and individuals substantial wealth, and an uncertain degree of political control over reservations. Just what this degree of control should be is so disputed in Congress and the courts that no simple summary can be given.

Outside the continental United States, there are other cases in which the boundaries of a state or territory coincide with or might have coincided with the boundaries of an ethnic group. Hawaii was originally occupied and ruled by Polynesians. But by the time Hawaii was annexed to the United States, it was politically dominated by a small group of American settlers, and contained twice as many Japanese as Hawaiians.[4] Hawaiians still have certain rights in Hawaii as the original inhabitants, but Japanese Americans completely dominate the state politically. Does Hawaii approximate, then, the kind of situation in which an individual political unit of a federal state expresses the distinctive ethnic characteristics and interests of a single group? In a sense it does, but in a very limited sense indeed. One has no impression or evidence that Hawaii is more pro-Japanese in its foreign-policy attitudes, for example, than other parts of the United States; indeed, one could argue the contrary, because Hawaii is most affected by Japanese tourism and Japanese investments, and this creates certain tensions. Rather, the character of Japanese American domination of Hawaii is of a peculiarly American form, owing to the almost complete as-‘ similation of the group to the general American political culture (not to mention American culture in other respects), its complete political divorce from the larger ethnonational group from which it is derived (Japan), its complete identification with the national political system, and its consequent failure to harbor suspicions and resentment of the federal center or other political units of the federation because of potential or actual infringements on ethnic rights. I will analyze what I call this peculiarly American relationship between ethnicity and federalism later.

Finally, I must mention Puerto Rico. If Puerto Rico were to become a state it would break the general pattern. This would have to be a Spanish-speaking state. It would be inhabited almost entirely by a single ethnic group. There would be little likelihood once it became a state that its dominant population would be diluted much by migrants from other parts of the United States, as happened in California, New Mexico, and Hawaii. Undoubtedly the fact that Puerto Rico would be such a state, distinguished in these respects from all the other states of the Union, would weigh heavily with Congress in accepting it as a state. For this and other reasons it is maintained in an ambiguous Constitutional status, one the Puerto Rican people and leadership prefer but one that makes it possible for enemies of the United States to call it colonial.

Should I add yet one more exception — Utah? Utah was settled by Mormons, a religious group, but one that imposed so many distinctive customs and practices on adherents to the religion, and in time created so distinctive a culture for them, that it might be considered an ethnic group. The relationship of Mormons to the political life of Utah resembles a situation in which one ethnic group is dominant, then challenged by immigrants of other ethnic groups, making the maintenance of predominance chancy.

Now that I have listed so many exceptions to the general pattern of the relationship between ethnicity and federalism in the United States, the reader may question the typicality of what I call the general pattern, that is, a broad distribution of ethnic groups, with concentrations in certain states, but concentrations insufficient to make ethnic and state boundaries and interests coincide. But I argue that this is indeed the general American pattern. We can see how general it is by comparing it with what might have been — Wisconsin a German state, Minnesota a Norwegian-Swedish state, Massachusetts an Irish State, Rhode Island an Italian state, New York a Jewish state, a block of black states in the South, of Mexican American states in the Southwest, and so on. This is not what happened; and it can no longer happen. As a multiethnic nation, we find our groups distributed so widely, and intermixed with so many others, that none can envisage any such result. In this condition, we differ from the multiethnic states of Eastern Europe (the U.S.S.R., Czechsolovakia, Yugoslavia), from the varied multiethnic states of the third world, from the old unified states of Western Europe that are now troubled by regional autonomy movements. Insofar as industrialization and urbanization mix the ethnic elements of other nations, they become more like us, but they are still very different.

Our pattern is what we may call "new world ethnic diversity," in which a founding element has been rapidly joined by substantial numbers of immigrants from varied nations to create ethnic diversity with only moderate regional concentration: Australia, Canada (outside French Canada), Brazil, Argentina, Uruguay. Even so, the conditions and national traditions of each of these countries are so different that it is doubtful that comparative exercises will get us far.

How has our federalist system responded to the distinctive

situation of ethnicity in the United States? I have already suggested the general pattern that relates ethnicity and federalism. To be more specific:

1. Ethnic groups do not have a "homeland" within the borders of the United States to which they are potentially attached and whose rights they want to see expanded — there are no Scotlands or Catalonias in the United States. American Indians are the only exceptions here.

2. Nor are they closely attached to homelands outside the borders of the United States to the point where "irridentism" is an American issue: The Spanish-speaking Mexican Americans of the Southwest and the French-speaking Canadians of Northern New England do not demand or expect that the boundaries of Mexico or Quebec will be extended so as to make them members of a majority rather than a minority.

3. Ethnic groups in the United States are fairly rapidly assimilated to the national political culture, and to the national culture in other respects as well. Thus, even when numerous in a state — as in the case of the Japanese Americans in Hawaii — they are rarely inclined to express ethnic interests that would place them in sharp opposition to other states of the union.

4. In any case, their concentration within any state is generally insufficient to give them a majority, and thus the power to express a variant interest. Even the Japanese Americans of Hawaii are less than 40 percent of the state's population. Only the original English Protestant settler group forms majorities in states, and it does not conceive of itself as a distinct ethnic group; this is after all the founding element.

5. But these concentrations are sufficient so that certain reflections of distinctive ethnic interest do help form the political culture, the laws and customs of given states, though the influence of the ethnic element, as against other influences on state political culture (regional, religious, time of organization), is not easy to disentangle.

Because of the first three characteristics, it is not possible to talk of most ethnic groups in the United States as one might speak of the Quebecois, Scotsmen, Flemings, and many other groups established on their own territory, with a strong corporate self-consciousness, potential or actual, with the opportunity of establishing political rights outside their areas of concentration as ethnic groups. Ethnic groups in the United States are much hazier entities, rather more shadowy, which rapidly lose the concrete characteristics of their ethnicity — in particular, language, which goes rapidly. They are maintained by small self-conscious elites who only occasionally find a response from the large mass of those who on occasion consider themselves of that group. Their edges or boundaries are indefinable owing to acculturation and intermarriage. This is a very different matter from the ethnic groups involved in a variety of thrusts to autonomy that we see around the world in different nations organized on a federal basis.

How therefore properly to characterize ethnic groups in the United States becomes a permanent dilemma of and challenge to social scientists, and it is very easy to get it wrong. Thirty years ago I referred to ethnic groups in the United States as "ghost nations," maintained more by ideology than by national culture.[5] This was perhaps overstating the case: they were also maintained by distinctive characteristics of social structure (such as occupation); they were supported by distinctive religions or variants of religion; they developed particular political interests, sometimes around the rallying cries of the nation from which they stemmed, more likely on the basis of their distinctive religious and cultural orientations and the interests flowing from their occupational and social structure. But the general picture remained true: ethnicity in the United States, for most ethnic groups, had become a symbolic matter. Groups demanded respect from others but rarely put forward concrete ethnic demands of the type we might see in nations where ethnic groups formed more compact, self-conscious, culture-maintaining entities.

But while this was the way most ethnic groups — those of European, and latterly of Asian, origin — behaved, there remains the complication that there were also the native American Indians, blacks, Mexican Americans, and Puerto Ricans, who possess much more in the way of national characteristics. Possibly these groups, with proper public policies to stamp out discrimination and inferior status and to encourage acculturation and assimilation, will become not very different from the European and Asian ethnic groups, the ghost nations, bound by nostaligia and sentiment and only occasionally coalescing around distinct interests. But it is also possible — with other public policies — that they will increasingly be defined as distinct groups in law, with distinctive rights, which would strengthen their group political consciousness and hamper or prevent them from becoming the same kind of groups that the European ethnic groups have become. And there is a final complication: If the public policy gets turned around to the point where, rather than trying to suppress or ignore the existence of the ethnic group as a distinctive element in American society and polity, it acknowledges a distinctive status for some groups and begins to attach rights in public law to membership in them, will that not react on the others, halfway toward assimilation, and will they not begin to reassert themselves so that they will not be placed at a disadvantage?

This perspective suggests three phases in the relationship between ethnicity and federalism in the United States, which can be arranged roughly chronologically:

1. The first phase is that of the dominance of the white English-origin pioneers and settlers. They have been the creators of every state as a political element, writing its Constitution, establishing its laws, ignoring the previously settled American Indians, refusing to grant any rights to blacks, and making only slight concessions to French and Spanish speakers in a few states. Rights of subordinate groups were held at the sufferance of the dominant English-origin founding element, and the former were deprived of the right even to maintain schools in their own languages. European immigrant groups might also hold certain rights, varying from state to state depending on their numerical strength and local political circumstances, but these rights, too, were held on sufferance.

So one could see, for example, in the right to use a language in the schools, the influence of large German migrations. Thus such rights were incorporated in state law in Ohio and Pennsylvania in the 1830s; German-language schools were accepted in Wisconsin; there were German public schools in other states. Subsequent waves of bigotry — against immigrants and against Catholics — led to attacks on the use of German in public schools, particularly in the 1880s. Even when German-language instruction then shifted to parochial schools these came under attack in heavily German-populated states. The First World War led to further legislation against German. In 1903 only fourteen states required that instruction in the elementary schools should be in English; by 1923, thirty-four states had such provisions.[6]

Concentrations of a group within a single state could lead to that state's adopting or tolerating practices that the group favored, as in the case of German in the schools, but it could also lead to counteraction by the dominant original-settler group and its later allies. Indeed, the larger a group within a state and its potential influence, the stronger might be the reactions against any public acknowledgment of its rights. The most vivid reflection of this of course is the situation in states (and parts of states) with large black populations, where, because blacks were deprived first of liberty and later of political rights, their suppression was most complete. And one could make the same point for states with large concentrations of Mexican Americans, American Indians, Chinese, and Japanese.

The relations between ethnicity and federalism imply the opportunity for a dominant majority — dominant generally in numbers, but it would be enough for it to be dominant in political power — to repress the rights of ethnic minorities. In this situation, the federal power generally stood aside, though there were important interventions to limit what states could do to suppress minorities.

This first phase is the phase of white settler dominance; it is also the phase when the cultural characteristics of immigrant ethnic groups, in particular the German, but also the Irish, Norwegians, and others were strongest. Thus on the one hand there was the strongest motivation for these groups to establish separate schooling, maintain church services in their own language, establish and maintain newspapers, and so on; at the same time there was the greatest likelihood of strong nativist reactions to and suspicion of such separate enterprises. There were great differences between what Southern states did to blacks, Western to Chinese and Japanese, and Midwestern to European immigrants: All attempts to generalize involve the suppression of unique and in some other perspective crucial differences. But for purposes of characterizing the relations between federalism and ethnicity, we may describe this phase as one of dominant states' rights and of politically dominant English-origin elements within the states. But since it is a period of states' rights, it is also a period of great diversity in state legislation.

2. The second phase is one in which the ethnic groups have become numerous and politically active and as a result can express their interests through state power. Once again, I must refer to the general picture of ethnic groups given before: They vary in the degree of attachment to ancestral homelands and languages, in the degree to which they lose the concrete content of distinctive culture. They have many other interests besides ethnic interests: economic interests stemming from occupation, wealth, income, property ownership; regional interests, whether expressing the orientation of a large region, or the part of a state they inhabit, or rural and urban distribution; religious interests, which in the case of the Jewish group are hard to distinguish from interests of a single ethnic group since the religion is composed of one ethnic group, but which generally coincide with the interests of a group of ethnic groups.

The extent to which the ethnic elements find expression in state constitutions and legislation is a subtle question. One can ask, is New York a leader in antidiscrimination legislation and free abortion because of the high concentration of Jews, with their liberal political outlook? Was Wisconsin a leader in social legislation because of the strong German-Scandinavian concentration? Is there an ethnic component in the fact that Minnesota, which has eliminated preregistration in voting and presumably feels fraud is not much of a problem, is heavily Scandinavian, and we know how law-abiding their distant cousins in their home countries are? Can we detect an ethnic pattern in the variable state responses to the death penalty, abortion, prohibition, and other issues that are seen as basically moral, and therefore dominated by religious teachings and world outlook? To all these questions I would answer, yes, to some extent, but to what extent it would be hard to say.

Daniel Elazar has done the most to link up political culture, as expressed in city and state politics, to ethnic factors, by way of the three large political cultures of moralism, individualism, and traditionalism. Each is linked to a major migratory stream, stemming from New England, the middle states, and the South, respectively. The middle states' stream is ethnically the most mixed. Ethnic determinants are not the only ones in creating these three cultures and their variants, but they play a very large role indeed, with different ethnic groups carrying different world outlooks and values more or less confluent with one or another of these cultures.[7]

Elazar presents the interesting case of how the various states stood in antidiscrimination legislation in 1961, before national legislation. The chief determinant was of course sectional — the Southern states (also traditionalist) had no such legislation, except for "semi-urban Kentucky and unionist West Virginia . . . and highly urban Missouri." Presumably the percentage of blacks should have affected the degree to which other states had acted to outlaw discrimination:

Eight of the ten northern and western states with the largest black populations had full or substantial coverage, among them four predominantly of the moralistic political culture, and three of the others with substantial moralistic minorities. But seven states with few blacks had coverage equally comprehensive, five of which were dominated by the moralistic culture and the other two, originally dominated by that political culture, with substantial moralistic minorities . . .

In every one of the foregoing fifteen states it was a combination of the moralistic culture plus the existence of a high degree of ethnic diversity that led to this kind of legislation. The ethnics affected, in effect, challenge the majority to live up to the demands of their political culture and virtually embarrass them into doing so.[8]

The states with the fullest coverage were Massachusetts, Connecticut, New York, Pennsylvania, Minnesota, Colorado, Oregon, Rhode Island, New Jersey, Michigan, Indiana, Illinois, Wisconsin, Washington, and California. The following states had tiny Negro populations: Massachusetts, Minnesota, Colorado, Oregon, Rhode Island, Wisconsin, and Washington. There are some strong differences among them. It is, for example, Minnesota that has voting without preregistration, and it is Rhode Island and Massachusetts officials who fear an epidemic of fraud if it is implemented in their state by national legislation. The varying ethnic concentrations and cultures from state to state help explain these differences. The moralism, individualism, and traditionalism found in different states, in Elazar's analysis, seem to me to vary considerably, depending on which ethnic groups have contributed to these political cultures.

But it is not necessary here to argue the details by which ethnic concentrations affect the political characteristics of various states of the union. The point is there is such influence. And this influence is exercised both through legislation to achieve specific ethnic aims (for example, teaching one or another language in the public high schools) and through the general culture each group brings, which often aggregates with the cultures of other groups into a large and significant influence.

3. The third phase is that of federal standards for the protection of the rights of minority groups and ethnic groups; and here some important and troubling questions affecting the relations between ethnicity and federalism come to the fore.

The most important federal intervention, dwarfing all others, was the Civil War and subsequent Reconstruction. After a long hiatus, the federal power again moved against the South, led by the federal courts, and has achieved political equality for blacks. But there have also been other federal interventions: to protect the rights of Chinese and Japanese in California, and of other ethnic minority groups, as in the Supreme Court case of *Meyer v. Nebraska* in 1923, which struck down extreme limitations on teaching in a foreign language. In general, during periods of state excesses in suppressing minority rights, it has been the federal power — particularly the courts, but often the national administration — that has protected minority rights, if they were to be protected at all. Federalism, despite the opportunities it gave ethnic groups to conduct some of their affairs as they wished through state and local influence, offered more opportunity to the dominant Anglo-Saxon whites to impose their will on ethnic minorities.

Federalism permitted diversity and taking account of ethnic concentrations among constituent units, whether for good or bad. The central power of a diverse nation could not make the same accommodations to diversity. If states responded to diversity by depriving minorities of rights, one could only applaud federal intervention: It was federal intervention that ensured voting rights for minorities, banned discrimination in employment and public facilities, opened housing to minorities throughout the nation. But this larger picture should not obscure the variety of the state picture: Many of these rights were guaranteed in many states long before federal action by courts or legislature or administration made them national. The adoption of national legislation in these areas has tried in measure to take account of state diversity: State commissions against discrimination in employment, education, and housing still operate, with federal funds and with some powers defined in federal legislation and administrative rules, but of course the replacement of the primary state role by a federal role does sap the significance of state action, as is true generally where state functions undertaken by progressive states (in welfare, for example) become national functions. The role of the states has been not only to defend what we see as backward and parochial values, but also to experiment in proposing and extending progressive and liberal values — and which role a given state plays is strongly affected by its ethnic constitution.

The federal power by the late 1970s, after many decades of the extension of national governmental scale and power, found it easy to lay down uniform rules for the nation. But as federal power expands, one also sees the possibility of its overriding those specific state rules and orientations which reflect the values of their specific ethnic concentrations. The national power, when it prohibits diversity among the states, may raise social conflict to an undesirable level. For example, the Supreme Court took it upon itself in 1973 to outlaw just about all state legislation on abortion. This legislation was already showing considerable diversity among the states, with New York — in this, as in other areas, a leader in expressing cosmopolitan values — having achieved almost abortion on demand, undoubtedly reflecting to some degree the high concentration of Jews and cosmopolitan Protestants. The abortion issue remains one that arouses passion, and contributes to strains in the political order. In establishing a new definition of freedom, one that is attractive to some strata of the population (the better-educated middle classes in particular, and markedly liberal Protestants and Jews), the Supreme Court offends deeply other groups (working- and lower-middle-class, Catholic and conservative Protestant) who might have been able to satisfy themselves with state legislation expressing their values.

Abortion, like temperance and prohibition, deeply divides the nation, along ethnic and religious lines as well as class lines. Under such circumstances, when the nation is divided over matters which touch deeply held values that arouse passion, it would appear that a federal system in which constituent units can respond differently to different values could accommodate the variety of interests with the least strain. It undoubtedly appeared irrational in the days before Prohibition (and once again now that the control of alcohol is back in the hands of the states) that one state should make it hard to get a drink under certain circumstances, others easy. But having tried national legislation — indeed constitutional prohibition — we have decided that on this issue we prefer to live with the irrational rather than a national, uniform standard that some of us simply cannot accept. Abortion — seen as the right to freedom by many, the right to immorality by many others — might also best be handled by not elevating it, whether enabling it or banning it, to the national level.

We find the same development in areas of direct interest to ethnic groups, such as bilingual and bicultural programs. I have pointed out that until the 1880s there were public schools conducted entirely or partly in foreign languages in parts of the country where there were strong ethnic concentrations. These then were challenged in various state laws and constitutions during periods of antiforeign and anti-Catholic sentiment, in some states even when these educational practices retreated to the private and parochial schools. In the 1920s the Supreme Court limited the degree to which states could ban such practices, and for the next few decades practices varied. In 1923 thirty-four states prohibited teaching in elementary schools in any language but English. Even before World War II, multicultural education and the teaching of tolerance for other groups were beginning to replace the previous intense Americanization efforts. With World War II and the revulsion against Hitler's racism, there was a strengthening of such tendencies, though they were still very modest. The civil rights revolution of the 1960s, which encompassed Spanish-language groups and led to reverberations among other groups, revitalized these tendencies. Then a concern for the educational achievement for minority groups and a proud self-image for ethnic groups was added, which led to proposals and demands for bilingual and bicultural education.

There was a variable but substantial state response to these developments. In 1971 twenty-two states still mandated English as the language of instruction, except in foreign language courses, in public or private schools, and none required bilingual or bicultural education. By 1974–75, only ten prohibitory laws still stood, and ten states had by law provided some degree of mandatory bilingual education under certain circumstances.[9]

The states that still had prohibitory legislation were Alabama, Arkansas, Delaware, Idaho, Louisiana (except for French), Nebraska, North Carolina, Oklahoma, and West Virginia. One notes that they include states that never had concentrations of foreign-language-speaking minorities, or states that clearly had reacted against large German-speaking minorities. The states with mandatory bilingual education were Alaska, Illinois, Massachusetts, Michigan, New Jersey, Oregon, Pennsylvania, Rhode Island, Texas, and Wisconsin. These are states with substantial minorities speaking foreign languages, or states with a strong liberal tradition.

Under these circumstances, one could have concluded that federalism was working properly. However, when the Supreme Court ruled in the *Lau* case that a Chinese-speaking student in San Francisco was entitled constitutionally to some appropriate remedial education, the Office for Civil Rights of the Department of Health, Education, and Welfare ruled that school districts must conduct censuses of possible need, that they must undertake "affirmative steps" defined by a special task force, and that compliance reviews would take place to see that they had complied. This unfortunately defines the pattern whereby national mandates — generally deriving from a combination of judicial interpretations and administrative agencies' reinterpretations, both often independent of statutory law — replace local determinations.

Inevitably the question must be raised, in connection with policy on bilingual and bicultural education as well as in connection with policy on issues rooted in cultural values such as abortion, temperance, and the death penalty, whether national norms or state variation under federalism are to be preferred. Federal uniformity has undoubtedly prevented bigoted or malicious legislation and administrative action against distinctive ethnic groups; but it also, one would think, inhibits the opportunity of each of the various autonomous units of the federal system to adopt diverse policies that would better suit the ethnic mix that has come to make up the population of the state.[10]

[1977]

15

Europe's Ethnic Problem

THE AMERICANS, in their misery, now have company in their major form of domestic social distress: the interaction of race and social problems. In Britain, France, West Germany, and the smaller countries of Western Europe there are now established permanent settlements of people of non-European background—West Indians, Indians and Pakistanis, North Africans, Turks—who differ in race, or religion, or ethnic background from the native populations of Western Europe. This melding of old populations and new that differ in descent and in culture demonstrates that American problems are not America's alone. They are the problems of all multiethnic societies. Is there anything someone from the New World, where this mixing of peoples into new societies has gone on more vigorously than anywhere else (and, I would argue, in the end more successfully), has to say to the Old?

The United States has one advantage over the countries of Western Europe: Legally, there is no ambiguity about the suitability of anyone, of any racial background, of any religion, of any language, of any level of cultural development (assuming for the moment that differences in culture can be arranged in stages) for full participation in American society, as a citizen, with exactly the same rights as Anglo-Saxons who have descended from the first seventeenth century settlers at Plymouth or Jamestown.

Even our conservative President Reagan insists that "anyone" can be an American, and "as good an American as any other." Can one imagine an English, French, or German Prime Minister saying, as Ronald Reagan did when he accepted the Presidency:

only a Divine Providence placed this land — this island of freedom — here as a refuge for all those people in the world who yearn to breathe free . . . Jews and Christians enduring persecution behind the Iron Curtain, the "boat people" of South-East Asia, Cuba, and Haiti, the victims of drought and famine in Africa, the fighters in Afghanistan, and our own countrymen held in savage captivity.

Leave aside the anti-Communist and anti-Soviet thrust, the mixed reference to the Iranian hostages, the fact that victims of drought and famine in Africa will not be able to engineer an easy passage to the United States, or the fact this quotation is cited in the latest report on American immigration, a report that tells us that we must *control* immigration in the light of American needs. The fact remains that the United States, almost alone among the countries of the world, sees itself as a natural home for people of any religion or race, any language or culture. Even the candidate of the Republican Party, a party that draws little support from immigrants and minority races, will proclaim this as a national virtue. And indeed the report tells us that the United States took in 800,000 immigrants in 1980, expects 700,000 in 1981: all *legal residents*, and most expected shortly to become citizens.

Should one expect the ancient countries of Western Europe — densely populated as they are, and with historic traditions that link them for many centuries with one ethnic group, of one language — to achieve any such simple solution to the questions of the legal status of peoples of very different race, religion, culture, and history? The Western European concept of *nation*, which has spread all too easily and without analysis to the rest of the world, implies a state with a homogeneous population, sharing a common history, a sense of common descent from revered ancestors, common institutions, generally a common language. Much of European history has involved the effort, through war and rebellion, to forge such nation-states, bringing together into a single political entity the members of the common nation-family, expelling those who do not belong. How does such a nation-state accommodate to the permanent presence of large communities of people who share none of these commonalties?

Western European nations have not, in general, seen themselves as "countries of immigration." Indeed, until recently they were countries sending large numbers of emigrants to the true countries of immigration, the "empty lands" of the New World and Australia, which welcomed immigrants and absorbed large numbers of them. The immigrants of the postwar period to Western Europe have come into a different political setting, one that raises, to begin with (and not least important), serious questions of their legal status in these countries, of what role they may legitimately claim in states that have for so long been almost synonymous with a single national group. As the eminent Swiss sociologist H. J. Hoffman-Nowotny writes:

It is the very paradox of European migrations today that millions of people who are living in foreign countries are not designated as "immigrants"; nor do these countries see themselves as immigration countries. And vice versa, very few of the countries that send millions of their citizens to work abroad consider themselves "emigration countries" in the narrow sense. Instead of the term "immigrant," words such as "foreign worker," "guest worker," "foreign employee," or "migrant worker" are used.[1]

Britain is something of a European exception. Its postwar immigrants are true immigrants. But now Britain struggles with the problem of just who is a British national or subject. It must deal with the heritage of colonialism; and it must deal, too, with the concrete reality that Britons never conceived their country as a "country of immigration," of people of varied background and race. The making of the British people was substantially complete by the twelfth century. Whatever additions later were made to the British people—of Flemings, or Jews, or Huguenots, or Italians, or political refugees—were small in number and merged more or less into the body of Britons. Scottish and, later, Irish immigrants were more numerous but were seen in time as not very different from Englishmen—and the term "Briton" was devised to cover Scots and Welshmen and assimilated immigrants. To think of Britain as now becoming multiethnic and multiracial — including more than the related Scots and Irish, and small streams from Europe — creates a certain difficulty. That is not what Britain was, or wants to be; but it is what Britain is, and cannot help becoming. The British family has been expanded to include very distant relatives. The fragments of the old British Empire still bound to Britain offer the possibility still of (for example) a mass migration of Chinese from Hong Kong — or so the ambiguities of citizenship and subjecthood permit. .

Just as Britain must struggle with the consequences of various kinds of rights to citizenship and entry, so must France and Germany.

France, also an ex-imperial power, has special arrangements with the countries of North Africa and the francophone countries of West Africa that it formerly governed, and special ties to formerly French Indochina. The German empire (which came late) was small, and was taken away after the defeat of 1918, and Germany therefore does not have the problem of how to deal with ex-subjects, and what special status to offer or allow them. But because of its membership in the European Economic Community — and its need for foreign labor, for which it has had to reach beyond the EEC — it, too, now deals with populations of different or ambiguous status, some who have free right of entry, some who do not. And the status of "German citizen," which has in the past covered Germans by ethnicity almost exclusively, is very difficult to attain for almost anyone of foreign birth.

Thus in terms of basic law as well as in terms of dominant conception, the countries of Europe now deal with large resident populations of ambiguous status in law or in settlement as to suitability for full equality.

The contrast with the clear-cut situation of the United States is striking. "We are all immigrants," John F. Kennedy proclaimed, and it was more than rhetoric. Whatever the social advantage of being a descendant of prerevolutionary settlers (and we still do retain the term "settler" for those who were here before the Revolution), only the American Indian can claim not to be the descendant of an immigrant. And the law makes no difference between the *Mayflower* descendant and the newest citizen, though there have been some vagaries in the past and some still remain, distinguishing the native-born from the immigrant citizen. (Thus, only a native-born citizen can become President, according to our Constitution: Dr. Henry Kissinger can aspire no further than, for example, getting elected a senator.) But there are basically no classifications of citizens, and there are no classifications of foreigners in terms of suitability to become a citizen.

Indeed, some of the most agitating American questions now revolve around the opposite question: the degree of preference for employment and college and university entry for U.S. residents (whether citizen or not), who are black, of Hispanic or Asian background, or American Indian. Policy even attempts to reduce the handicap of foreign language. Thus bilingual programs in the schools as frequently try to maintain a non-English language as to teach English (and in some programs *more* effort is devoted to the former than the latter); and the citizen who speaks Spanish or an Asian language must be given special assistance in voting, by means of the translation of necessary information into his language.

U.S. citizenship is thus now radically divorced from race and ethnicity. Whatever the degree of social prejudice — and much of that is beyond the reach of the law — blacks, Asians, and Latin Americans know that they can aspire to the highest offices (short of the reservation of the Presidency to the native-born); for the ideology of our race-blind polity is now backed by the presence of members of these groups in such offices.

Thus there may be clear advantages to having had to deal with these matters for centuries rather than decades; and there is the further advantage of a constitution and a constitutional system which, through design or good luck, can be used as the basic law of a multiethnic and multiracial society.

I begin with law as a means of considering the status of the large new immigrant groups of Western Europe because, while law is only formal and may well diverge from sentiment, it is also a good index to sentiment.

It is hard for homogeneous and old nations to contemplate turning into nations of a different sort, marked by increasing heterogeneity of race, culture, language, religion. A nation in a sense is an extension of a family, or a tribe. It is often thought of as such, and sentiments of kinship are appealed to in times of war or disaster. Not that the ties of humankind are limited by nations or ethnic groups, but clearly one feels more strongly for people of one's ethnic group and nation, as one feels more strongly for members of one's family. The family is defined by blood relationship, and ethnicity by a putative blood relationship. We have been embarrassed by these ties of "blood" (as we now know, more properly genes) because of the terrible consequences of an extreme attachment to those of one's group and hostility to those of another. But loyalty to country and kin is surely not in its nature a reprehensible sentiment. It helps guide us in the degree of attachment we should feel for others; and there are good moral grounds for asserting that our responsibility for those closer to us is greater than for those more distant. It is true that political rather than ethnic status is the basis generally on which we limit or grant rights and duties; but it is normally expected, in countries of homogeneous character such as those of Western Europe, that almost all of those defined by law as citizens will have also been defined by history and relationship as members of the same group.

When political bounds and ethnic bounds fail to coincide, we have in the past expected problems. Thus, the history of Europe in one respect has been, until recently, a history of efforts to make ethnic and political boundaries coincide. The solution to "irredentism"—movements to bring those of one's own ethnic group under a common rule—was considered by liberals in the past to be shifting state boundaries, not preaching a universalistic ignoring of all ethnic differences.

Ethnically defined states were created after the cataclysm of World War I out of the debris of the Austro-Hungarian and Russian Empires; and that was considered sound and good. Boundaries were moved to arrange that Italians live under the political rule of an Italian state, unfortunately adding a good number of Austrians and Slavs to become "irredentist" in their turn. In the aftermath of World War II, action to make ethnicity and state boundaries coincide became even stronger, with the expulsion of great numbers of Germans from Poland and other countries. It seemed as if the vision of the nineteenth century, and of Woodrow Wilson, was coming to pass.

It is interesting to reflect upon the period after World War II, in which old states were either ethnically homogeneous (as the states of Europe) or new countries made up of immigrants from many, but with one dominant and exclusive language and culture drawn from one colonizing power, as was the case in the New World. Where there were other independent states in the world, such as Japan, they seemed to fit the European model.

Then two things happened; and the idea that nation and state could or should coincide was blasted. Scores of new states became independent, emerging from the British and French and Belgian and Dutch and Portuguese colonial empires. Almost all were ethically diverse, and possessed boundaries that had been drawn up with no regard for language, or culture, or ethnicity. As we learned more about the ancient empires trying to become modern states — China, India, Iran, Turkey — we discovered how ethnically diverse they were, and how difficult it was to keep all their parts together in harmony. And in Europe, which had become the model of the kinds of states the developing Third World was trying to build, the coincidence of state and ethnicity began to break down as the heritage of colonialism and economic need for immigrant workers opened the way to a radically new diversity created by immigration.

Nowhere has this adjustment been easy. And early optimistic assumptions have had to be revised even in Western Europe.

Britain, despite its magnificent traditions of hospitality and equal rights before the law, must still deal with prejudice. It has not been easy for Britain to turn into a multiracial country. To be sure, it has been, of all Western European countries, most open to granting full citizenship to immigrants of different race and culture, and in this respect it most closely resembles its offspring of the New World and Australia that have adapted — I would argue — most successfully to multiethnicity and multiracialism. But it still faces the complex problems of internal prejudice and discrimination and the inevitable differentiation of "new immigrants" and the "new communities" they create socially and economically from the native population. Its most difficult problem is how to forge an immigration policy that does not explicitly differentiate by race; for Britain is not happy to see its population of West Indians and Indians and Pakistanis expand from its present modest percentage. This is the problem that the United States and Australia have faced in the past. Both countries in the postwar epoch gave up efforts to differentiate among immigrants by race. The racial distinctions were totally abandoned in the United States in 1965; and as a result of that, among the most rapidly growing immigrant ethnic communities in the United States are now Korean, Filipino, Indian, and Chinese, all of whom may expect, after the easy preliminary steps that are required to become citizens, to enjoy full U.S. citizenship.

France and Germany, despite their careful efforts to limit full citizenship, and to exclude their North Africans and Turks from attaining it, now must confront the reality of large permanent settlements of non-Europeans, with second generations growing up to reach their teens — and the age of job-seeking and delinquency. In this respect, they join the second generation of the non-European communities in Britain, and despite the difference in legal status, one fears the reality in terms of social strain and conflict will be the same. Nor can the small states of Western Europe, now with substantial non-European communities, escape from these dilemmas. The ties of kinship still seem to make the problems of assimilating those of more closely related ethnicities easier. One suspects Sweden will have less difficulty with its Finns than its Turks; and Switzerland — despite the fact that it has by far the largest foreign working community proportionately in Europe — will have less difficulties with its predominantly Italian foreign population than Germany with its Turks and Yugoslavs.

What stands behind this nearly universal difficulty? Certainly it is not simply the arrogance of Europeans, or Western Europeans, or white Europeans. Indeed Europe and its offspring come off best in the postwar world in their management to date of problems of multiethnicity.

In Africa and Asia, there have been murderous ethnic wars in Nigeria and the Indian subcontinent, and in other countries the expulsion with great cruelty of communities dubbed "foreign." Within India, the demand for the exclusive right to Assam by Assamese — and this has been preceded by other movements claiming the right to jobs and higher education and residence for various "sons of the soil" — makes the modest restrictions on working and residence that affect foreigners in Western Europe seem almost benign. It was not possible for Indian census-takers to enter Assam: it was not possible for oil to leave it. It is not possible often for any non-Assamese with business in Assam to leave the blockaded airport. And the unbending demand of the protesters — that all "foreigners" (that is, principally Bengalis) be expelled from the state — is impossible for the central government to accept. Yet Assam is only the most extreme example of growing movements in India to reserve jobs, educational opportunities, and the right to purchase land for the "sons of the soil," the ethnic group dominant in a given state. In India, generations are required before an immigrant group can be accepted as assimilated to the native ethnic group, leaving aside the question of whether immigrants and their descendants find such assimilation desirable in a society in which caste, linguistic, and cultural differences, including details of dress and cuisine and script, are given great significance.[2]

In Africa it is not only Indians who have been expelled (as from Uganda). Blacks of different tribe and citizenship have been pushed from one country to another, as each — within its quite artificial boundaries created by European empires — tries to reserve jobs and privileges for those who are considered "native." The oil-rich states of the Middle East, hungry for manpower, import it — as did the United States, Canada, and Australia in their days of expansion; but they deny citizenship even to those of closest kin, making a mockery of any idea of an "Arab nation," let alone of the idea of a Muslim, or a Third World, "brotherhood." Tribe is dominant — or, if not tribe in any reality, the new tribes created by boundaries drawn across the sand by Western powers.

In such cases, it is hard to make any sense of "racist" explanations, even if one is willing to include among racists non-white peoples. Social scientists tend to adopt a more sophisticated formulation. The conflict is over scarce goods everywhere — over jobs (and in particular good jobs); over access to housing and social services; over access to education. Depending on the relative position of native and migrant groups, these conflicts will center on different goods. In Western Europe, it seems, the issue of conflict over jobs is not so severe — the ethnic division of labor often means that natives and immigrants do not compete for the same jobs. The conflict over access to education has not yet developed: the immigrants' children are not yet numerous enough, or accomplished enough, to arouse any anxiety over competition for higher education. One wonders whether there is even conflict over elementary education, though when the numbers of immigrant children become too large in a given school, there is a tendency for the native Europeans to depart. Is this because they see the quality of education decline, or because they simply do not want their children to interact with immigrant children? There *is* conflict over social services — not because immigrants compete for social services, but because they may consume too large a share. Grumbling becomes overt and serious when there is a sudden influx of impoverished immigrants — as in the case of the Ugandan Indians in England.

It would appear at first blush that there is also conflict over housing. But is there? In each country, the immigrants inhabit different housing and different quarters from the natives. In France, they are to be found in the new housing projects on the outskirts of Paris; in Germany they are concentrated in old housing in the central cities; in England they are to be found in older council housing, or buying up poorer housing, or renting it, and are more in competition with each other than with Britons, who have better access to the modern council-housing stock.

In developing countries — in India, Africa, the Middle East — one sees clearer conflicts: over jobs and access to higher education in India (which has led to demands for reservations of public jobs and positions in colleges and universities for natives);

over land for housing. The conflict spreads into arguments over language. If English is used in government offices and higher education, all compete equally; if the native language replaces English, the migrants from other states are at a disadvantage. In Africa there are also conflicts over trading and job opportunities. In the Middle East, the huge returns from oil are reserved for the natives; and they are not willing to share their good fortune, even to build up the population of the state with other Arabs.

In the developing Third World incoming migrants often take the higher positions. They are the more energetic traders, the harder workers, the better-educated who take clerkships, posts with foreign firms and governments; and their children have opportunities at home and in background that make them superior competitors in education. The native population has the political power, and protects itself not simply by insisting on the rights of the "sons of the soil," but by exaggerating the differences in culture that justify the exclusion of newcomers.

In Western Europe, by contrast, most of the migrants take inferior positions. They do not compete for the better housing, or for subsidized housing (or only begin to do so after the native population is satisfied). The jobs they take are those the natives spurn. Their children are not yet ready to compete in school, and indeed present problems of educational backwardness rather than forwardness. Under these circumstances, why the conflict between old and new populations, natives and immigrants?

Social scientists are endlessly energetic in finding a hard material base to any conflict, and they have come forward to tell us that the cultural differences are really epiphenomenal. There is, they feel, "something else" at the "root" of the matter; and in this case it is not a less well endowed native population protecting itself against those who are better able to compete and may be dubbed "foreigners," but a better endowed native population exploiting less well endowed immigrants to preserve its superior access to scarce goods.

It is the scarcity, and the resulting conflict, this theory asserts, that accentuates the ethnic differences, which may be quite minor or hardly noticeable. But if a native group wants to reserve jobs, education, land, political power then it will exaggerate the differences that divide it from the immigrants; and the immigrants, often in self-defense, will exaggerate their own distinctions. Both will ascribe the cause of their conflict to cultural differences, when it is basically an issue of who will be getting access to scarce goods. Ethnic differences are one way of defining a restricted group that has the right to a reserved share of these scarce goods. "In short," writes Myron Weiner, describing the situation in India, "nativist movements convert cultural differences into cultural conflicts. Cultural conflicts should be viewed as the effects, not the cause of nativism."

Does this obtain in Europe? I do not think it does.

The areas of conflict over interests are hard to define or find, when there are such different paths and experiences for work, education, and housing for natives and immigrants; and the two rarely come into direct competition. But the absence of these direct conflicts does not prevent the rise and popularity among social scientists of "interest-conflict theories" to explain the strained relations between natives and immigrants.

The most popular theory asserts that the newcomers are victims of an "internal colonialism," and are now exploited by the advanced colonial powers in the metropolitan homeland, as they were when they inhabited the distant colonies. The chief exponent of the theory of internal colonialism is Michael Hechter, who has written a subtle and sophisticated book on the relations between Englishmen and the periphery of Scots, Welshmen, and Irish. He has developed a theory that is easily applicable to the current situation of natives and immigrant workers in England, or any Western European country. His aim is to explain regional conflicts within the countries of Western Europe; but the theory works as well to explain conflicts between any two ethnically discernible groups divided by different jobs, education, and residence. For we want to explain not only Welsh and Scottish nationalism, but the conflict between immigrant communities and native populations. Hechter writes:

The spatially uneven wave of modernization over state territory creates relatively advanced and less advanced groups. As a consequence of this initial fortuitous advantage, there is crystallization of the unequal distribution of resources and power between the two groups. The superordinate group, or core, seeks to stabilize and monopolize its advantages through policies aimed at the institutionalization of the existing stratification system. It attempts to regulate the allocation of social roles such that those roles commonly defined as having high prestige are reserved for its members. Conversely, individuals from the less advanced group are denied access to these roles. This stratification system, which may be termed a cultural division of labor, contributes to the development of distinctive ethnic identification in the two groups. Actors come to categorize themselves and others according to the range of roles each may be expected to play. They are aided in this categorization by the presence of visible signs, or cultural markers, which are seen to characterize both groups. At this stage, acculturation does not occur because it is not in the interests of the institutions within the core . . . [3]

The presentation is somewhat abstruse and involuted, but the argument leads to one conclusion: Welshmen and Scotsmen in the past — and West Indians, Pakistanis, and Indians today — do not become Englishmen; North Africans do not become Frenchmen; Yugoslavs and Turks do not become Germans — because it is not in the interests of the natives that they should. Now clearly this is a rather limited explanation of the reasons for the resurgence of ethnic identities and the heightening of ethnic tensions and conflicts; and Professor Hechter might agree that to some extent, this assimilation does not take place because the migrants to the core simply do not want to give up their identity. The "visible signs" or "cultural markers" of identity not only serve to mark them for positions inferior to the natives of the advanced center of these societies, but also serve as a means of mobilization. On occasion, indeed, the people of the periphery develop some advantage over the center — Scots because of the presence of offshore oil; Basques and Catalans because it is in their areas that Spanish industry has most effectively taken root. In these cases the "visible signs" and "cultural markers" serve to *defend* the interests of the peripheral groups, rather than to mark them off for "exploitation."

But is this what the whole matter of ethnicity reduces itself to? For one great tradition in contemporary social analysis, I am afraid it does. Incapable of dealing with culture or psychological factors except in the crudest fashion, Marxists and neo-Marxists (and many related traditions of social analysis) do see absolutely nothing else. The workers from the periphery are exploited, just as the workers of the center are. But under conditions of imperialism and colonial expansion it is possible to exploit one's own native workers somewhat less because colonial workers are being exploited more. A conflict of interest is built up between workers in imperialist states and in the colonies, in which the former see their advantage in keeping the latter down. And then the markers of ethnic identity will play a role in setting the boundaries between "less exploited" and "more exploited."

This familiar explanation undoubtedly contains a measure of truth; it is what it does not contain that makes me uncomfortable and makes the approach oversimple. Are the present migrant workers of Europe in truth "exploited"? If they are, they are just about the least exploited workers in history; and it makes one wonder about the sheer usefulness of the term. They come voluntarily; they leave areas which offer few good jobs, and have no or low social benefits and only limited education; and they come to countries where, as far as working conditions are concerned, they are put on the same level as native workers, in terms of wages and hours, social benefits, unemployment insurance, child allowances.

The language of "exploitation" is popular among Western social scientists. But it is hard to see how it applies to the guest-workers of Germany, or to the new immigrant communities of England, or even to the immigrant workers of France. It is true these workers take jobs native Western Europeans do not want; but these are not by their nature inferior jobs; and in any case, they are the jobs that limited training, or education, or facility in the language of the country make necessary or inevitable. It is always a matter of wonder to the American visitor to Europe that these "inferior" jobs consist of driving a bus in London, cleaning the parks in Paris, working on construction in France, cleaning the streets in Germany, working on the assembly lines of automobile plants. All of these jobs happen to be, in the

United States, because of their good pay or long-term security, very desirable. Exploitation? Whatever meaning one gives the term it is hard to see how it applies to voluntary choices, made by people who have other choices—for example, the choice to stay at home.

One can of course make a more elaborate analysis to shore up the exploitation thesis—for example, that West Indians, Indians, Pakistanis, Portuguese, Spaniards, Italians, Greeks, Yugoslavs, and Turks must leave their homes because of the general exploitation by the more advanced countries, who either held them as colonies or exploit them through unfair terms of trade, or the like. But it is hard for me to accept this unlikely and far-fetched analysis. Portugal, Spain, and Turkey until recently had their own empires; and if they are badly off it may be less because they are exploited by today's neocolonialists than because they allowed their empires to drain and divert them. And Sweden and Switzerland, devoid of colonies or imperial adventures (for the last few hundred years, in any case) have very large concentrations of foreign workers. Have these, too, been driven by exploitation into the arms of new exploiters?

But what is perhaps most difficult to accept in the theory of ethnicity as evoked and supported by conflicts of interest between more or less exploited workers is that there are such real and hard phenomena as cultural, religious, and linguistic interests—and these are interests taken seriously by people.

And on both sides. The Turkish workers want to maintain the religious upbringing of their children; the Indians and Pakistanis are concerned about retaining language and religion (and modesty for girls); and so it goes for each and every group.[4] In the event that the two cultures are very far apart, with migrants differing from those among whom they live in language, in religion, and also in race, then there is a strong feeling of threat. But even Portuguese and Spanish workers in France, who are Catholic in religion, and who do speak a related Romance language, find there is much that they value and would have to give up in order to become assimilated Frenchmen. Even more unhappy, of course, are North Africans and Turks.

And on the indigenous side, is it only the sense of threat to established material interests that disturbs native Europeans? A near majority of Swiss were ready to vote for extreme measures to expel foreign workers, an expulsion that would undoubtedly have hurt the Swiss economy rather than helped it. The German parent who sees his child in a classroom with increasing numbers of foreign children worries about how good an education the child will really be getting. The Frenchman, no matter how liberal and enlightened, is concerned over how well his child will be learning French in a classroom dominated by foreigners.[5]

Nor is this all. European natives can see clouds on the horizon, clouds that have precious little to do with competition over concrete interests. What of the second generation? The immigrant parents want their children to learn ancestral languages and traditions; but progress in their new countries demands effective education in those countries' language and customs. How can, how do, the schools manage both? And if they do not, and cannot, and if the children begin to drop out of school without credentials, will not Europe in the 1980s be somewhat in the position of the United States in the 1950s, when the "social dynamite" of black youth (growing up in Northern and Western American cities, and to new aspirations) created an explosive situation?

What happened in the United States — and turned large parts of our American cities into wastelands of arson, drugs, and crime — must surely be of concern in Europe.

Alas, while the United States offers a terrible example, it has little to suggest as to means to avoid it. Ray C. Rist, who has studied problems of school integration in the United States, has also studied the guest-workers of Germany, concentrating on educational issues. One would think our own multicultural and multiethnic country would have at least something to offer Germany, and Rist is quite convinced it does; but it is not at all clear what he is proposing. His argument is that Germany must accept the American model, or so I understand it: "Succinctly, it is the basic thesis of this book that Germany has become a multicultural society with an ever growing number of persons who claim social and cultural identity-traits from their mother country as well as from Germany, the country of immigration. What have emerged are people who are Turkish-German, Yugoslav-German, Greek-German, and the like."[6] There is nothing odd about Turkish-American, Yugoslav-American, Greek-American. We are, after all, a multiethnic country in which "American" has no distinctive and unique ethnic meaning any more; and thus any kind of American is as good as any other, as even President Reagan has assured us. But *Turkish-German, Yugoslav-German, Greek-German*? I suspect it will sound as odd in German as it sounds in English.

And how does one adapt to this multiethnicity, particularly in dealing with that most difficult problem, the second generation? The first generation, after all, has come basically for self-improvement; it does not expect, I would hazard, a full identity with the country of immigration, and it is satisfied with the opportunity to work, to earn money (and send remittances home), with basic social benefits, and with elementary justice and protection, all of which Europe generally provides.

The second generation is a different matter. It expects more. But how to satisfy these expectations is not simple. Will an education identical to that given natives satisfy them? Not likely. Though some immigrant children, either because of class or culture, do as well as natives or better—Jews, Japanese, Chinese, and now Vietnamese in the United States, for example; the children of political refugees almost everywhere; perhaps the children of Indians in England—most immigrant children fall behind. Should it, then, be an education that emphasizes the native language in the expectation (or hope) that these children are still only "temporary" settlers? Not too wise. Whatever their parents may think, they are probably not going back. Can it, then, be a training that combines both? But does not that load so much on the children that they will fail at both?

If these alternatives are unsatisfactory, what is not? This is Professor Rist's dilemma. He is censorious of *all* German efforts to deal with the education of immigrant children. Thus, he suggests four possible options: (1) define the children as "guests" who will return to their homeland, and educate them for that;

(2) define them as "new Germans," and give them a fully German education; (3) define them as "hyphenated Germans" (the concept of "hyphenated American," in the form of "German-American," and so on, is common in the United States), and seek some synthesis of the first two extremes. And then he presents a last option (which seems to me not very different from the third): "There is a fourth policy option, one that seems untenable. This is to approach the education of the children as if two spirits and selves were within one body. Unfortunately that is precisely what seems to be the thrust of current German educational policy. The children are considered Germans for the period of German instruction and foreigners for the instruction of the mother tongue and life in the homeland."[7]

Rist seems to believe there is a way of blending the two elements that avoids options one, two, three, and four, that avoids the danger too of overloading the students, and that gives the best chance of avoiding an undereducated, barely employable, discontented, and dangerous second generation. One must, in all fairness, point out that many Germans he quotes are equally critical of whatever Germans are trying to do in this difficult situation.

But it does seem hard on Bavaria, for example, which offers all possible options (German, foreign or mixed education), that Rist should be strongly critical of all. One wonders what could be considered satisfactory? His model for Germany is the United Statess; not just as it exists, but as its most progressive exponents of meticulous sharing of rights and benefits equally among all groups would want it to be. And yet I note that when Europeans do what is applauded for the United States, Rist is still censorious. Thus, he writes of one Bavarian program: "To assume that taking no more than eight hours a week of German as a foreign language will prepare the student for moving into German-language classes and functioning on a par in content and curriculum with German age-mates is questionable, to say the least. More likely, it is a pedagogical disaster."[8]

This struck me with particular force because I had just visited bilingual programs for the children of Spanish-speaking parents in New York City, programs mandated under a U.S.

court order at the demand of representatives of the Puerto Rican community — and these programs also require no more than eight hours a week of English. Are they, too, a mandate for disaster? I think so. But I wonder whether Rist would think so, when these are after all the programs that have emerged from what, as far as we can tell, are the actual demands of the leaders of the Puerto Rican community in New York?

The whole issue is certainly more complicated for Germany and for France than it is for the United States. Many of the immigrants will "go back" — or so they say. Should this be taken seriously? Or should they be released from the limbo that progressives decry? Should Europe begin to model itself on the United States, so that the status of Briton, Frenchman, or German is no longer an ethnic status, but only a formal political status? And even if Europe should adopt this course, can it fulfill it?

In another place Professor Rist writes that, from the point of view of the schools, "there is little that can be done to make one a Bavarian if he/she is not already . . . " One senses a criticism of the schools, and their too moderate ambition. But how *does* one make a Bavarian of a Turk or Yugoslav — when it is no simple matter even to make a Bavarian of a Swabian, a Rhinelander, or a Prussian? The identities we deal with are multiple and complex, and if some are identified with the core of the nation — its culture, its history, its language, and its dialects — then the problem of the status of immigrant groups is clearly far more than a matter of (as Hechter argues, and Rist suggests) maintaining an "exploited group" in a "lower status."

And so we are left with the dilemma. Should European countries change, and begin to model themselves on the United States, Canada, Australia, in dealing with multiethnicity and multiracialism? (Note that the terms "New Canadian" and "New Australian" seem to be accepted with full assurance both by immigrants of any ethnic group or race and by natives.) Can they? It seems to be countries of Anglo-Saxon origin that are able to perform this extraordinary trick, and Britain seems to be closer to doing it than France or Germany. But even if Europe succeeds, does that solve its problems? If cultural distances are too great, prejudices too widespread, levels of training and education too diverse, do we not have "a recipe for disaster," whatever the schools try to do, whatever the laws dictate for equality and more than equality?

This is the chilling prospect before Europe as it looks at the United States. Whatever our success in overcoming the legal presumption of ethnic superiority for one group, we have not been able to bring all groups to a level of approximate social and economic equality. European immigrant groups, even those from traditional peasant backgrounds who came without skills and education, now participate on an equal level in all aspects of American society. Older Asian groups (Chinese, Japanese) now do so; and the newer Asian groups (Indian, Korean, Vietnamese) seem to be following in the path of the old. Blacks do not. Puerto Ricans do not. Whatever the reasons — prejudice, discrimination, experience, expectation, resentment — Europe must fear that even if it succeeds in "assimilating" the children of immigrants of distant cultures to a common political status, it will be no simple matter to make them "equal" in other crucial respects.

Perhaps Europe can learn from the United States what we have not yet learned from our own experience and our own efforts. As for the rest of the world, in which multiethnic states, new and old, are struggling with the problem of cultural and economic conflict, it still has much to learn from the Western democratic commitment to fairness and equality which, with whatever difficulties, prevails within the liberal constitutional framework of the developed First World.

[1981]

V

AMERICA NOW

16

The Politics of a

Multiethnic Society

IN 1970, viewing the condition of politics in New York City for the second edition of *Beyond the Melting Pot*, Daniel P. Moynihan and I described two paradigms, which we dubbed for convenience a Northern and a Southern. We might more specifically have defined them as the Northern urban pattern and some selected aspects of Southern political reality as it emerged between the end of Reconstruction and the success of the Civil Rights Act and the Voting Rights Act in bringing blacks into the pattern of Southern politics. We described the two patterns— and it should be recalled that we were writing in the midst of the explosion of racial violence in Northern and Western cities that marked the later 1960s and that only came to an end at the beginning of the 1970s—as follows:

We now have as alternatives two models of group relations, which we will name the Northern and the Southern. Both reject a total assimilation in which group reality disappears. In the Southern model, society is divided into two segments, black and white. The line between them is rigidly drawn. Other groups must choose to which segment they belong, even if . . . they do not really want to belong to either. Violence is the keynote of relations between the groups. And "separate but equal" is an ideology if not a reality.

The Northern model is quite different. There are many groups.

They differ in wealth, power, occupation, values, but in effect an open society prevails for individuals and for groups. Over time a substantial and rough equalization of wealth and power can be hoped for . . . and each group participates sufficiently in the goods and values and social life of a common society so that all can accept the common society as good and fair. There is competition between groups, as between individuals, but it is muted, and groups compete not through violence but through effectiveness in organization and achievement. Groups and individuals participate in a common society. Individual choice, not law or rigid custom, determines the degree to which any person participates, if at all, in the life of an ethnic group . . . This is at any rate the ideal — prejudice and discrimination often force people into closer association with groups than they wish.[1]

I will not suggest that there is anything timeless about this contrast: as I have indicated, it was written, if I may be hyperbolic, in the blaze of Northern urban ghettos, and at a time when the slogan "separate but equal," under which whites had kept down blacks, had been startlingly resurrected by Northern blacks under the cry "black power," which in its concrete details emphasized both separation from all whites, even potential allies, and an insistence on a turf in which blacks could wield independent power.

And yet, despite the limitations of our now twelve-year-old formulation, there is much merit in it, if one replaces the emphasis we placed on *violence* in our description of the Southern pattern by another feature that equally connects the pre-civil-rights-revolution South and the post-civil-rights-revolution United States: *law*. Law today specifically defines the rights and privileges and burdens of two groups, which are assumed to encompass all of society: One is a favored group, the other a disfavored one. Pre-civil-rights Southern law protected the privileges of the white group; post-civil-rights national law protects the interests of the black group, and some others. With this modification, I will argue that one can see the present situation in group relations as one that is still understandable in terms of a conflict between the two patterns, with the rise, in the sidelines, of what we may murkily discern as a third, complicating pattern.

We have thus seen an evolution of the Southern pattern, in the 1970s, into a rather more benign form, but still one marked off from the Northern urban pattern. But we are now moving into a situation in which a third pattern is emerging — shall we call it the Western? — and we may expect now a tripolar struggle between different ways of conceiving and adapting to American ethnic diversity.

One possible pattern, a model to which liberals and nationalists once aspired — that of assimilation, pure and simple, in which racial group is a matter of indifference to government and scarcely salient to actors in politics — simply does not seem to be in the cards for a while. Each of the three patterns that have replaced it operates instead on the reality that we are not a homogeneous society, ethnically or racially or religiously, and that the conflicts of class and interest that dominate all democratic politics are in the American situation affected by a clash of ethnic and racial and religious interests which are not simply reflections of economic position. They are interests that in part are based on the dominant socioeconomic characteristics of each group but which also reflect in varying degrees values of each group which themselves become interests. In what way, for example, can we interpret the now severe conflicts over abortion and school prayer, or over school busing, as conflicts based on *economic* interests? Indeed, on occasion we see people acting directly against their economic interests to realize their value objectives. The opponents of abortion are predominantly white upper working class and lower middle class, and the supporters are the more educated and more liberal parts of the population. Yet opposition to government-funded abortion means more infants added to the welfare population, and higher taxes for the working and middle classes. Thus opponents of government-funded abortion act against their economic interests. But this has hardly moderated the intensity of opposition to abortion. Similarly, the intensity of passions over such value issues as prayer and gun control can hardly be given an economic meaning, and there is only limited economic significance to the fierce opposition to busing that rends many communities.

But to return to our two patterns: The Southern pattern takes for granted the primacy of *one* central division in society, between white and black. The white South was ethnically much more homogeneous than the rest of the country, with only moderate infusions of European immigrants and very few Chinese and Japanese immigrants to complicate the stark black-white division. Where there were European ethnic groups (for example, Italians in New Orleans, Jews in many cities) they simply became part of the white majority, willy-nilly. They shared in the advantages given by legal segregation and formal discrimination, and similarly American Indians and Chinese were assimilated by white prejudice and insistence into the lower black caste.

Inevitably such a stark division in society meant that every issue had to be seen in black and white terms, in both senses, and since one group was held down in an inferior position, violence, whether exercised legally as in the practices of the police force or illegally through lynching and threat, was part of the political reality. When we argued in 1970 that the Southern pattern was moving North, we had in mind the spread of inter-racial violence as exemplified in the riots. But this was not an essential part of the Southern pattern. What was essential was the sharp division of society into two groups, and the significance of law in defining the rights and privileges of each. Law in the South codified relations; we now have a national system of law affecting the relations of groups in various spheres. But looking back at the original distinction we made, I would argue that one evidence of the migration of the Southern pattern into the North and West is that intergroup relations, once regulated by custom, and custom that hardly dared to pronounce publicly the specific roles and expectations that guided intergroup relations, is now defined in law. The law in question is very different from the law that governed black-white relations and kept blacks in an inferior position in the South: It is a law designed to achieve equality and not to ensure dominance. But it shares one thing with that earlier law: It names groups, and because the groups are named, individuals inevitably become beneficiaries or nonbeneficiaries of law specifically because of group membership. As that previous Southern law did, it defines who has the right to claim the benefits of membership in a group, and who must accept the lack of benefit because he is defined as part of another group. The Southern pattern to my mind is exemplified by the fact that there are two groups, one a group that is to be benefited, another a group that is to be deprived of benefits.

The complication created in the North and West (and, with increasing immigration and economic growth, in the South, too) is that as against simply two groups, there are in reality many groups. There are thus groups that must be added to the benefited group (Asians, Hispanics) whose "right" to be so included is challengeable; and groups incorporated into the nonbenefited category who attack and criticize their placement (Italians, Poles, Jews) and indeed some of whom are able to get themselves shifted from the nonbenefited to the benefited group (Asian Indians).

I suggest the term "Western" (or "Southwestern"?) pattern for this developing situation of *two* groups of groups, the benefited and the nonbenefited, because it is in the Western states that the first complications of applying the Southern pattern first came into view. Thus, quite early in desegregation cases the question arose, are the Hispanics to be considered majority or minority? If the first, then it was possible to have "desegregated" schools in which black and Hispanic together made up the entire student body. If the latter, there were new complications. When the groups to be desegregated rose to three, two of which were themselves a combination of other groups (the Hispanic and the Asian, as in San Francisco) the problem became even more complicated.

Let me summarize the three patterns in terms of the way they envisage the group structure of society. The Northern pattern sees American society as a mixture of many groups, which can be ranged along many spectra, of which perhaps the most significant are those of income and occupation. But there are other spectra, too—for example, political influence. It was characteristic of the developing urban political patterns in the North that groups that were far from the top in occupational status and income did become dominant — for example, the Irish in Boston and in other cities. Associated with this multigroup spectrum was a system of law that did not recognize differences among groups, a system of law that aimed at formal blindness to ethnic, racial, and religious difference. This is not to say that the law was not used to advance the interests of one group or another. In Boston, when the Irish became politically dominant, the state legislature, still dominanted by Yankee Protestants, created the Finance Commission to watch closely the operations of Boston city government, and deprived Boston of a considerable measure of self-government. One could say that Yankee Protestants were through law reducing the power and independence of Irish Catholics — but the law itself adhered to universal forms and did not specify Irish Catholics as the deprived, Yankee Protestants as the benefited. In one case law did differentiate among the various groups by name — in immigration law — but that was considered, from the 1920s on, an egregious case of group discrimination, finally removed in 1965. The Northern pattern, then, assumes a spectrum of groups, and law that is blind in distinguishing among them.

The Southern pattern, in contrast, envisages two groups, and the law has never been blind between them. For centuries the law specified an inferior position for one group, and then, almost immediately, with no period of color-blindness intervening, it specified a position of special protection. Perhaps this was inevitable. Since blacks had been separated from whites in schools, there might have been no other way of overcoming that heritage of separation than by specifying the proportions of white and black that would be allowable in each school. Or, since blacks had been deprived of political representation, there might have been no other way of assuring political representation than by requiring close federal examination of every state and local action affecting elections. Whether or not in these two cases this was the best course, or the right course, it was the course that came into existence and in varying degrees spread throughout the country.

I have argued that we now see emerging a Western or Southwestern pattern, one that is distinguished from the Northern pattern with its spectrum of groups. If there are more than one or two disfavored groups, complications arise that mean the Southern pattern cannot apply. One reason is that the disfavored are disfavored in varying degrees, on the basis of different histories, and different legal statuses. The American Indians have a unique status in that they are the only group with a sharp definition and a governmental policing of its boundaries. American Indians may these days be the beneficiaries of substantial sums in compensation for having been deprived of their land. Tribes may possess important natural resources. Who is an Indian, and who is not, and of what tribe, becomes important in defining these beneficiaries. They are also beneficiaries of affirmative action policies, but these pale in significance when compared with the substantial sums to which individuals may have a legal claim as a consequence of tribal membership.

Hispanics are a congeries of groups, each with different legal, social, economic, and political characteristics. The Puerto Ricans are in an ambiguous condition of citizenship: They are full citizens on the mainland, but of a special status if they live in Puerto Rico—and a simple passage in either direction shifts them from one to the other, and as often as they move from island to mainland, so often is their political status changed. Mexican Americans have various statuses—from old settlers (some with special treaty protection), to recent immigrant citizens, to immigrants legally domiciled, to illegal immigrants. As a group they stand higher than the Puerto Ricans economically and exercise more political influence. Cubans are another special category, perhaps closest to earlier European immigrants. They began as political refugees, and their middle-class social status (and perhaps the additional benefits they receive from government as favored political refugees) has rapidly moved them above Puerto Ricans and Mexican Americans, in occupation, income, and, where they are sufficiently concentrated, political influence. It is unnecessary to move through other groups of Hispanics who are becoming numerically important in one or another part of the country—Dominicans, Nicaraguans, Salvadoreans, Colombians, and others, for each of whom a slightly different story must be told.

And finally, consider the multiplicity of Asian groups and their varying socioeconomic positions and histories. Asians were first included in affirmative action programs because there had been a history of severe legal discrimination against Chinese and Japanese, and because they, like blacks, were of nonwhite race. Presumably consistency required that all nonwhite races that had suffered official discrimination be included among the protected groups. I am less clear about why they were included as protected groups in the renewal of the Voting Rights Act of 1975, since there was, I believe, no evidence that where their numbers permitted (as in Hawaii) they suffered from political discrimination or underrepresentation.

Whatever the justification for including Asians as beneficiaries of legislation and regulation that was devised along the Southern pattern primarily to raise the position of blacks, matters become much muddier when we add to the Chinese and Japanese — who were almost all the Asians we had at the time of the major civil rights legislation of the mid-1960s — substantial and rapidly growing communities of Filipinos, Koreans, Asian Indians, Vietnamese, and some smaller Asian groups, of varying legal status and socioeconomic position.

Thus the first distinguishing characteristic of the new Western or Southwestern pattern is that we have swept up under the rubric of the protected group a range of groups, some of whose rights to special benefit and protection are disputed by others, both among the protected and the nonprotected. This differentiates the new pattern from the Southern pattern.

And differentiating the Western from the Northern pattern is the fact that these new ethnic strains added to our national mix do not form a part of a single multiethnic spectrum: Both because of law and because of other factors that I will explore, there is a break between the white majority, whatever the number of ethnic groups into which it can be divided, and the new immigrant groups of different race and cultural background.

This break reflects the fact that the dominant European ethnic groups completed their immigration to this country almost sixty years ago. European immigration then came to a halt for more than two decades. When it resumed in the years after World War II, it was moderate in size, and the new immigrants — Irish, Germans, Italians, Jews, Poles, Ukrainians — in large measure either affiliated themselves with the ethnic groups that had been established here decades before, or rapidly assimilated. In the old immigrant areas of first settlement in the Northeastern cities there were indeed new immigrants in the 1950s and 1960s from the countries of Europe that had fed the immigration before the 1920s, but these new arrivals did not become nationally visible, and there was no reason to think that the forces of economic and political mobility and cultural and religious change that had affected earlier immigrants from their countries and made them into assimilated Americans would not operate on them.

The situation since the mid-1960s that has strengthened a nascent Western or Southwestern pattern is of a different type. The figures themselves tell the story. In the 1960s there were 1.6 million European and Canadian immigrants, and in the 1970s only 957,000, while Asian immigration jumped from 362,000 in the 1960s to 1.5 million in the 1970s. Immigration from Mexico rose from 432,000 to 624,000, immigration from South America only from 219,000 to 266,000 — but we are all aware that substantial numbers of illegal immigrants have come from Latin America. Even immigration from Africa, only 33,000 in the 1960s rose to 87,000 in the 1970s.

The point of these figures is that the shift from European and Canadian sources of immigration to Latin American, Asian, and African must create a new and different multiethnic pattern. The new pattern mirrors neither the Northern, which had as its social base European immigrants, who expected to and were expected to assimilate, nor the Southern, with its stark black-white gulf based on the history of slavery and casteism.

What are the consequences of this change for the American political pattern? Large consequences I will leave for my conclusion. But one consequence is the clash between at least the first two conceptions, with equally indignant responses by those raised in the Northern pattern and those who are utilizing the

new conceptions that arose out of the Southern pattern to over-
turn Northern assumptions and practices. A revealing conflict
took place over the redistricting of council seats in New York
City in 1981, which led a federal court to suspend New York's
primary election and the Supreme Court to confirm this judgment on the very eve of the election. There have been many
suspensions of elections in Southern cities over similar
issues — how to redistrict to guarantee a certain number of seats
for blacks, or conflicts over at-large and district seats, or
conflicts over annexations that could dilute black votes. They
received little national attention. It was understood that in the
context of the Southern pattern, where white stood arrayed
against black and national power was inserted to help blacks,
such conflicts should occur, with interventions to increase black
power and reduce white power (I leave aside the question of
whether this assumption was always justified).[2]

The North is a rather more complex matter, as I have
argued, and its complexity, when the Voting Rights Act was
used to cover three of the five counties of New York City, was
already revealed when Hasidic Jews charged that a redistricting
intended to increase the number of black congressional seats
from Brooklyn had, by splitting the Hasidic community into
two districts, reduced *their* political power: A third party had
entered the suit (any close study of the situation would undoubtedly have revealed many more groups with the potential
to enter). In the event, the Supreme Court upheld the redistricting, a new district designed to produce a new black congressman came into being — and this district then regularly
voted into office a Jewish manufacturer, even though on occasion excellent black candidates attempted to replace him. The
stark black-white conflict had been complicated not only by the
Hasidic community but by the fact that white candidates could
appeal, against the assumptions of the Southern pattern, to
black voters — just as in North and West the reverse has occurred, with black candidates winning in majority white districts.

The present New York City situation is even more complex.
There are in play not only a variety of racial and ethnic groups

(blacks and Puerto Ricans in particular) but also strictly political considerations, such as the desire of incumbent councilmen to preserve their seats under redistricting. The New York City council redistricting was a classic case of black, white, and Puerto Rican incumbents defending themselves against challengers, black, white, and Puerto Rican, by using the time-tested forms of gerrymandering, a technique that goes back to Massachusetts long before there were immigrant communities, blacks, or Puerto Ricans to complicate the issue. The mayor of New York knew that in the new situation he had to protect his flank against minority attacks—and did, or so he thought. Leading blacks, including Congressman Charles E. Rangel, Kenneth B. Clark, a distinguished community leader, and Herman D. Farrell, the Manhattan Democratic leader (the successor to the great Tammany chieftains), all supported the redistricting, as did the Puerto Rican Councilman Gilberto Gerena-Valentin. Gerena-Valentin changed his mind and sued (as did others) on grounds of violation of the Voting Rights Act.[3]

What is clear in the New York City case is that there was no simple ganging-up of whites against blacks—the characteristic situation the Voting Rights Act was designed to prevent. What happened was a new chapter in the lengthy and complex interplay among ethnicity, political interest, and public interest in New York City. It was claimed that the percentage of seats that would go to blacks and Puerto Ricans would be too small under redistricting in view of their substantial increase as a proportion of the population of New York City in ten years, and that the percentage of seats that would go to whites would be too large in view of the fact that *their* proportion in the city population had dropped greatly since 1970.

The law permitted these challenges, the suspension of elections at a cost of millions of dollars, and the introduction of a great deal of confusion that would undoubtedly—against the very intention of the law—*reduce* substantially the numbers voting in the primary or primaries when they eventually took place. The situation to which it was applied had nothing to do with the intention of the law, and was covered by what can only be considered accident. The law set a simple statistical standard for federal intervention, 50 percent of eligibles voting in a presidential election. But because low proportions of blacks and Puerto Ricans register and vote in New York City, it is very difficult for the high-minority boroughs to show 50 percent of eligibles voting. Thus they fall under the act.

But there is a serious problem when the act is employed. There is no way of guaranteeing that almost *any* percentage of blacks or Puerto Ricans will produce a black or Puerto Rican candidate. Councilman Theodore Silverman was chairman of the committee that approved the new districting; he himself represents a district that is majority black and Puerto Rican. Three adjacent districts, represented by two blacks and one Puerto Rican, had lost population. His had gained (a characteristic pattern for the 1970s, for while the black and Puerto Rican population had *increased*, the population of black and Puerto Rican districts had *declined* as blacks and Puerto Ricans spread to new sections of the city). Silverman asked, "So what would you add to those other districts? . . . Some blacks from Mr. Silverman's district? or some whites?" He had given up some blacks, he said, and the result had been to leave him with a district that was 60 percent black and Hispanic. "The rule-of-thumb minimum for a black or Puerto Rican district is 70 percent, according to the council's map-makers."[4]

This rule of thumb is dependent on two factors: First, there is a huge age difference between white and black and Hispanic populations in New York City and in other central cities, children under eighteen cannot vote, and young people generally in their twenties and thirties do not vote as much as older people. But secondly, there are great differences in proportions of each group enrolled, and fewer voting-age blacks vote in New York than in Mississippi. This is an old story, known to every politician, long preceding the Voting Rights Act and quite impervious to its intentions or assistance. Arthur Klebanoff points out in an unpublished paper that between 1950 and 1965 blacks and Puerto Ricans increased from 9 to 29 percent of the Brooklyn population, but this had almost no impact on representation: "The remnants of the older political machinery, once broad-based, continued to control Brooklyn politics as late as

1966. Jews and Italians ran the stores, owned the apartments, and filled the political clubhouses. This was to be expected. The surprise was the absence of any competing Negro or Puerto Rican organizations. Jews and Italians continued in office long after the districts they represented became predominantly Negro and Puerto Rican."[5]

What is even more surprising is that further massive increases in the percentage of black and Puerto Rican population in the fifteen years since 1966 have not been accompanied by any substantial increase in minority representation. The roots of this phenomenon must be explored, and they cannot be overcome by the brute intervention of a hardly relevant Voting Rights Act. The realities that have created this situation are the demographic characteristics of minority and white populations, the failure for whatever reasons of blacks and Puerto Ricans to equal the economic and skill resources of the old immigrant populations, and perhaps some problems in organization in these communities that have cultural and historical roots. The Irish got into politics immediately and with great effect. Jews did not, and only in recent decades have they been playing a substantial political role in the city in which they were for a long time the largest ethnic group. (Abraham Beame, elected in 1973, was, astonishingly, the first Jewish mayor of New York.) There are reasons for these substantial differences. They have no relation to the assumptions of the Voting Rights Act.

And the situation Klebanoff described in 1966 persists. *The Wall Street Journal* asserted in an editorial in 1981: "Last year, 59.5% of all voting-age blacks in Misssissippi voted, as did 51.3% of all voting-age blacks in South Carolina. The comparable figures were 40.4% for New York, and 38.4% for Massachusetts."[6] Thus, even under the best of intentions to increase black and Puerto Rican representation, and it is agreed that these intentions were hardly dominant, it would be hard to see what kind of voting system in New York City could represent blacks and Puerto Ricans in any proportion within hailing distance of their percentage of the city population. If redistricting was arranged to concentrate minorities up to 70 percent, it could be argued they were being concentrated in classic fashion

to reduce their influence. And even if such redistricting occurred, and if Puerto Ricans and blacks were divided in the
district, what was to prevent a politically astute white with
money or political attractiveness or both from gaining the seat?

The New York Times in an editorial in 1981 pointed to the
complexities of determining what was fair, or indeed what was
effective, in redistricting. Silverman had given up some blacks
in his new district.

Was the change intended to promote a white man's chances for re-
election? Without the change, the district would have become even
more black. Or was moving the black voters to the adjacent district
intended to promote a black woman's chance for re-election? Many
whites have moved into her district since 1970, reducing the black
plurality that had elected Mary Pinkett.

Should fairness be measured by how many districts are likely to
elect minority candidates, or by how many contain more nonwhites
than whites? The two can be quite different. Poorer black and
Hispanic voters concentrated in some areas are less likely to vote than
middle-class voters in others. And minority voters who do turn out
may prefer a white candidate. Despite efforts to create a black state
assembly seat in central Harlem, Edward Sullivan, a white, keeps on
winning.[7]

The newspapers explored well the complexities involved in
applying the Southern pattern to the Northern mosaic, but even
so they left aside three other complexities: splits within each of
the groups,[8] splits between the two minority groups, and differential interests among the whites. It is hardly likely that in the
complexities of New York City politics the issue in the city
council was seen as one of only "whites" against "minorities." It
could not have been a matter of indifference whether that white
was Jewish, Italian, or Irish. But since all whites had been reduced by the Southern simplicities of the Voting Rights Act to
the position of homogeneous defendants, no one explored these
complexities. They were not at issue legally, significant as they
may have been in affecting some of the redistricting.

Is the distinction between the Southern pattern and the
Northern pattern more than academic? Is it of significance for

the actual condition of blacks and Hispanics that a Southern mode overtakes a Northern mode? I believe it is. The Southern mode forces everything into the courts and into a context of rights and wrongs: In the courts one side is right, and the other is wrong; there are no alternatives. Outside the courts, there is bargaining and negotiation. How does a minority bargain, one might ask. The fact is, in the Northern pattern each group is a minority among other minorities. And no minority, in a situation where procedural equality prevails, where all have access to the ballot, where all have access to the schools and colleges, and in particular the law schools, is fully powerless. There are areas in which a group, even a small group and a poor one, is dominant, and has influence — like the Hasidic Jews in Williamsburg. To push the question of the practical significance of the two patterns further, which is more helpful: a decision from a court that one is right, or an outcome to a negotiation in which one gets something — a new housing project or school, a nomination for an assembly seat, a promise of a job as an assistant D.A.? I have described the common coin of the Northern pattern. Negotiation is not ruled out in the Southern pattern. One can still negotiate before, during, and after a court decides one is right or wrong. But this pattern does encourage a different kind of combat, a different kind of stance. An adversary lawyer working for a foundation- or public-funded legal defense organization is a very different kind of battering ram with which to expand the opportunities of a group than a community leader. For one thing, he is likely to be of a different ethnic group, not to live in the community, to have a rather abstract idea of how it may be advanced, and not to make it easy to negotiate and compromise.

Clearly, in the South of the 1940s, 1950s, and 1960s, and perhaps even the 1970s, that is just what was wanted: Since negotiation and compromise in a situation of political powerlessness would get nowhere, it was essential to appeal to Constitution and law, to fight the crucial issues through the courts, and one wanted the best lawyer, rather than the best representative of the people (not that there is necessarily a division between the two — it depends on the circumstances).

I believe the political process that in the end made way for the Jews, the Italians, the Poles, and the other immigrant groups of the second immigration would in time, did in time, make way for the blacks and the Puerto Ricans. The process will not come to an end because we now have national laws based on the experience of the South to which new groups can appeal. But it is also true that when another and apparently more effective way is opened up, an older way tends to fall into a certain degree of disuse. And that will have consequences, too.

The political problem of Northern blacks today is not a problem of formal inequality through rule, or actual inequality through custom. The polls are open, the courts are open, the civil service is open — indeed, under the new affirmative action measures of recent years, more than open — the colleges and law schools are open. Despite all this, there is a severe problem, one best symbolized by the remarkably low registration and voting figures of blacks in the Northern cities, much lower, as we have seen, than the percentages in the South. The matter is mystifying. It cannot be explained by the fact that the blacks are such a small minority in the Northern cities that politics are for them a futile path to the advancement of group interests. Indeed, blacks form as high or higher a percentage of the population in Northern cities as in Mississippi and South Carolina, where they are far more active at the polls. Nor is the problem poverty: The blacks of the Southern states are no more prosperous. Nor is it poor education: The blacks of the North are better educated. Nor is it that there are no models to encourage political participation: There have been major models in the form of prominent black congressmen, assemblymen, councilmen, state officials for a good forty years or more.

I hesitate to suggest reasons for this remarkable phenomenon. Perhaps one reason is the rise of federally funded poverty organizations in the 1960s which were for the most part limited to blacks and minorities, and which gave jobs and access to federal funds. These may have been seen as a more desirable way of advancement, and traditional politics as a result may have been neglected. As these programs decline in access to funds and are wound down, we may see a new rise in involvement in traditional politics. Perhaps, too, another factor that discouraged involvement in local politics was the fact that the national government for twenty years was the standard-bearer of minority rights: The federal largesse was such that it seemed more valuable to enter the federal civil service in the newer programs than to start out on the hard career of local political representation. A leadership cadre that had been available to earlier ethnic groups in the days when the federal government did almost nothing for the cities may have been drawn off into federal office holding. Once again, the refusal of the Reagan administration to continue in the line of the Kennedy, Johnson, Nixon, Ford, and Carter administrations may force a rebirth of black and Hispanic participation in local politics.[9]

I have suggested that a third pattern is visible on the horizon, which I have dubbed Western or Southwestern. What are the characteristics of this pattern?

1. The newer groups are more distant in culture, language, and religion from white Americans, whether of the old or new immigration, than these were from each other. We now have groups that are in American terms rather more exotic than any before. Added to the Chinese and Japanese are now Filipinos, Koreans, Asian Indians, Vietnamese, Cambodians, Laotians, Pacific Islanders, many of them speaking languauges unconnected to the languages of Europe, many practicing religions that have had very few representatives in this country (though there are many Christians among them), and most of racial or ethnic stocks distant from the European. The largest of these new groups is the Mexican, which does not qualify as exotic in these ways, but when one takes into account the substantial Indian component in the Mexican immigration, this does add an element of distance. Mexican culture itself, because of the Indian-Spanish mix, strikes Europeans and Americans as something quite different from that of overseas European societies.

2. For this new immigration, issues of legality of immigration loom large. This was never an issue for the old immigration. Immigration to this country was in effect almost unregulated until the early 1920s, getting citizenship was easy, and thus almost everyone was legal. Certainly the question of legality

which hangs over many of the new groups of the West and Southwest affects deeply their ability to participate in politics.

3. The new groups enter a situation in which the differences among groups — in income, occupation, educational achievement, language, and voting participation — have become national political issues. They have a right to bilingual education — whether they want it or not (and if they have a right to it, many in the group will find it to their advantage to claim the right, at least for the others). They have a right (many of them) to assistance in voting in their own language, if they become citizens. They are protected by antidiscrimination legislation, as are all Americans, but they further have varying claims to special consideration under affirmative action requirements.

4. I sense a remarkable diversity among them in their capacity to take advantage of American economic and educational opportunities for upward mobility. The differences in this respect among the older immigrants (Irish and German, Italian and Jews), did not lead to marked political conflict between them. I fear we may see something new among the new immigrants. Some show a surprising mobility. Some of course come fairly highly educated and achieve professional status (Asian Indians, for example), some show remarkable ability in small business (Koreans), some already show considerable success in educational achievement. But the gaps that these differential achievements open up between these groups and the two great minorities, black and Hispanic (or, specifically, the Mexican and Puerto Rican element among the Hispanics), suggests conflict among new immigrant groups, as well as between them and older Americans. The matter becomes more delicate insofar as these differences are seen crudely as the result of differential discrimination, which is the effect of antidiscrimination and affirmative action legislation and regulations, and the way they are interpreted by courts and regulators. A competition over who is more discriminated against, who more worthy of federal or other protection, may well develop, with nasty overtones.

5. Finally, there is an important international dimension to the new immigration that must be considered. A few years ago,

after hearing testimony on immigration to the United States, a congressman commented. "We have been told that by the end of the century there will be 140,000,000 Mexicans and half of them will be living north of the Rio Grande." Perhaps those figures are too high — perhaps there wil be only 100 million and only a third of them will be living north of the Rio Grande. I leave it to demographers to figure out which is the more likely prospect. But we will have on our southern border a neighbor, still poorer than we are by a considerable margin, with enough reasons, old and new, for resentment at the United States; and within the United States an enormous minority with the right to be educated in American schools in language and loyalty to Mexico, in its history, its culture, its customs. (I speak only of the *right*, now fairly well established — many things may come to pass before it is fully exploited in all respects, including some narrowing of the right.) Recall that a few hundred thousand Japanese, with their homeland seven thousand miles away, helped give rise to a great fear of the "Yellow Peril." (The actual growth of Japanese power was a more substantial factor.) The situation is potentially delicate, and neither the old nor the new immigrations from Europe, or from Canada, raised any parallel issue.

Further on the international dimension: Two substantial new communities in the United States — Cubans and Vietnamese — have been created not as a result of our will, but as a result of decisions of foreign powers over which we had no control. In both cases, we responded in accord with old traditions, newly strengthened, of offering asylum to refugees and a place to live to immigrants. But recall that that tradition suffered a substantial interruption of at least fifty years in the middle of this century, and that some groups — Chinese and Japanese — were basically barred from immigration for very much longer periods. There are many countries in the world in which the expulsion of large parts of their population — ethnic or racial minorities, political dissidents — may seem desirable in decades to come. This possibility of expulsion of immigrants to the United States is not an unlikely one, and we must consider how it will complicate intergroup relations in the United States.

These five factors to my mind create a heady brew, and turbulent as was the assimilation of the new European immigrant groups, the tensions of these five factors suggest a more turbulent period for the new groups. They will, on the one hand, form more obvious targets for attack; they will, on the other, find easier access to legal protection, and to legal rights that are unique in the experience of older Americans and will create resentment. The combination to my mind spells a good deal of trouble, which we have not yet seen, but which in the absence of good sense and adaptability may yet come.

The Northern pattern of race relations found a resolution, at least in the case of the European immigrants. Whatever the intensity of conflict among immigrant groups, in time a modus vivendi was worked out. While each group maintained its attachments to its culture and its homeland to some degree (in the case of Israel, it amounts to an overriding political commitment), each was able to find a place in American economy, society, and polity. If these groups had analyzed the statistics, they might have found much to grouse about. Since the Irish dominated electoral politics, all other groups were by that token "deprived." Since the Jews were the most successful in terms of high occupational status, all the others were by that token "deprived." Yet that is not the way the political debate went, and all the European ethnic groups believed they had done well in America, and there is scarcely a one that bears grievances.

The Northern pattern might well have accommodated the blacks as they moved north, the Puerto Ricans as they emigrated to the mainland, the Mexican Americans as they moved into the cities of the West. It has not been successful in doing so, in the perception of minority leaders, and of leaders of opinion for the majority. Actually, the success of the Northern pattern, of accommodation and mobility independent of direct public assistance, was greater than is generally realized.[10] I will not rehearse the facts of black and other minority-group political, economic, and educational status, but every average, we must realize, conceals within it substantial groups well above the average. The fact that young black families do almost as well in income these days as young white families seems to me a substantial achievement, and it was already becoming apparent when Moynihan and I were writing the introduction to the second edition of *Beyond the Melting Pot*, in 1970.[11]

In saying that what we have had is in part a failure of perception, I do not dispute that there is a failure in reality in bringing blacks into the mainstream of American society and opportunity: But the failure is not only one in reality. The partial successes of reality are now swept away by prevailing perceptions: These perceptions shape the actions of major government agencies, the interpretations of the television networks, of the major organs of the press. They are now as much reality as any reality. And as a result, the Southern pattern has become, in its new formulation in which law is designed to raise the lower caste rather than to keep it down, the national pattern.

I have argued that this new national pattern will be challenged as a new wave of immigration reshapes American cities. The new wave will raise many questions. Does it deserve the same benefits as the protected classes of the 1960s? How will the borders of protected classes be set? If nonwhite immigrants have greater benefits in law than white natives, what will that do to the willingness to allow immigration to continue at the rate of the 1970s? As some of these immigrants show success in economic activity and in achieving political representation, what will that do to the viability of the Southern pattern?

Beyond all three patterns is one I have not even mentioned, the ideal of the period of Americanization of World War I, the 1920s, and 1930s. This ideal was one of full assimilation of all immigrant groups to a common national type, so that ethnicity would play a declining role in individual consciousness, groups would not be formed around ethnic interests, "hyphenated Americanism" would be a thing of the past, and the United States would be as homogeneous in its Americanness as the nations of the old world were once in their Englishness, their Frenchness, their Germanness, their Italianness. Leave aside the fact that the old Americans did not hold this ideal in full consistency: They expected abandonment of difference, but would not reciprocate with full acceptance of those who had given up their difference. Leave aside the fact that even the nations of the old world have lost their homogeneity, to the extent they had it, under the impact of the economic changes of the past three decades (see Chapter 15). Leave aside the realism of expecting people to give up ethnic attributes, attachments, and loyalties within any brief period of time. This still is an ideal that is worth holding in mind. Difference, alas, is always liable to become a source of conflict. Assimilation has already proceeded so far with some groups, specifically the European ethnic groups, that it is not an unreasonable hope. If this original hope offered the best chance of a society in which ethnic and racial rivalries and conflicts could be laid to rest, there is no reason why it cannot still be held up as an ideal. Instead, it has been driven from the field of discussion of ethnic issues. The "melting pot" is now attacked not only on the empirical ground that it really didn't melt that much or that fast, but on the normative ground that it should not have been allowed to do so. And on the basis of this attack, Americanization becomes a dirty word, and bilingualism and biculturalism receive government support.

I doubt that this is wise. Without endorsing the rigors of the Americanization programs of World War I and the succeeding decades, I can still see the virtue of forging a single society out of many stocks, and can still see that this process deserves some public guidance. Beyond the Northern, Southern, and Western patterns, there is still, or should be, the possibility of a more unified even though ethnically and racially diverse society. When every group insists it must match every other group in economic resources, occupational status, and political representation, and that public power be used to attain these ends — and to maintain the existence of the group as a separate group, to boot — we have a sure recipe for conflict. We will have to do better, and one way of doing so is to explore whether the much maligned goal of assimilation does not still have much to teach us.

[1982]

Notes

INTRODUCTION

1. U.S. Commission on Civil Rights, "The Federal Civil Rights Enforcement Budget: Fiscal Year 1983" (Washington, June 1982), p. 6.

2. Those writings include a monograph, "Social Characteristics of the American Jews, 1654–1954," in the *American Jewish Yearbook* for 1955; *American Judaism* in 1957; *Studies in Housing and Minority Groups* (edited with Davis McEntire) in 1962; and *Beyond the Melting Pot* (with Daniel P. Moynihan) in 1963. In a series of essays I had developed my sense of the meaning of ethnicity in American life: "Ethnic Groups in America: From National Culture to Ideology," in *Freedom and Control in Modern Society*, ed. Morroe Berger, Theodore Abel, and Charles H. Page (New York: Van Nostrand, 1954); "The Integration of American Immigrants," *Law and Contemporary Problems* 21 (Spring 1956): 256–259; "The Immigrant Groups in American Culture," *Yale Review* 68 (Spring 1959): 382–397.

3. Charles B. Keely, "Immigration and the American Future," in *Ethnic Relations in America*, ed. Lance Liebman (New York: Prentice-Hall, 1982), p. 32.

4. "Minority Status Asked in a Petition to SBA," *India Abroad*, May 21, 1982.

5. "$30 Billion Is Reserved for SBA," *India Abroad*, August 13, 1982.

1. THE PEOPLES OF AMERICA

1. Samuel Lubell, *The Future of American Politics* (New York: Harper and Row, 1956).

2. Will Herberg, *Protestant, Catholic, Jew* (Garden City, N.Y.: Doubleday–Anchor Books, 1955).

3. Ruby Jo Reeves Kennedy, "Single or Triple Melting Pot? Intermarriage Trends in New Haven, 1870–1940," *American Journal of Sociology* 49 (January 1944): 331–339.

2. Negroes and Jews: The New Challenge to Pluralism

1. Kenneth Clark, "Candor on Negro-Jewish Relations," *Commentary*, February 1946.

2. James Baldwin, "The Harlem Ghetto: Winter 1948," *Commentary*, February 1948.

3. Howard Brotz, *The Black Jews* of Harlem: *Negro Nationalism and the Dilemmas of Negro Leadership* (New York: Free Press of Glencoe, 1964).

3. E. Franklin Frazier and the Negro Family

1. E. Franklin Frazier, *The Negro Family in the United States* (Chicago: University of Chicago Press, 1939; 2nd ed. 1966).

2. E. Franklin Frazier, *The Negro Family in Chicago* (Chicago: University of Chicago Press, 1932); idem, *The Free Negro Family* (Nashville: Fisk University Press, 1932).

3. T. W. Adorno, E. Frenkel-Brunswik, D. J. Levinson, and R. N. Sanford, *The Authoritarian Personality* (New York: Harper, 1950).

4. Thomas F. Pettigrew, *Profile of the Negro American* (Princeton: Van Nostrand, 1964).

5. E. Franklin Frazier, *Black Bourgeoisie* (Glencoe, Ill.: Free Press, 1957).

6. Frank Riessman, *The Culturally Deprived Child* (New York: Harper and Row, 1962).

4. Ethnic Groups and Education: Toward the Tolerance of Difference

1. For a review of this work, see Alex Inkeles and Daniel J. Levinson, "National Character," in Gardner Lindzey, ed., *Handbook of Social Psychology* (Cambridge, Mass.: Addison-Wesley, 1954), pp. 977–1020.

2. See, for example, Marvin K. Opler, *Culture and Mental Health* (New York: MacMillan, 1959); Anthony de Reuck and Julie Knight eds. *Transcultural Psychiatry* (New York: Little Brown, 1965).

3. On this specific point, see Moses Rischin, *The Promised City: New York's Jews, 1870–1914* (Cambridge, Mass.: Harvard University Press, 1962).

4. Nathan Glazer, "Social Characteristics of American Jews," in Louis Finkelstein, ed., *The Jews*, 3rd ed. (New York: Harper and Row, 1960), p. 1705. See also Meyer Weinberg, "A Yearning for Learning: Blacks and Jews Through History," in *Integrated Education 7* (May-June 1969) 20–29.

5. The Census of 1950 showed Japanese in the state of California with more years of education than any other racial group, including whites. The observation of the Universtiy of California is based on estimates of students there. For a general view of the Japanese American experience as a case of success under adverse conditions, see William Petersen, "Success Story, Japanese-American Style," *New York Times Magazine*, January 9, 1966. See also Petersen's book *Japanese-Americans* (New York: Random House, 1971).

6. Leonard Covello, *The Social Background of the Italo-American* School Child (Leiden: E. J. Brill, 1967).

7. Arthur Jensen "How Much Can We Boost I.Q. and Scholastic Achievement?" *Harvard Educational Review 39* (Winter 1969): 1–123. See the critiques of his work in the *Harvard Educational Review* (Spring 1969).

8. Mark Zborowski and Elizabeth Herzog, *Life Is With People* (New York: Schocken, 1962).

9. For the dispute surrounding Moynihan's report on the Negro family, see Lee Rainwater and Martin Yancey, *The Moynihan Report and the Politics of Controversy* (Cambridge, Mass.: M.I.T. Press, 1967).

10. The chief critics are Edgar Friedenberg, *Coming of Age in America* (Random House, 1965) and other books and Paul Goodman, *Compulsory Miseducation* (Horizon Press, 1964) and other books. But their thinking is now diffused to the high school level, and below.

11. I am referring to the argument of Robert Theobald (in many books) that expectable and near technological achievement will make the need to work for most people unnecessary.

12. Susan Silverman Stodolsky and Gerald S. Lesser, "Learning Patterns in the *Disadvantaged,*" *Harvard Educational Review 37* (Fall 1967): 546–593.

5. BLACKS AND ETHNIC GROUPS: THE DIFFERENCE
AND THE POLITICAL DIFFERENCE IT MAKES

1. This position is presented more fully in Glazer, "Ethnic Groups in America: From National Culture to Ideology," pp. 158–173 idem, "The Integration of American Immigrants"; idem, "The Immigrant Groups and American Culture"; and Nathan Glazer and Daniel P. Moynihan, *Beyond the Melting Pot*, 2nd ed. (Cambridge, Mass.: M.I.T. Press, 1970).

2. Covello, *The Social Background of the Italo-American School Child*; Glazer, "The Immigrant Groups and American Culture."

3. See George De Vos and Hiroshi Wagatsuma, *Japan's Invisible Race* (Berkeley: University of California Press, 1966).

4. See chapter 9, "Comparing the Negro and Immigrant Experience," in *Report of the National Advisory Commission on Civil Disorders* (New York: E. P. Dutton, 1968).

5. Nathan Glazer, "Slums and Ethnicity," in Thomas D. Sherrard, ed., *Social Welfare and Urban Problems* (New York: Columbia University Press, 1968), p. 91.

6. *New York Times Magazine*, September 11, 1966.

7. Robert Blauner, "Internal Colonialism and Ghetto Revolt," *Social Problems* 16 (Spring 1969): 397.

8. Ira De Augustine Reid, *The Negro Immigrant* (New York: Columbia University Press, 1949), pp. 235, 237.

9. How large this limitation is is not simple to determine. There are varying positions: Karl E. Taeuber, in "The Effect of Income Redistribution on Racial Residential Segregation" *Urban Affairs Quarterly* 4 (September 1968): 5–14, presents data to show that it is quite small and that black residence is affected overwhelmingly by discrimination and much less by economic factors. Anthony H. Pascal, using a different model in *The Economics of Housing Discrimination* (Santa Monica, Calif.: Rand Corporation, 1967), concludes that economic factors explain 50 percent of the variance in percentage of blacks in Chicago and Detroit neighborhoods. For a discussion and an effort at reconciliation, see Karl E. Taeuber, *Patterns of Negro-White Residential Segregation* (Santa Monica, Calif.: Rand Corporation, 1970).

10. Nathan Kantrowitz, "Segregation in New York City, 1960," *American Journal of Sociology* 74, no. 6 (May 1969): 685–695.

11. Erich Rosenthal, "Acculturation without Assimilation?" *American Journal of Sociology* 66 (1960): 275–278.

12. See Glazer and Moynihan, *Beyond the Melting Pot* p. 318, table 2.

13. W. Lloyd Warner and Leo Srole, *The Social Systems of American Ethnic Groups* (New Haven,: Yale University Press, 1945).

14. Eugene P. Foley, "The Negro Businessman in Search of a Tradition," *Daedalus* 95 (Winter 1966): 107–144.

15. For a particularly impressive analysis of low black participation in small business, which ascribes major weight to factors of internal organization and cohesion, formal and informal, familial and extrafamilial, see Ivan Light, *Ethnic Enterprise in America* (Berkeley University of California Press, 1972).

16. For the best account of this struggle, see W. E. B. DuBois, *The Philadelphia Negro: A Social Study* (Philadelphia: University of Pennsylvania Press, 1899). See also Herman Block, *The Circle of Discrimination* (New York: New York University Press, 1969). [More work has been done since on the question of the relative rates of economic and political progress of blacks and white and Asian immigrants. See, in particular, Stanley Lieberson, *A Piece of the Pie: Blacks and White Immigrants Since 1860* (Berkeley: University of California Press, 1981). This recent research persuades me that I underestimated the difference in degree of discrimination met by blacks and white and Asian immigrants in northern and western cities. But the question remains whether it is this difference that explains differences among the three groups, or whether we must go to other causes, such as the unexpected consequences of the social policies of the late 1960s and 1970s. —N.G., 1983]

17. For the disorganization that may afflict an immigrant ethnic group, see, for example, W. I. Thomas and F. Znaniecki, *The Polish Peasant in Europe and America* (1918–1920; New York: Dover, 1958); W. I. Thomas, *The Unadjusted Girl* (Boston: Atlantic–Little Brown, 1923); and Oscar Handlin, *Boston's Immigrants* (Cambridge, Mass.: Harvard University Press, 1941).

18. For an account of a ferocious battle to gain representation for Italians, see Humbert S. Nelli, *The Italians in Chicago, 1880–1930: A Study in Ethnic Mobility* (New York: Oxford University Press, 1970). The Italians lost, which simply goes to make my point that groups other than blacks do lose.

19. Arthur Klebanoff, "The Demographics of Politics: Legislative Constituencies in the Borough of Brooklyn" (Senior honors thesis, Yale University, 1969).

20. See *Abstracts of Reports of the Immigration Commission*,

Senate Document 747, vol. 1 (Washington, D.C., 1911), pp. 485–487.

21. John P. Gavit, *Americans by Choice* (New York: Harper, 1922).

22. Jack Elinson, Paul W. Haberman, and Cyrille Gell, "Ethnic and Educational Data on Adults in New York City, 1963–1964," mimeographed (School of Public Health and Administrative Medicine, Columbia University, 1967), p. 155.

23. Nelli, *The Italians in Chicago*, pp. 75–77.

6. The Problem of Ethnic Studies

1. The main themes of cultural pluralism were presented by Horace Kallen and Randolph Bourne in magazine articles published during World War I, and reprinted in Horace M. Kallen, *Culture and Democracy in the United States* (New York: Boni and Liveright, 1924), and Randolph Bourne, *The History of a Literary Radical and Other Papers* (New York: Russell and Russell, 1956). The best account of the development of American attitudes to diversity since the turn of the century is in John Higham, *Send These to Me: Jews and Other Immigrants in Urban America* (New York: Atheneum, 1975).

2. See, for example, Louis Adamic, *What's Your Name* (New York: Harper, 1942) and *A Nation of Nations* (New York: Harper, 1945). Henry Arthur Christian has compiled a bibliography: *Louis Adamic: A Checklist* (Kent, Ohio: Kent State University Press, 1971).

3. Ronald K. Goodenow, "Progressive Education, Race and Ethnicity in the Depression Years: An Overview," *History of Education Quarterly* 15 (1975), is a good acount of the intercultural education movement's links to progressive education. See also William E. Vickery and Stewart G. Cole, *Intercultural Education in American Schools: Proposed Objectives and Methods* (New York: Harper, 1943). It lists in its introductory pages eight other books that were being prepared for the Service Bureau of Intercultural Education. A unit dealing with Intergroup Education in Cooperating Schools, located in the American Council on Education, also published a number of books, all with Hilda Taba as first author.

4. Vickery and Cole, *Intercultural Education in American Schools*, pp. 34–35.

5. Goodenow, *Progressive Education, Race and Ethnicity*, pp. 375–376.

6. Higham, *Send These to Me*, p. 208.

7. Judith Herman, ed., *The Schools and Group Identity:Edu-*

cating for a New Pluralism (New York: Institute on Pluralism and Group Identity, 1974), p. 27.

7. AMERICAN PLURALISM: VOLUNTARISM OR STATE ACTION?

1. These documents are quoted from *Bilingual-Bicultural Education: A Handbook for Attorneys and Community Workers*, a convenient compilation made by the Center for Law and Education, Cambridge, Mass., published in December 1975.

2. Herman, *The Schools and Group Identity*, p. 77.

3. Ibid., pp. 58–60.

4. National Advisory Council on Bilingual Education, *Second Advisory Report*, 1976, p. 85.

5. Ibid., pp. 40, 80.

6. Higham, *Send These to Me*, pp. 242–243.

8. BILINGUALISM: WILL IT WORK?

1. "Sweet Houston Sound: Vietnamese Language," *New York Times*, March 4, 1979.

2. "Elmhurst Flourishes as Melting Pot," *New York Times*, April 4, 1979.

3. See Noel Epstein, *Language, Ethnicity, and the Schools: Policy Alternatives for Bilingual-Bicultural Education* (Washington, D.C.: Institute for Educational Leadership, George Washington University, 1977).

4. "High Court Upholds Denial of Teaching Posts to Aliens," *New York Times*, April 18, 1979.

9. AFFIRMATIVE DISCRIMINATION: FOR AND AGAINST

1. Such programs also set statistical goals for women (and men) but they are not the subject of the present discussion. "Affirmative action" refers not only to employment, of course, but to other forms of action by institutions to raise the position of minorities. In this article I limit myself to employment issues. The setting of statistical goals to eliminate segregation of students and faculty in elementary and secondary schools could be called affirmative action, but the term is not generally applied to such policies even though they are very similar to the employment policies. Programs to increase the number of minority students admitted to institutions of higher education are sometimes

called affirmative action. For example, the case of Bakke against the medical school of the University of California at Davis was generally considered an affirmative action case. *Regents of the University of California v. Allan Bakke*, 98 S.Ct. 2733 (1978).

2. Thomas Sowell, "'Affirmative Action' Reconsidered," *The Public Interest*, no. 42 (1976), p. 48.

3. Frank C. Morris, *Current Trends in the Use (and Misuse) of Statistics in Employment Discrimination Litigation* (Washington: Equal Employment Advisory Council, 1977).

4. Conference Board, *Nondiscrimination in Employment: Changing Perspectives, 1963–1972* (New York, Conference Board, (1973) , pp. 28, 29.

5. Subcommittee on Equal Opportunities, *Staff Report on Oversight Investigation of Federal Enforcement of Equal Employment Opportunity Laws*, U.S. House of Representatives, 94th Congress, 2nd sess., 1976, pp. 61–87.

6. Ibid., p. 69.

7. Harry T. Edwards and Barry L. Zaretsky, "Preferential Remedies for Employment Discrimination," *Michigan Law Review* 75 (1975): 30.

8. Marilyn Gittell, "The Illusion of Affirmative Action," *Change*, October 1975, pp. 39–43.

9. Sidney Hook and Miro Todorovich, "The Tyranny of Reverse Discrimination," *Change*, December-January 1975–1976, pp. 42–43.

10. National Association of Manufacturers, *Equal Employment Opportunity Reform: An NAM Analysis and Proposal* (Washington, n. d.).

11. Richard Freeman, "Changes in Job Market Discrimination and Black Economic Well-Being," in Michael B. Wise, ed., *Beyond Civil Rights: The Road to Economic Security* (Notre Dame, Ind. University of Notre Dame Law School, Center for Civil Rights, 1976).

12. Andrew F. Brimmer, "The Economic Position of Black Americans," Special Report no. 9 of the National Commission for Manpower Policy (Washington, 1976), pp. 26–28.

13. Richard B. Freeman, *Black Elite; The New Market for Highly Educated Black Americans* (New York: McGraw Hill, 1977); Reynolds Farley, "Trends in Racial Inequalities: Have the Gains of the 1960's Disappeared in the 1970's?" *American Sociological Review* 42 (1977): 189–208.

14. See the summary in Phyllis A. Wallace, "A Decade of Policy Developments in Equal Opportunities in Employment and Housing,"

in Robert H. Haveman, ed., *A Decade of Federal Anti-Poverty Programs: Achievements, Failures, and Lessons* (New York: Academic Press, 1977).

15. Theodore V. Purcell, "Management and Affirmative Action in the Late Seventies," in Leonard J. Hausman and James L. Stern, ed., *Equal Rights and Industrial Relations* (Madison: University of Wisconsin, Industrial Relations Research Association, 1977).

16. Work in America Institute, Inc., "Sears: The Largest Voluntary Affirmative Action Program," *World of Work Report* 2 (April 1977): 38–40.

17. Richard B. Freeman, "Changes in the Labor Market for Black Americans, 1948–1972," *Brookings Papers on Economic Activity* 1973, no. 1, pp. 67–120; Robert E. Hall and Richard A. Kasten, "The Relative Occupational Success of Blacks and Whites," *Brookings Papers on Economic Activity* 1973, no. 3, pp. 781–797.

18. *New York Times*, May 1, 1977.

10. Who's Available?

1. Sheila Johnson, "It's Action but Is It Affirmative?" *New York Times Magazine*, May 11, 1975, p. 18.

2. "A Unique Competence," A Study of Equal Employment Opportunity in the Bell System, EEOC Pre-Hearing Analysis and Summary of Evidence, 1971, p. 212.

3. Orley Ashenfelter, *Minority Employment, 1966* (Washington: EEOC and Department of Labor, 1968), as reported in Wallace, "A Decade of Policy Developments in Equal Opportunities in Employment and Housing," pp. 338–339.

4. Freeman, "Changes in the Labor Market for Black Americans," p. 118; Hall, and Kasten, "The Relative Occupational Success of Blacks and Whites," pp. 785, 791–792.

5. Richard B. Freeman, *Black Elite* (New York: McGraw Hill, 1977), p. 31.

6. Eleanor Meyer Rogg, *The Assimilation of Cuban Exiles* (New York: Aberdeen Press, 1974).

7. Betty Lee Sung, *Chinese American Manpower and Employment* (New York: Praeger, 1976), p. 7.

8. Calvin F. Schmid and Charles E. Nobbe, "Inter-Ethnic Differences among Nonwhite Races," *American Sociological Review* 30 (1965): 909–922.

9. David H. Rosenbloom, *Federal Equal Employment Opportunity* (New York: Praeger, 1977), pp. 6–7.

10. S. M. Lipset and E. C. Ladd, Jr., "Jewish Academics in the United States," *American Jewish Yearbook* 72 (1971) 89–128.

11. Freeman, *Black Elite*, p. 3.

12. E. P. Hutchinson, *Immigrants and Their Children, 1850–1950* (New York: John Wiley and Sons, 1956).

13. Glazer and Moynihan, *Beyond the Melting Pot* (see tables derived from U.S. Census on pp. 322–323, comparing the occupations in 1950 of immigrants and their children from Italy and the U.S.S.R., predominantly Jews).

14. Charles E. Johnson, Jr., "Consistency of Reporting of Ethnic Origin in the Current Population Survey," U.S. Bureau of the Census Technical Paper 31, February 1974.

15. "Rise in Black Students Brings Disputes on Law School Recruiting," *New York Times*, April 7, 1974, p. 48.

16. Ivan Light, *Ethnic Enterprise in America* (Berkeley: University of California Press, 1972), pp. 4–5.

17. "Vegetable Stores Provide a New Start for Korean Immigrants," *New York Times*, June 25, 1977, p. 21.

18. Freeman, *Black Elite*, p. 153.

19. Rosenbloom, *Federal Equal Employment Opportunity*, p. 7.

20. P. J. Bichel, E. A. Hammel, and J. W. O'Connell, "Sex Bias in Graduate Admissions: Data from Berkeley," *Science* 187 (February 7, 1975): 398–404.

21. Herbert Gans, *The Urban Villagers* (Glencoe, Ill.: Free Press, 1962).

11. Liberty, Equality, Fraternity — and Ethnicity

1. One should, in any full discussion of the role of fraternity in America, take account of Wilson Carey McWilliams's enormous and comprehensive book, *The Idea of Fraternity in America* (Berkeley and Los Angeles: University of California Press, 1973), although the relevance of the book is limited here because McWilliams does not get to the issues raised by the newer developments in the efforts to achieve equality between ethnic and racial groups, and he goes into many problems that are not at issue here.

2. *Science* 192 (May 14, 1976): 660, in a review of Phyllis A. Katz, ed., *Toward the Elimination of Racism* (New York: Pergamon, 1976).

3. C. S. Jencks, *Inequality* (New York: Harper and Row, 1972), and many other sources.

4. For examples both of this economic success and of the barriers such groups have faced and do face in developing countries, whether under colonial rule or independent, see P. T. Bauer, *Dissent on Development* (Cambridge, Mass.: Harvard University Press, 1972).

5. Such examples may be found in my book, *Affirmative Discrimination* (New York: Basic Books, 1976).

6. The matter is far too complicated for any simple set of references to suffice, but see *Human Diversity*, ed. Bernard D. Davis and Patricia Flaherty (Cambridge, Mass.: Ballinger, 1976). for a broad range of data and points of view.

7. R. B. Zajonc, "Family Configuration and Intelligence," *Science* 192 (April 16, 1976): 227–236.

8. Samuel Bowles and Herbert Gintis, *Schooling in Capitalist America* (New York: Basic Books, 1976).

9. John Rawls, *A Theory of Justice* (Cambridge, Mass.: Harvard University Press, 1971).

10. See Bertrand De Jouvenel, *The Ethics of Redistribution* (Cambridge: Cambridge University Press. 1951).

11. Bauer, *Dissent on Development*, p. 197.

12. Two recent news items bear on this point: "The regional office of the U.S. Department of Housing and Urban Development (HUD) plans to extend its affirmative action employment plan to Polish Americans this summer. It is believed to be the first time a federal agency has agreed to actively seek a proportionate representation of a white group in its work force." "HUD Will Extend Job Plan to Poles," *Cleveland Plain Dealer*, April 14, 1976, p. 80.

"Members of the various Indian organizations in the New York area held a meeting at the Tandoor restaurant, 40 E. 49th St., St., on February 14 to discuss issues concerning the ethnic classification of Indian immigrants in America. The Federal Interagency Commission, an ad hoc committee on racial and ethnic definition, classifies Americans under five categories: American Indian or Alaskan Native; Asian or Pacific Islander; Black/Negro; Caucasian/White; and Hispanic. The Caucasian/White category includes persons whose ancestry is traced to Europe, North Africa, the Middle East or the Indian subcontinent. By definition, therefore, the Indians are classified as 'White' and are not eligible for minority consideration in affirmative action programs . . . at least one person expressed reservations against taking any affimative action. Dr. Ambuj Mukherjee, representing the Tagore Society of New York (an Indian cultural organization), opined: 'Indians should make it a point to be judged on merit alone, wherever they are.' Dutta replied: 'I endorse your views, but the tragedy is that the slate is not clean. The distinctions have been made, and we have to face it.'" "Indian Organizations in U.S. Seek To Reclassify Immigrants," *India Abroad*, February 27, 1976, p. 6.

12. THE UNIVERSALIZATION OF ETHNICITY

1. They have been described in the fascinating book by George De Vos and Hiroshi Wagatsuma, *Japan's Invisible Race* (Berkeley: University of California Press, 1966), a work that argues that one can find some remnants of caste in most East Asian countries.

2. Rupert Emerson, *From Empire to Nation* (Cambridge, Mass.: Harvard University Press, 1960), pp. 95–96.

3. Clifford Geertz, *Old Societies and New States* (New York: Free Press, 1963), p. 108.

4. Frances R. Hill, "Genesis of a New Exodus," *Harvard Political Review*, Spring 1973, p. 9. [In 1983 the world was shocked by the precipitous expulsion of huge numbers of Ghanaians from Nigeria—N.G., 1983]

5. See E. J. B. Rose et al., *Colour and Citizenship* (London: Oxford University Press, 1969), and Anthony Lester and Geoffrey Bindman, *Race and Law in Great Britain* (Cambridge, Mass.: Harvard University Press, 1972). I point out these American influences in reviews of these two books in *Sociology* 6 (January 1972): 97–100, and in *Harvard Civil Rights–Civil Liberties Law Review* 9 (March 1974): 403–411. See, too, my article "The Scarman Report—An American View," *Political Quarterly* 53 (April-June 1982): 111–119.

6. "Dr. Obote names both Libya and the Palestinian Liberation Organizations as among those assisting in killings in Uganda . . ." "Ex-Ugandan Head Charges Genocide," *New York Times*, May 27, 1973.

7. "Australia Plans Croatian Inquiry," *New York Times*, May 29, 1973.

13. INDIVIDUAL RIGHTS AGAINST GROUP RIGHTS

1. Vernon Van Dyke, "Justice as Fairness: For Groups," *American Political Science Review* 69 (1975): 607.

2. See Glazer, *Affirmative Discrimination*, pp. 40–43; Chapter 9 of this volume; Freeman, *Black Elite*.

3. See Nathan Glazer, "Why Bakke Won't End Reverse Discrimination," *Commentary*, September 1978, pp. 36-41.

4. Gordon P. Means, "Human Rights and the Rights of Ethnic Groups — A Commentary," *International Studies Notes* (1974): 17.

5. Robert L. Hardgrave, Jr., "DeFunis and Dorairajan: 'Protective Discrimination' in the United States and India," paper delivered at the 1976 annual meeting of the American Political Science Association, Chicago, Illinois, September 2-5, 1976.

14. Federalism and Ethnicity: The American Solution

1. See Cynthia Enloe, *Ethnic Conflict and Political Development* (Boston: Little, Brown, 1973), pp. 84-158, which has the best treatment I have seen of these varying approaches.

2. This early history of the rights of Spanish-speaking persons in various spheres is indeed complex; for a summary and introduction, see Arnold H. Leibowitz, *The Imposition of English as the Language of Instruction in American Schools* (Ponce, P.R.: Revista de Derecho Puertorriqueno, 1970), pp. 199-208, and references therein.

3. For a full treatment of the problem of black nationalism insofar as it looked to separate political entities, see Theodore Draper, "The Negro Question," in *American Communism and Soviet Russia* (New York: Viking, 1960), pp. 315-357; idem, "The Fantasy of Black Nationalism," *Commentary* 48, no. 3 (September 1969): 27-54; idem, *Commentary* 48, no. 6 (December 1969): 14-18.

4. Leibowitz, *Imposition of English*, p. 187.

5. Glazer, "Ethnic Groups in America: From National Culture to Ideology," p. 172.

6. Leibowitz, *Imposition of English*, pp. 179-183.

7. See Daniel J. Elazar, *American Federalism: A View from the States* (New York: Thomas Y. Crowell, 1966), pp. 85-141; ibid., 2nd ed. (1972), pp. 83-154. "Ethnic group," and some specific groups such as German American, Irish American, Italian American, and others appear in the index to the second edition, but not the first, showing the greater salience ethnicity had developed by 1972. But the text of the first edition makes clear — if not as clear as the second — the ethnic component in the shaping of the three political cultures. This is shown even more sharply in idem, *Cities of the Prairie* (New York: Basic Books, 1970), pp. 153-205; see, for the specific relationship of various groups to the three cultures, p. 474. For a treatment of ethnic elements in regional politics based on Elazar and other sources, see Raymond

D. Gastil, *Cultural Regions of the United States* (Seattle: University of Washington Press, 1975), pp. 55-70.

8. Elazar, *American Federalism*, 2nd ed., pp. 150-152.

9. National Advisory Council on Bilingual Education, *Second Advisory Report* (1976), pp. 85-88.

10. For a description of this process in a variety of areas of policy, see Glazer, *Affirmative Discrimination*; for a discussion of the bilingual case in particular, see Chapter 7 of this volume.

15. EUROPE'S ETHNIC PROBLEM

1. "European Migration after World War II," in *Human Migration*, ed. William H. McNeill and Ruth S. Adams (Bloomington: Indiana University Press, 1978), p. 86.

2. For an excellent treatment of the conflicts created by migration in search of jobs in India — conflicts among citizens of India, rather than between Indians and foreigners, but no less severe for all that — see Myron Weiner, *Sons of the Soil: Migration and Ethnic Conflict in India* (Princeton: Princeton University Press, 1978).

3. Michael Hechter, *Internal Colonialism*: The Celtic Fringe in British National Development, 1536-1966 (Berkeley: University of California Press, 1974), p. 9.

4. Thorny constitutional issues often arise here, where church and state separations (as in West Germany) preclude "religious education" in the public school system.

5. See Mavis Gallant, "Paris: The Taste of a New Age," *Atlantic Monthly*, April 1981.

" 'My daughter,' says a solemn man at a dinner party, 'has to go to school with children of Spanish and Portuguese concierges . . . My daughter has no contact with her own culture.'

"He is left-leaning and would never object to his daughter's mingling with the foreign children . . . [But] he is afraid that his daughter's prolonged contact with Spanish children will affect her French."

6. Ray C. Rist, *Guest Workers in Germany*: The Prospects for Pluralism (New York: Praeger, 1978), p. xi.

7. Ibid., p. 192.

8. Ibid., p. 217.

16. THE POLITICS OF A MULTIETHNIC SOCIETY

1. Glazer and Moynihan, *Beyond the Melting Pot*, 2nd ed. pp. xxiii-xxiv.

2. Abigail Thernstrom, "The Odd Evolution of the Voting Rights Act," *Public Interest*, no. 55 (Spring 1979), pp. 49–76.

3. I base this account on news items in the *New York Times*, September, 1981.

4. "Two Councilmen Debate Redistricting Issue," *New York Times*, September 12, 1981, p. 27.

5. Quoted in *Beyond the Melting Pot*, p. xix.

6. "The Vote Prevention Act," *Wall Street Journal*, September 11, 1981, p. 30.

7. "The Week of the Un-election," *New York Times*, September 12, 1981, p. 22.

8. Kenneth Clark testified in favor of the redistricting but, as reported in the *New York Times*, "Mr. Clark said his statement was actually written by his son, Hilton Clark, a Democratic leader in Harlem." "Some Pointed Questions on Primary Raise a Phalanx of Pointed Fingers," *New York Times*, September 11, 1981, p. B8.

9. I include the Nixon-Ford administrations in this sequence because from the point of view of federal programs aiding minorities there was no break in growth, whether in money distributed or positions funded, during those years. Indeed, those were the years when affirmative action and the agencies enforcing it (Office of Federal Contract Compliance, Equal Employment Opportunity Commission) were unchecked.

10. See Thomas Sowell, *Ethnic America: A History* (New York, Basic Books, 1981).

11. *Beyond the Melting Pot*, 2nd ed. p. xcii, n. 6.

Credits

Chapter 9 appeared under the title "Affirmative Discrimination: Where Is It Going?" in the *International Journal of Comparative Sociology*, March-June 1979, a special issue edited by William Petersen.

Chapter 10 was published as "Issues on Availability," in *Perspectives on Availability* (Washington, D.C.: Equal Employment Advisory Council, 1977), copyright © 1977 by the Equal Employment Advisory Council.

Chapter 11 was published in *Daedalus*, Fall 1976.

Chapter 12 was published in *Encounter*, February 1975.

Chapter 13 is from *Human Rights*, ed. Eugene Kamenka and Alice Erh-Soon Tay (London: Edward Arnold, 1978).

Chapter 14 was published under the title "Federalism and Ethnicity: The Experience of the United States," in *Publius*, Fall 1977.

Chapter 15 appeared as "The Ethnic Factor" in *Encounter*, July 1981.

Chapter 16 is from *Ethnic Relations in America*, ed. Lance Liebman, copyright © 1982 by The American Assembly, Columbia University; it is reprinted here by permission of the publisher, Prentice-Hall, Inc.

Index

Addabbo, Joseph P., 10
Adamic, Louis, 103
Adorno, T. W., 48
Affirmative Discrimination (Glazer), 161
American Association of Colleges of
  Teacher Education, 107
American Communist Party, 278
American Council on Education: Center
  for Intergroup Education in
  Cooperating Schools, 104
American Jewish Committee, 39, 181
American Jewish Congress, 181
American Telephone and Telegraph
  Company (A.T.& T.), 172, 180, 187,
  192
Amin, Idi, 247
Anti-Defamation League of B'nai B'rith,
  181
Ashenfelter, Orley, 188
Authoritarian Personality, The, 48

Bakke, Allan, 181, 265–266, 270
Baldwin, James: on integration, 51
Bauer, P.T.: on merit and reward, 221
Benedict, Ruth, 46, 58, 62
Beyond the Melting Pot, 315–316
Bilingual Education Act, 131, 132, 135,
  139
Blauner, Robert, 80, 82, 83, 88; on in-
  ternal colonialism, 79, 87
Boas, Franz, 62
Bourne, Randolph, 98, 102
Bowles, Samuel, 220
Brimmer, Andrew: on black employ-

ment, 170–171
Brown v. The Board of Education, 259
Bureau of the Census, 197
Burgess, Ernest W., 44, 52

City College of New York, 59
Civil Rights Act of 1964, 1–2 , 4; and
  color-blindness, 7, 126, 159; and
  Immigration Act, 8; and cultural
  pluralism, 127; Title VI of, 132, 133;
  and multicultural education, 135,
  136, 139; and affirmative action, 162,
  165–166, 168, 190; amendment of
  (1972), 163, 177; Title VII of, 169,
  187; and discrimination, 211–212,
  224, 254–255, 262, 263; and individual rights, 257, 259–260, 271; and
  politics, 315
Clark, Kenneth B., 325; on black attitude toward Jews, 29–30
Cole, Stewart G., 104, 106
Commentary, 4, 29, 30
Commission for Civil Rights, U.S., 113,
  179
Common Council for American Unity,
  104
Commons, John R., 99
Constitution: amendments to, 2, 7, 256–
  257; color-blindness of, 4, 177; and
  cultural pluralism, 127; and affirmative action, 168, 183; and individual
  rights, 265; and multiethnicity, 297;
  and political powerlessness, 329
*Contractors Association of Eastern Pa.
  v. Secretary of Labor*, 166